CW01019958

Light and Shade

Hong Kong University Press thanks Xu Bing for writing the Press's name in his Square Word Calligraphy for the covers of its books. For further information, see p. iv.

For my grandchildren Alexandra, Antonia,
David, Jonathan and Rachel, with love

Light and Shade

Sketches from an Uncommon Life

Solomon Matthew Bard

香港大學出版社

HONG KONG UNIVERSITY PRESS

Hong Kong University Press
14/F Hing Wai Centre
7 Tin Wan Praya Road
Aberdeen
Hong Kong

ISBN 978-962-209-949-4

Secure On-line Ordering
http://www.hkupress.org

British Library Cataloguing-in-Publication Data
A catalogue copy for this book is available from the British Library

Printed and bound by Liang Yu Printing Factory Ltd., in Hong Kong, China

Hong Kong University Press is honoured that Xu Bing, whose art explores the
complex themes of language across cultures, has written the Press's name in
his Square Word Calligraphy. This signals our commitment to cross-cultural
thinking and the distinctive nature of our English-language books published
in China.

"At first glance, Square Word Calligraphy appears to be nothing more unusual
than Chinese characters, but in fact it is a new way of rendering English words
in the format of a square so they resemble Chinese characters. Chinese viewers
expect to be able to read Square Word Calligraphy but cannot. Western
viewers, however are surprised to find they can read it. Delight erupts when
meaning is unexpectedly revealed."

— Britta Erickson, *The Art of Xu Bing*

CONTENTS

PREFACE

"Nothing you write, if you hope to be good, will ever
come out as you first hoped."

Lillian Hellman (1905–1984)

Several friends in the past had suggested that my background and life
experiences were unusual and interesting enough to write about. I was not
so sure. There have been dozens of books by and about people with similar
stories to tell – uprooted by events beyond their control, migrating to new
lands, learning a new language, and embracing a new culture and country. It
was not until Dr Colin Day, of Hong Kong University Press, showed interest
in the idea, that I was persuaded to write this book. I am very grateful to
Colin, for without his continuing encouragement and forbearance at the
slow rate of, and frequent long gaps in, my writing, this book might not have
been written.

The book is not an autobiography, although the sketches in the first part,
covering in sequence my childhood and adolescence, might suggest this. It
is, as the title conveys, a collection of autobiographical sketches or episodes
drawn from my life. In each I attempt to present a broad picture of the subject
against a background of historic events and persons, occasionally including
my own observations. Is there a central thread uniting these sketches into
a notion, a viewpoint? I did not intend one, but if there is, it may perhaps
be one of wonder at the extraordinary range of human endeavour, with the
lowliest to the loftiest of motives, be it the slaughter of war, the ruthless
efficiency of the Incas, the silent majesty of the Easter Island statues, or the
sublime artistry of Maria Callas.

Looking back at my life, I have been lucky to be able to pursue three
occupations — medicine, music and archaeology — the last two initially as
hobbies, later to become full-time professions. I enjoyed the challenges they

offered, and the ever-expanding horizons of my experience. At the same time I am fully aware how much I owe my fortune to chance, to being in the right place at the right time. For example, when I retired from my medical post at Hong Kong University, at the requisite age of sixty, had I been offered an extension, which was suggested but later withdrawn, I would have accepted it and missed the opportunity of taking up a full-time position with the Antiquities and Monuments Office. The latter gave me the opportunity, and immense satisfaction, of being the first government officer charged with the all-important mission of identifying and protecting Hong Kong's rich heritage.

I am relatively a newcomer to the art of writing. I am very grateful to Dr Tatiana Jelihovsky for reading thoroughly the manuscript and for making useful suggestions on many aspects of the text. Dr Jelihovsky and John Wisely also skilfully improved some of my old, faded, and hopelessly inadequate colour prints and slides.

I am grateful to my brother Leo, six years my senior, whose impeccable memory helped to verify or correct some details in my story. My family in Sydney and London were supportive throughout my writing.

My thanks are due to Hong Kong University Press for accepting the book for publishing, and to the Hong Kong Museum of History and the Antiquities and Monuments Office, both of the Leisure and Cultural Services Department, for allowing me to use photographs from their collections. I am also indebted to Geoffrey Bonsall, one-time colleague at Hong Kong University, for information on the Sino-British Club; to Andy Neilson, my fellow-officer in the Royal Hong Kong Regiment (The Volunteers), for allowing me to reproduce his powerful painting *The Lasting Honour*; to Tim Ko, for generously allowing me to use some rare photographs from his own collection; to Robin Hutcheon for permission to quote from his book *Shanghai Customs*; to James Hayes for advice on Hong Kong Volunteeers; and to Jennifer Day for helping with the title of the book.

My encounters over the years with diverse events and people have enriched my life. It is my earnest hope that the reader will find these sketches enjoyable and even informative. I have certainly enjoyed recounting them.

PART 1

1

SIBERIAN CHILDHOOD

"One day in the depths of a winter most cruel
I came from the forest. 'Twas frosty and still,
I saw an old horse with a sledge-load of fuel
Come painfully dragging its weight up the hill"

Preamble

This stanza, sensitively translated by Juliet M. Soskice, comes from an enchanting poem "Peasant Children" by the Russian poet Nicholas Nekrassov.[1] As a child of three or four I had often and with great gusto declaimed these lines to the delight of my parents and occasional guests. Although not a peasant child, I felt deeply the words. Images of cold, frosty and interminably long winters, of great forests and white snow-covered plains, were never far away from where I was born, on 13 June 1916, in Chita, a small thriving town in Siberia, a remote and inhospitable eastern region of Russia.[2]

A child's recollection may not always be accurate. Sometimes it is hard to tell how much may have been added to the story by later information. However, I believe that my first memory, at the age of two and half, of a very sad and tragic event, is true: it was the funeral of my eldest brother David. I see myself on the windowsill being held by my nanny and looking through the window at the snow-covered yard outside. People are moving about and a coffin is being placed on a hearse. Although I could not have understood what was going on, the scene has remained in my mind ever since.

---

1. *Poems by Nicholas Nekrassov*, Oxford University Press, 1929.
2. Russia at that time still adhered to the old calendar. The Gregorian or Western calendar, which became known as the New Style, was adopted by the Soviets on 31 January 1918, as part of the Regime's reforms. The calendar was advanced thirteen days and my birthday became 26 June.

Go East Young Man

Both my parents came from the western parts of Russia: my father from Poland, at that time ruled by Russia, my mother from the Crimea, on the Black Sea. What then brought them to Chita thousands of miles away from home? I should have liked to imagine my father as a pioneering adventurer seeking fortune in new, as yet little explored lands. It was only partly true. Coming from a poor family with a large number of siblings, father was apprenticed at the age of thirteen or fourteen to a watchmaker and silversmith somewhere in Poland.[3] Then, at the age of seventeen, he moved to Sevastopol, in the Crimea, to work for his uncle. There were few prospects for quick success in Sevastopol for a young watchmaker with few connections and no money. Moreover, he was courting my mother, three years his junior. No doubt father was looking for an opportunity for a quicker and shorter way to prosperity than that offered by his current position. This came unexpectedly from a distant relative in Chita who needed an assistant in his expanding shop; it was specified that the new assistant must be married! My parents arrived in Chita and were married there in 1906. My father was twenty-one, my mother eighteen.

Chita

It is said that Chita owes its origin to an enterprising Cossack chieftain as far back as the 17th century, when it was probably little more than a camp. Mineral resources, especially silver and gold, discovered in Siberia in the 18th century, advanced Chita's position, but its political history was made in 1827 when a number of early Russian revolutionaries, known as the Decembrists, who included leading intellectuals and academics, were exiled to Siberia.[4] Many were placed in Chita, no doubt raising this small Siberian town to at least a minor cultural centre.

Chita's next important phase came with the construction of the Trans-Siberian Railway, built in stages between 1891 and 1916. This nine-thousand-kilometre railway, linking Moscow in the west to Vladivostok in the east,

---

3. "Watchmaker" is not an entirely accurate translation from Russian. The Russians use the word "master", in the sense of a master craftsman, in describing one who repairs and maintains watches and clocks, but not necessarily makes them.

4. The Decembrists were a group of army officers who led an uprising against Imperial Russia in 1825. It was regarded as the earliest Russian revolutionary movement against the autocratic repressive government. Because the uprising occurred in December, rebels were called the Decembrists.

passed through Chita. In 1901 the town became a junction station for the new East Chinese Railway linking the Trans-Siberian Railway with the Chinese province of Manchuria, further boosting Chita's place in the wilderness of Siberia.

Early Success

My father, realizing that there were better prospects in Chita than working for his relative, left his employer after less than two years. Using every penny (sorry, kopeck) they saved, my parents opened their own watches-and-jewellery shop, called somewhat pretentiously "Renaissance". They lived in the spacious premises at the back of the shop; both worked at the counter, and the shop was doing very well. Their success in a relatively short time was not surprising. Chita, while not exactly a frontier town, was a boom town. Private gold and silver prospectors and hunters for valuable furs came to Chita to sell their spoils and buy luxuries such as watches and jewellery and other consumer goods. My eldest brother David was born in 1908, then Leo in 1910. By the time I was born six years later, we had become a well-settled, moderately prosperous family.

Clouds Gather

Those early years in Chita must have been very rewarding for my parents who were bringing up a family and working hard to build for us a comfortable and prosperous life. The harsh Siberian climate, the frugal life-style, and the great distance from their families were not serious problems for the young couple. But far away in the west, sinister events were gathering momentum towards a global conflagration. In 1914 the Great War started in which Russia played a major role. In 1915 my father was called up to serve in the army but was spared active service at the front because of severe myopia (shortsightedness). He spent the next two years as an army clerk mostly in Irkutsk, Siberia, and so was able to come home on leave from time to time. Mother was now fully occupied with looking after the shop, my brothers were nearly old enough to look after themselves, but when I was born a nanny was engaged to look after me. She was Polish and spoke to me mostly in her language. She looked after me until I was four and I was told that my first spoken words were in Polish. I remember my nanny and the thick Polish potato soup she cooked which I loved, but nothing whatever of the Polish language. Apart from the strain imposed on mother by father's absence, our life was relatively unaffected until 1917.

The War and the Revolution

After initial successes against Austro-Hungary, the Russian armies suffered a series of crushing defeats at the hands of the Germans in 1915. There were huge casualties. As the Russian front gradually disintegrated, there were widespread discontent and early signs of an impending popular uprising. Revolutions were not new to Russia. The Decembrist uprising of the 1820s was mentioned earlier. In 1905 a revolution sparked by the failure of the government to put into effect reforms it had promised earlier was crushed within a year, but some reforms, notably the establishment of the Duma, a legislative body, were forced from the government. My mother's sister Luba, who was an active participant in the revolutionary movement, was exiled to Siberia. Unlike the Decembrists, political prisoners of this period were no longer sent to Chita, but imprisoned in much harsher conditions in the far north of Siberia. She was freed when the 1917 Revolution had finally succeeded. Sadly, although we were in Chita at the time, my mother was either unable or not allowed to visit her sister.[5] The February 1917 Revolution appeared to have achieved moderate results with the abdication of the Tsar and establishment of the provisional government, but it was a case of "too little too late". Eight months later, in what is known as the "Great October Revolution", the Bolsheviks seized power, abolished the provisional government and set up the Marxist Soviet regime.[6] While this was the end of the old regime, it was also the beginning of the civil war which lasted for another four years.

The cataclysmic events of the Revolution were as yet too far away to seriously affect our life in Chita. Many, like my parents, were convinced that the forces of the old regime, often referred to as Whites, in contrast to the Red forces associated with the communist movement, would prevail.[7] This belief was reinforced by the Allied Intervention which began in 1918 and involved

---

5. I am not sure of the dates when aunt Luba was exiled and released, probably sometime between 1910 and 1917. She was a social democrat, and although released by the Revolution as a political prisoner, would have had no part to play in the Bolshevik government which was strongly opposed to social democrats. On release, she married a Latvian, settled down in Latvia and had three children, but maintained little connection with her family. Her health was undermined during the exile, and she died at a relatively young age.

6. The date, 25 October, became 7 November, New Style, (see note 2) and was subsequently celebrated in November.

7. White Army: An umbrella term for the various counter-revolutionary armies that fought the "Bolshevik" Red Army in the Russian Civil War. The name "White Russian" has also been used to describe Russian emigrants, or émigrés, who fled Russia

several foreign powers. These occupied portions of the Russian territory in the west and in the east, including Siberia. Surely the optimists reasoned, the Revolution could not succeed in the face of such opposition. However, some of the effects of the Revolution soon began to reach our region, such as devaluation of the currency and resulting inflation. My parents decided on what seemed to be the only plausible course: in 1917 they bought property and we soon moved into it. In retrospect this proved to be a big mistake, for contrary to most predictions, the Reds were getting the upper hand, and as the Revolution rolled steadily east with the Whites in retreat, property too lost its value and in any case was difficult to sell. We were tied to it and in the end had to give it up and leave, but this part of my story is still to come.

New Home and Tragic Loss
It was a substantial piece of property, centrally placed and comprising four houses, spacious grounds and a garden, all in one block, at No. 5 Argunskaya Street. I remember it well, the main house — our residence — was an attractive solid stone-and-brick building which stood in the middle of the compound facing a wrought-iron ornate gate and the street beyond. Two houses abutted the street while the fourth, the smallest of the four, stood at the back. Gradually we acquired an ample household staff, some with children; I also recall hens, ducks and geese at the back of the yard, and a large dog of uncertain pedigree called "Yellowpaws" (for obvious reason). There were fruit trees in the garden, but we, the children, much preferred small dark-coloured berries which grew on trees and which resembled blackberries; I think they might have been wild cherries. The echoes of the civil war were still too far away to affect us, and life in our new home during these early upheaval years of 1917–18 was uneventful and happy. My father had been released from the army and was back at the shop. Some years earlier, he brought his younger brother, Jonah, from Poland to Chita and helped him to open a stationery shop; I soon became uncle Jonah's favourite. Then suddenly tragedy struck. My eldest brother David developed a bone infection which spread to his blood; he died in December 1918 at the age of eleven. It was a cruel blow, which my parents tried to bear stoically, but which brought gloom and grief

as a result of the Revolution. According to the *Oxford Dictionary of Twentieth Century World History*, "Whites" has been used to describe those loyal to a monarchy, ever since the French Revolution (1789), when monarchist forces adopted the white flag of the Bourbon Dynasty as their symbol.

into our life and took a long time to heal. David was a gentle, loving boy. It is sad that I can only remember his funeral and know him only through family photographs.

My Mother — *The Good Samaritan*

An episode, of which I was completely unaware until many years later, occurred sometime in 1918. Many prisoners-of-war of the Austro-Hungarian forces captured by the Russians were sent to Siberia where some worked in private households or on farms. The surveillance was light as an escape from Siberia was regarded as unlikely. In the turmoil of the Revolution, some had tried to escape making their way east towards the sea hoping to reach their homeland by ship. One day a man, exhausted and hungry, turned up at our house. He admitted he was an escaped prisoner-of-war and asked for help. Mother took pity on him and kept him hidden on our property for two weeks while he was recovering his strength, then provided him with food, clothes and some money and sent him on his way. There is no doubt that mother's "Good Samaritan" deed was a risky action. It could also be regarded as foolhardy, though I prefer to think of it as brave. In the event, this single unconnected episode would have an unexpected sequel years later.[8]

The Civil War

The Revolution was opposed by the monarchist, counter-revolutionary forces — the White forces. By 1918 Russia was engaged in a ruthless, cruel civil war. Consisting mostly of regular army regiments, well-trained and organized, and Cossacks, the Whites were expected to defeat the Soviets and, indeed, they scored some initial successes. However, the tide later turned in favour of the Reds. Amazingly, although formed from scratch and led by the commissar of war, Trotsky, who was without any military training, the Red Army did turn the tables and by 1919 the Whites were in retreat. Admiral Kolchak, the main hope of the White movement, was retreating east and the ill winds of the civil war were now blowing across Siberia and were felt as far as Chita. After the relative calm of the two previous years, 1919 and 1920 were troubled years for Chita, which changed hands between Whites and Reds several times though little actual fighting took place in the city.

It was during a "White phase", in 1919, that three officers of the White Army were quartered in our house. I assume we had no choice, but in the

---

8. To be described in another essay.

event their stay with us seemed to have passed pleasantly. I am not sure how long they stayed, perhaps several months, but during that time they took a great liking to me and spoiled me atrociously. They took me with them when they rode to water their horses in the river, carefully holding me in front while I clutched at the horse's mane, giggling uncontrollably from pleasure all the way. On one occasion they dressed me up in their uniform, many sizes too big for a three-year-old child and took a photograph of me. They also taught me to swear like a trooper to the great distress of my mother, and the amusement of my father. Then suddenly the officers were gone and the city was occupied by the Reds. It soon changed hands again, but this time it fell to a White Cossack chieftain by the name of Semionov and his men, with a sinister reputation for lawlessness and strong anti-Semitism.[9] Many believed that Semionov was in this for his own power and gain rather than for the White cause. My mother related how the city lived in fear, not knowing what to expect, and how one day my father was taken away and locked in a railway car with several other local merchants, under threat of being blown up. Evidently some sort of ransom was expected. My mother rushed to Semionov's headquarters demanding to see him. To her utter surprise he received her courteously, listened to her plea and had my father released, reputedly in the nick of time. The other captives were released soon afterwards. I was never told whether in fact a ransom was paid, but I suspect it was.

By the end of 1920, the Whites were decidedly defeated, though sporadic skirmishes between small isolated groups continued until 1922. The fruitless foreign intervention fizzled out and the Allied troops departed, except the Japanese who remained in some parts of the Russian Far East until 1922.

The first Soviet government, established in 1918 as the Russian Soviet Federated Socialist Republic, or R.S.F.S.R, did not at once exercise central control over the whole of Russia. In our region, the Far Eastern Republic declared itself in 1920. Ostensibly democratic, it was nevertheless under Communist control. The D.V.R., as it was called (Russian initials for the Far Eastern Republic), lasted until the end of 1922, when Soviet power was finally established over the whole of Russia under the name of the Union of Soviet Socialist Republics, or U.S.S.R.

---

9. Semionov later found refuge in the southern part of Manchuria, which was under Japanese control, and there engaged in some, mostly ineffective, anti-Soviet activities. When the Soviet Army overran Manchuria at the end of the Second World War, Semionov was arrested, tried in the Soviet Union and executed.

Life at Home

In Chita by late 1920 conditions began to return to near normal. Although we were now under the rule of the D.V.R., my family was not as yet affected by the new regime. Father continued to run the shop. We could hear him coming home daily after work, always playfully scolding "Yellowpaws" and receiving happy barks in return. Mother was busy in the house, and my brother Leo was attending high school in his black uniform with shining brass buttons and smart peak-cap. Sometime after I had turned four, my nanny left, retiring to her native Poland. At the same time I began attending cheder, a Jewish primary school. Although the school was some distance away, I walked there alone carrying my books and an ink bottle tied to my wrist. On the way back from school I invariably stopped at my uncle Jonah's shop where I pretended to help him in return for packets of candy. In winter, although wearing thick woollen mittens, I recall coming home with my hands numb from the cold and tears running down my cheeks, having stopped at uncle Jonah's, to "warm up" I explained, though his shop was further away from school than my home. At school I learned almost nothing of Hebrew, but showed excellent progress in reading and writing Russian. Perhaps my parents were aware of this, for the following year, after I had turned five, I was enrolled in a Russian primary school.

Expropriation

As children, my brother and I were largely unaware of the momentous events unfolding around us. In spite of apparent normality, my parents must have been living in constant expectation of drastic changes in our life and fortunes, knowing that in the eyes of the Soviets they were the despised bourgeois — landowners and merchants — exploiters who must be eliminated.[10] The blow finally came in 1921, though I am not sure exactly when. I recall the scene as I stood with my mother in the hall of our house: two men in leather jackets, high boots and peak-caps, were informing mother that our immovable property — the houses — was being "expropriated" in the name of the Soviet government. My father was not present, he was probably at the shop. I believe my mother took it stoically, for I do not recall her crying or reacting with shock to the announcement. The blow was softened by the men further announcing

---

10. The term "bourgeois", which in French means mainly "middle class", in Soviet Russia acquired a somewhat different connotation — a derogatory term for the class enemy, or those who did not belong to the proletariat.

that we would be allowed to occupy the small house at the back without rent. The new regime was living up to its proclamation "all power to the Soviets". This was now a land for workers and peasants, and those who belonged to the upper and middle classes lost their property and were regarded at best as suspects, or at worst as enemies of the people.

Looking back at this turn of events in our life, I am amazed how quickly and realistically my parents accepted our new situation and adapted to it. In part this may have been due to the fact that they had been expecting this development for some time, that although dispossessed, we were not deprived of our personal possessions and were certainly not destitute, and that we were not alone in this condition. Moreover, somewhat contrary to their expectations, we were not subjected to any ill treatment. We moved into our new home, which we found big enough for the family and which proved comfortable and manageable. The entrance led, through a small hall, into the kitchen, where an enormous stove reaching to the ceiling helped to keep the whole house warm in winter. From the kitchen the door opened into a large sitting room which continued into a smaller dining room. Three bedrooms were all on the same side, separated from the sitting/dining rooms by a corridor. The other three houses in the compound were occupied by government agencies, the main building housing some sort of trading department. One of the remaining two houses was occupied, to our consternation, by the infamous "Cheka" — the Soviet State Security Organ — an early version of the KGB.

Winters

As the years 1921 and 1922 rolled on, and we settled down in our new home, our daily life continued in a near-normal way. Father still went to the shop, but I believe it was to wind up the business; Leo and I attended our respective schools. At the approach of winter, frantic activity would develop in our household. The entrance door was padded with felt on the inside to keep the cold out. The double window panes were sealed, leaving only a small hinged pane which could be opened for ventilation. Known as "fortochka", it is a feature in most Russian houses. One or two days were devoted to shredding and salting cabbage which was then stored in barrels. A favourite ingredient in Russian cuisine, the cabbage would be served throughout winter. Leo and I loved this ritual since we enjoyed eating the sweet, crisp left-over heads of the cabbage. Winter was also a time for cooking meat and cabbage pies, known in Russian as "pirozhki". Throughout my life I have retained a very strong fondness for Russian meat pies. Another favourite winter dish, especially popular in Siberia, was small boiled meat dumplings called "pelmeni". An entire meal would consist of "pelmeni", and partakers would often compete at eating the greatest number of them.

Winters were long and very cold, temperatures sometimes reaching minus 30 degrees Centigrade, but it is impossible not to admire and love the sight of a pure white, far-reaching snow carpet in the open countryside. For those who have never seen snow, the first sight of it must be an unforgettable experience. I remember how many years later my own children, who saw snow for the first time when already in their teens, rushed about madly throwing snowballs at each other in sheer exhilaration. Growing up in Chita, we were used to the snow and the cold and enjoyed our outdoor pastimes. We wore warm underwear, thick overcoats, hats with flaps to cover our ears, and felt boots. After school, Leo and I with our friends played in the snow or went sleighing or skating on our frozen river. Chita had two rivers — Ingoda, wide and swift-flowing, and its narrow quiet tributary called Chitinka (small Chita). Both froze in winter, but we skated mostly on Chitinka. Sleighing in winter was great fun, but not without its dangers, as I learned by bitter experience. It was during one of these rides that Leo, pulling the sleigh with me on it, ran fast over frozen ground and overturned the sleigh. I fell off, nearly biting off a slice of my tongue. Bleeding profusely, and Leo in a panic, I was brought home with fuss and alarm, but fortunately the damage was soon repaired. A faint scar on my tongue is still visible. There were days, however, so cold that we spent the time indoors, reading or playing with mostly home-made toys. Leo became quite adept at carving "soldiers" from spent wooden spools. Unlike the present age of mass productions, we had few toys, at least in Chita. Rarely, when we were given a real toy, it was an occasion for great jubilation, such as happened when a toy wooden cannon, which I had admired many times in a shop window, was brought home by my father and given to me. Siberian winter also brought some bizarre incidents such as when our watchman Alexander brought into our kitchen a goose which had its fleshy tongue frozen to its back where it had been licking its feathers. Soon unfrozen in the warmth of the kitchen, the poor bird seemed none the worse for its unpleasant experience and presently returned to the yard.

Summers

At the onset of spring, we would all go to watch the frozen river coming to life. Listening to the grinding noise of the breaking ice, as the large ice-floes begin to move, has always been an exciting experience. As much as we enjoyed our winters and springs, the short and hot summers provided us with different pleasures. On some holidays or Sundays, father would hire a large horse-drawn cart with a coachman, pile on old rugs, pillows, a hammock or two, and plenty of food and drink, and the family, often with friends, would go for a picnic in the wood by the Ingoda river. I looked forward immensely to these outings. There, in a Chekhovian atmosphere, in the shade of sweet-smelling pines, the older folk would relax on rugs or in hammocks, chatting, sipping tea or just sleeping, while the younger set and the children swam in the river or played games.

The near-idyllic picture I have drawn should not detract from the overall sad state of the country. The civil war left Russia exhausted and ruined. Nationalization of industry, suppression of private trade, and other drastic economic measures contributed to the breakdown of the economy. There were shortages of food and other commodities. Private land was confiscated and those belonging to the upper and middle classes suffered discrimination. The western regions of the country, with their larger population, were especially badly affected, but by 1921 Siberia too was experiencing shortages.

Armed Hold-Up

Although we belonged to a privileged class, despised by the new regime, we were not harassed and were largely left alone to get on with our lives. Since we did not seem to suffer any obvious privations, I assume my parents still had money and were able to keep their personal valuables. In 1922 father had wound up the shop and was able to spend more time at home. We had become accustomed to our new status and were comfortable in our new modest house. Life seemed almost normal: there were dinner parties with friends in our house although with less cognac and fewer cigars than before, but with the usual game of preference after dinner.[11] Leo and I were usually allowed to sit at the table with the adults, but after dinner were sent to bed. It was during one of these dinner parties that we had an armed robbery. At the height of the party, two masked men appeared in the dining room. Brandishing a revolver, one of the men ordered everyone to stand up and raise their hands. My father, thinking someone was playing a practical joke, said something to the effect: "stop fooling". The next command came in such a menacing tone that there was no longer any doubt that this was a real armed hold-up. Suddenly all was quiet. Everyone stood up with hands raised; I cannot remember whether I raised my hands, probably not. The ladies were then told to remain at the table but warned not to move, make any noise or raise an alarm.

---

11. Preference: a card game not unlike whist or bridge, which was very popular in Russia and generally in Eastern Europe.

The men, including Leo, were ordered into the bathroom where they remained guarded by one of the robbers. I suspect Leo was proud of the fact that he was counted as an adult. The other robber ordered mother to show him where money and jewellery were kept. I followed mother, the man paying no attention to me. I remember mother opening some drawers and I presume money and some items were taken. Strangely, I do not remember being frightened; perhaps I did not fully appreciate the situation.

Suddenly the loud sound of a shot fired was heard. Apparently one of our guests had tried to escape from the bathroom and the man guarding them fired his gun. Fortunately no one was hurt. Shortly afterwards the two men left after wishing us a "good night". We learned later that there were two other men — one was in the kitchen watching our domestics, and the fourth was keeping watch outside. A few weeks later we were told that the robbers were apprehended and mother was summoned to the police station to identify them. She did not; she was either unable or unwilling to identify them, I never learned which. There was still a good deal of lawlessness in Chita, some perpetrated by the former members of the White army, mostly destitute and desperate, who may have turned to crime. It was ironic that we were robbed under the very noses of the dreaded Cheka housed in our compound.

Home Life and Books

When I think of my home and family, I believe we were a happy close-knit unit with my memories predominantly of warmth and love. But punishment was also administered when deemed necessary: being placed in a corner facing the wall was the standard form for being naughty or disobedient; recourse to a belt was used but rarely. Leo, though always protective of me, preferred, understandably, to spend time with friends of his age: six years' difference at that age was a very wide gap. I think I grew as a quiet, shy, introspective boy prone to imagination, even some phantasy. I, too, had my own friends, but seemed to prefer books. By the time I passed my sixth birthday I was becoming a voracious reader. Fortunately, when my parents had bought the property, they also acquired with it a sizeable library. Apart from the Russian classics, there were translated works of foreign writers. There was also a marvellous set of four large volumes called "Wonders of the Universe" which Leo and I browsed through repeatedly, mainly for their fascinating coloured pictures. I recall that my favourite books were adventure novels by Jules Verne, Mayne Reid and Fenimore Cooper. They stirred my childish imagination and I often pictured myself in them. At one time our house was the Nautilus, of *20,000 Leagues under the Seas*, and I was its captain Nemo; at another it was the steam house, Jules Verne's fabulous steam engine in the shape of an elephant. I liked to share these adventures with my friends, and with our household domestics to whom I would excitedly relate the stories I had read.

Journey to Moscow and Sevastopol

As I was approaching my seventh birthday, I learned with surprise and much excitement that I was to embark on a real adventure, the greatest adventure of my childhood far surpassing my imaginary ones in the world of Jules Verne: a trip with my mother on the Trans-Siberian Railway across the whole of Russia to the Crimea. Mother had made this trip twice before, on both occasions taking with her my two elder brothers, and each time combining seeing her parents in Sevastopol with buying some merchandise for the shop. This time there would be no stock buying and I alone was to accompany her. No doubt, the thought of possibly leaving Russia in the near future and perhaps never seeing her parents again played a part in mother's wish to visit them. I was told later by my parents that around 1922 they began contemplating leaving Russia. We had no future in the new Soviet Russia, simply because we belonged to the wrong class — the despised bourgeois. Moreover, there were persistent rumours that emigration from Russia would soon be drastically restricted and even stopped altogether.

Mother and I left Chita in May 1923 for Moscow where we spent three weeks with mother's younger sister Sonia and her husband Grisha. Then, with Sonia, we travelled to Sevastopol and spent three months with grandparents before returning to Chita. The time for our journey was well chosen. The New Economic Policy, or N.E.P., introduced by Lenin in 1921, which relaxed many of the early drastic economic measures and even allowed a limited measure of private enterprise, had now reached our distant region. It was a welcome reprieve from previous hardships and shortages. Relaxation of restrictions on farming resulted in better supplies of food and other provisions. The N.E.P. was a great success, but after the death of Lenin, in 1924, it was effectively at an end, although not officially stopped until 1928. In the meantime travelling around the country was also made easier and we departed Chita full of cheerful expectations.

The journey to Moscow took seven days. During that time, we must have made not a few friends among our co-travellers, but curiously I remember little of the actual journey. Among my few recollections is that of the train passing through countless tunnels, I believe there were about forty, as the train rounded Lake Baikal, reputed to be the deepest lake in the world. The train stopped by the Lake and we were able to get off the train and walk for a few minutes along the shore; I stared across but could not see the opposite shore of this huge lake. I remember the rush for boiling water at every station and the hurrying back in constant fear of missing the train. I recall one unpleasant incident when the train ran over a cow. I suppose, excited as I was to be on this trip, much of the long journey had assumed a monotonous routine. In Moscow at last, we were met at the station by uncle Grisha and aunt Sonia, and driven home in a hired motorcar — my first experience of a motor vehicle. It was a very thrilling experience. Years later I could still remember the joy of this sensation, but could never recapture it, once it had become commonplace.

My uncle and aunt occupied a small flat of two rooms, one of which served as uncle's studio (he was an artist), the second room served all other purposes. Half of uncle's studio was now converted into mother's and my bedroom; the other half was crammed with canvasses and panels. To reach their flat one had to walk through a long winding corridor in almost total darkness. There was a communal kitchen which served several flats in the building. Every morning, it became my task to walk to a bakery one block away and buy the most delicious fresh raisin bread, which had only recently become available thanks to the N.E.P. Aunt Sonia was a large plump woman with a kind, always smiling face, but it was uncle Grisha who totally won my heart. He was a tall, thin handsome man with a serious face and an animated manner when he talked. He usually wore a wide-brimmed hat and dressed in a somewhat Bohemian fashion. This is, of course, a description by an adult; to me as a child, he seemed a large man, gentle and kind. As he confided to me later, his ambition to paint art-works was constantly frustrated by the government which employed him, and for which he had to produce stereotyped propaganda posters depicting happy wholesome-looking workers and peasants standing in defying poses with hammers and sickles in their hands. Grisha had taken a holiday for our visit, and while mother and Sonia had a lot to talk about, he spent most of the time with me, taking me on exciting trips all over Moscow, including many art galleries. He talked to me as if I were an adult and seemed to enjoy explaining and describing to me the things we saw and the places we visited. I remember vividly our visit to the famous Tretyakov Gallery which houses paintings by the great Russian masters like Repin, Vasnetsov and Levitan. It is difficult to describe adequately the overpowering effect I felt, transported from a small backward town into the largest city in the country: fine buildings and paved streets, the wonders of the Kremlin, the onion-domed churches, the river embankment and other wonderful sights — all made an unforgettable impression on me. Three weeks passed quickly and I was sorry to part from uncle Grisha, but I was excited at the prospect of visiting another city and meeting my grandparents for the first time. Soon mother, Sonia and I were on our way to Sevastopol — a three-day journey south by train. I remember nothing at all of this journey, probably because nothing much happened.

Sevastopol, located at the tip of the Crimean peninsula on the Black Sea, was founded by the empress Catherine the Great in 1783, though some might argue that the city had its origin in an ancient Greek colony Chersonesus as far back as the 5th century BCE.[12] Indeed, while in Sevastopol we visited the remains of the ancient Chersonesus located a short distance from the city. Sevastopol's more recent importance dates from the early 19th century when the city was fortified and used as a naval base. It played a central role in the Crimean War of 1854–55 when it was attacked by the combined British, French and Turkish forces. To the Russians, as I was soon to learn, it was not the eventual outcome of the war, which they lost, that mattered, but the glorious defence of the city which held out for eleven and a half months, and in which admiral Nakhimov, killed in action, and the troops under his command displayed outstanding courage and heroism. A statue of the admiral stands prominently in the central square of the city overlooking the sea. Years later I was able to appreciate the opposing side's view, which also had its gallant moments such as the British cavalry action at Balaklava, immortalized in Tennyson's "Charge of the Light Brigade".

We arrived at Sevastopol in the early evening just as it was getting dark and were met by my grandfather. Ourselves and all our baggage were placed in a long, open horse-drawn carriage with two central back-to-back benches, called, I subsequently learned, "lineika".[13] Instead of going home, we were first taken to a bath-house, no doubt to wash off the grime of the long train journey. Russians are very fond of these bath-houses in which a whole room serves as a steam bath, not unlike the present-day sauna. By the time we arrived home where grandmother was waiting with delicious hot dinner, I could hardly keep awake and was soon packed off to bed.

---

12. BCE = Before Common Era; CE = Common Era.
13. "Lineika" means (measuring) ruler. I have no idea why the vehicle I described should also be called by this name.

Grandfather

My grandfather was a short sturdy man in his late sixties. He had a beard and at home always wore a skull-cap. I suspect my grandmother wore a wig, as prescribed for married women by the Jewish religion, but I am not sure. Like so many others, my grandparents suffered hardships and privations in the early years of the Revolution when Sevastopol, like Chita, changed hands in the ensuing fighting. Their two sons, my mother's younger brothers, managed to escape to Greece, on a Greek destroyer, in remarkable circumstances. But now, the city had largely recovered and was enjoying the plenitude brought by the N.E.P. Grandfather ran a small business at home as a furrier, still apparently tolerated by the Soviet authorities. It seemed an unlikely profession in Sevastopol which has a mild warm climate.

He seemed always in a cheerful mood, his only worry being grandmother's health as she was suffering from diabetes. He and grandmother were obviously delighted to welcome their two daughters and discuss family matters with them, but after a few days grandfather devoted most of his time, when not busy with his furs, to me. One of our first visits was to a special museum housing the famous panorama painted on a huge cloth, depicting scenes of the defence of Sevastopol, 1854–55.[14] As in Moscow, what impressed me enormously were the paved streets and footpaths in contrast to Chita where there was mostly sand and mud. As I walked with grandfather, I admired the city's fine buildings and its many monuments, but the biggest thrill was the sight of the sea, the first time for me. The harbour, the pavilions on the waterfront, the warships anchored in the harbour, and people strolling on the promenade by the sea — for me these were scenes from a different world. One day grandfather took me to the beach and taught me to swim. I learned quickly and after that we went swimming often. It was so different from my home river Chitinka in which I was allowed to wade up to my knees but not to bathe because of the current and dangerous eddies. There were trips on a hackney-coach by the whole family to the neighbouring resorts of Yalta and Evpatoria to look at the beautiful "dachas", to have a picnic on a long sandy beach, and swim. Then the return journey, feeling tired but happy, through copses of walnut trees, with the coachman niftily knocking off walnuts with his whip into our laps.

---

14. This picturesque panorama, painted on a cloth by the artist F. F. Rubo, extends in an endless circle along the wall of a rotunda-shaped building.

Grandfather had interesting stories to tell about his life. Before becoming a furrier, he worked as a flautist and music teacher but found it difficult to make a living in that profession. Then a family secret was revealed: my father had taken violin lessons from him. "Your father had no talent and was not really interested in music," grandfather said, "it was a ruse to get close to my daughter, your future mother, because he had fallen in love with her". Grandfather learned to play the flute in the army. At the age of eighteen he joined the army in place of his elder brother who had recently married and was called up to serve shortly afterwards. Apparently such "replacements" were quite common and legal. Unfortunately for my grandfather, just as he was completing his normal four-year army service, in 1877, the war between Russia and Turkey had broken out. There was no discharge from the army, and grandfather soon found himself marching under the Russian general Skobelev, popularly known as the "White General" because he always rode a white horse. They reached Turkey and, grandfather declared with some pride I thought, laid siege to the Turkish fortress of Plevna.[15] Serving in the band did not offer any protection; on the contrary, my grandfather explained, bands in those days marched in front of the troops and were therefore exposed to the first volleys from the enemy.

I listened fascinated to the stories of his war experience. The one I liked best, and wanted to hear again and again, was the story of the "restless pillow": after marching the whole day in hot weather (it was June, there was no transport for infantry in those days), they stopped for the night in a field. Grandfather was very tired. As it grew dark, he folded his greatcoat, put it on the first large stone he saw and using it as a pillow went to sleep. During the night he felt a strange sensation that his pillow was moving, but too tired to get up, he went on sleeping. In the early morning as he got up to the bugle call, he lifted his greatcoat to discover to his amazement that the "stone" turned out to be a tortoise, which obviously was not amused at being used as a pillow! In another war story, my grandfather with several of his comrades went on a food-foraging expedition. They climbed a steep hill and as they reached the crest they came suddenly face to face with a small party of Turkish soldiers, obviously on a similar mission. "What happened,

---

15. Actually the war was with the Ottoman Empire, often referred to as the Turkish Empire or simply as Turkey. Plevna (or Pleven) is in present-day Bulgaria, at that time part of the Ottoman Empire. Unlike the Crimean War of 1854–55, the 1877–78 war resulted in a decisive Russian victory. However, under pressure from the Western powers, Russian gains in the subsequent peace treaty were significantly reduced.

grandpa?" I cried excitedly. "Did you fight?" "No," he replied, "we looked at each other for a moment, then turned and went our separate ways." One day, at my request, grandfather took out his flute and began to play. Music so far had not played any part in my life or in that of my family. The piano at home was merely a piece of furniture, though mother occasionally would sit at it and improvise, rather poorly, some familiar tunes. Now, suddenly I wanted to learn to play the flute and to start at once. But grandfather said that I was too young to learn a wind instrument, but he would teach me when I was old enough. He did, years later when he came to live with us after the death of grandmother.

Return to Chita

With so much to do and to see, the three months soon passed and it was time to leave. We stopped in Moscow on the way back for a few days and then embarked on the long journey back to Chita. I recall nothing of the return trip. Chita seemed dreary after Moscow and Sevastopol, but it felt good to be home with father and Leo. I soon realized that my parents were now making firm plans to leave Russia. Our destination was Harbin, a city in Manchuria (now called Heilongjiang), the northern province of China, two days' journey from Chita on the Chinese Eastern Railway. Harbin had become a regular destination for émigrés from Soviet Russia. The Railway was managed jointly by China and Russia, and the former Russian technical staff had not yet been replaced by the new Soviet personnel. Thousands of Russians, before the Revolution, had settled comfortably in Harbin, many fine schools had been established and a rich cultural life had developed with theatre, symphony orchestra and other fine amenities. It was decided that father and Leo would leave first, to find accommodation and father to explore business and work prospects in Harbin; mother and I would then follow. In retrospect it was a dangerous plan since the Soviet authorities were rapidly shutting down emigration from Russia and there was a real possibility of our family becoming split. About two months after our return from the Crimea, in the early autumn of 1923, father and Leo left Chita for Harbin. Leo was very sad at leaving his dog, a black mongrel called Mishka. Shortly after they left, mother and I moved from our home into a boarding house. Before leaving, father advised uncle Jonah to follow us to Harbin but Jonah, now married, decided to stay. The government allowed him to continue running his shop provided he did not employ any staff.

Farewell to Russia

In January 1924 Lenin, the all-powerful leader of the Soviet Union, died.[16] The whole country was plunged into mourning. In Chita everybody, it seemed, was wearing a black armband. With Lenin's death, the benefits of the N.E.P., his creation, were beginning to disappear, and leaving the country was becoming more difficult by the day. In the boarding house many, like us, were also apparently waiting for exit visas. Mother now began her regular visits to the government department and dealing with rigid, unsympathetic officials in the visa section. Fellow boarders kept telling mother that our chances of leaving the country were extremely small. In spite of the prevailing gloom on the subject of exit permits, there was a great deal of partying at the boarding house, perhaps born of general desperation, or the Russian spirit which finds reasons for having a good time under any circumstances. I stopped going to school and spent time with the children at the boarding house or reading the few books we took with us. There was a little girl of my age at the boarding house with whom I played a curious game. In it we alternately sentenced each other to hard labour and then pardoned. Psychologists would have had a field day trying to understand our minds. Looking back, although I find it a very odd game for children to play, I am certain there was nothing sinister or cruel in our minds, for I recall distinctly that we both experienced pleasure in the pardoning, not the sentencing. Occasionally I went to our old compound on Argunskaya street where the domestic staff, now working for new employers, welcomed me with my favourite meat pies. I would eagerly relate to them a story from one of my favourite books. I recall that on one of my last visits it was *The Last of the Mohicans*.

At the boarding house the residents seemed to be like one, though not always happy, family, and celebrated every successful granting of an exit visa. Then, one late afternoon mother returned from her usual visit to the visa office holding in her hand, and waving triumphantly in the air, her passport, and everyone knew that she had at last the precious exit visas for us. That night there was a big celebration at the boarding house, everyone congratulating mother and wishing us good luck. We left Soviet Russia for Harbin at the end of June 1924. I had just turned eight; we were heading for a new country, new home, and a new life.

---

16. V. I. Lenin, leader of the Bolshevik party and the supreme head of the Soviet Union, died on 21 January 1924 at the age of fifty-four. The death was regarded as due to a series of strokes possibly aggravated by the injury sustained in an assassination attempt in 1918.

2

MANCHURIAN ADOLESCENCE

"Whither, oh whither have you gone,
Golden days of my spring?"

Poet Lenski's lament from
A. S. Pushkin's *Eugene Onegin*[1]

These words of a young poet are very moving. Were they only the foreboding of his impending death in the duel, or more than that — a recollection of cherished hopes and noble ideas which remained unfulfilled? As I begin writing about the long-gone "golden days" of my adolescence, I am filled with sweet sadness when I recall the unfulfilled aspirations, the lost friendships that were to last forever, and the joy and pain of early love. But I also feel immensely grateful for the lasting gift of music and its magic, and my life-long love of it.

Departure and Arrival

At the end of June 1924, shortly after my eighth birthday, mother and I left my birthplace Chita, in Soviet Russia, to join father and my elder brother Leo in Harbin, in China's northern province of Manchuria (now called Heilongjiang). Father and Leo had gone there the previous year to prepare the ground for the whole family. Although we left the country legally, still in possession of Soviet passports, technically we were refugees — dispossessed though not destitute — émigrés from a communist state which regarded my parents' merchant and landowner status as undesirable, putting it mildly. We left of our own free will, because there was no conceivable future either for my parents or for us, their children, in the new regime.[2]

---

1. My translation from the Russian.
2. Described in my "Siberian Childhood" essay.

We were now in a foreign land, but it did not seem foreign: there were Russian-speaking people everywhere, shop signboards and street names in Russian, and the architectural styles of buildings were either Russian or Western, at least in the area of Harbin where we were to live. There were, of course, also many Chinese people on the streets and, as I learned later, a district of Harbin, called Fu Dzia Dian, inhabited entirely by Chinese. My first impressions of Harbin were very favourable: wide cobble-paved streets with fine buildings. The main street of our district had many shops displaying a wide variety of attractive items in their windows. Father had arranged for us to stay temporarily with old friends of the family. After two or three months we moved into a flat which we shared with another family who had one son, slightly younger than I. Father found a job as a bookkeeper, a new profession for him, in a firm dealing with cutlery and kitchenware. Leo had already started to attend the First Railway School taken over by the Soviets from the former Russian Railway administration. The choice was surprising in view of our status, but Leo persuaded our parents. I believe he had already made good friends with two or three boys who were attending that school.

Harbin

Harbin is located roughly in the centre of Heilongjiang Province of China (formerly Manchuria), on the right (south) bank of the Sungari River. The city's importance dates from the construction of the Chinese Eastern Railway (CER), 1897–1901, an extension of the Trans-Siberian Railway linking the latter with the southern Manchurian city of Dairen. The CER was built by the Russians but administered jointly by Russia and China. Passing through Harbin, previously hardly more than a village, the CER transformed it into a thriving modern city and the administrative centre of the CER. The Railway brought large numbers of Russian technical staff into the city, and following the Revolution of 1917 another influx of Russian émigrés, both White Russian and Jewish Russian. All contributed greatly to the development of the city as a major commercial and cultural centre. Following Russia's defeat by the Japanese in the Russo-Japanese War (1904–05), Japan took control of the southern portion of the CER. Curiously, the administration of the northern portion of the CER continued under the former Tsarist staff until 1924–25 when it was finally replaced by Soviet staff.

Harbin was divided into a number of districts, of which Pristan (which means "Wharf"), where we lived, was especially popular with the Jewish community. Other districts were Novyi Gorod (New Town), Old Harbin, Modiagou (Chinese name) and Fu Dzia Dian, a predominantly Chinese district.

The climate was only slightly milder than in our former home, Chita: winters were long and cold, when the Sungari River froze, and summers short and hot. Spring, especially late April and May, was very pleasant. The population was essentially divided into Russian (Christian and Jewish) émigrés, Soviet citizens, mostly engaged in working for the CER, the Chinese, and a small number of other nationals, such as English and German, running businesses or banks. In my recollection, there was free mixing among the émigrés, but only limited with the Soviet community whose members congregated around the Railway Club. Intercourse with the Chinese community seemed confined chiefly to dealings with artisans, such as carpenters or tailors, manual or skilled workers, and itinerant pedlars whose distinctive cries could be heard every day as they moved from street to street. It was sad that only the very occasional non-Chinese Harbin resident bothered to learn Chinese. Children, however, easily picked up Chinese swear words in the street.

Schooling

In Chita, before coming to Harbin, I did not attend school for several months while we were waiting for our exit visas. Presumably I was somewhat behind with my studies, since a tutor was engaged to prepare me for entrance examinations into a school. The one chosen for me was not Leo's school but a small popular school called the First Harbin Public Commercial School. Conveniently, it was located immediately opposite the house where we lived in our shared flat. Like most Russian schools it had three preparatory (preps) and seven high school classes, a total of ten years, at the end of which one was deemed ready to proceed to tertiary education. My tutor had advised my parents that I should aim at the upper prep class, suitable both for my age and my level of knowledge, and take examinations the following year in time for the beginning of the term in September 1925. However, after six months of tuition, the tutor declared that I was good enough to skip the prep class and aim for the 1st Form. His forecast was correct: I passed the entrance examination for the 1st Form and was duly admitted. I shall never forget my first few days at school which were something of a disaster. Mother took me to the school on the first day, which caused me acute embarrassment, as most children arrived without their parents. It soon became apparent that they were continuing from the upper prep class and were familiar with the school. I felt a total stranger as I saw them greeting each other, laughing and chatting. Within minutes of my arrival, with mother still around, I had a fight with one of the boys, a red-haired lad, who was probably taunting me as mummy's little boy (we became good friends later on). The second day passed without incident, but on the third day there was a class test in biology, and I could not understand the way the questions were distributed. I sat at my desk feeling terribly unhappy and unable to write anything, whereupon the teacher, well known as a harsh disciplinarian, came across to my desk, but instead of helping me, angrily drew a large mark "1" on my blank exercise book — the lowest mark one can possibly get, and generally regarded as a mark of contempt or derision.[3] It says something for me that I did not burst out crying but grit my teeth and sat gloomily until the end of the class. It took a week or two before I began to feel at home and make friends with my classmates.

The school was co-educational, about one third of the pupils being girls. The pupils were mostly children of Russian émigrés, about half of them Jewish and half Christian with a few Tatar (Muslim) children.[4] Parents, especially the mothers, were very active in school activities, including serving delicious sausage rolls for school lunches. It was a progressive school in which discussion, individual initiative and resourcefulness were encouraged.

The Russian school educational system encompassed a wide range of subjects. My graduation certificate contained thirty-three, including such diverse subjects as astronomy, jurisprudence, botany, and, being a "commercial" school, knowledge of merchandise, elementary bookkeeping, economics, and business correspondence. Because of the large number of subjects, some were dropped after a few years and replaced by others; for instance, arithmetic was dropped after the 3rd Form and replaced by algebra and geometry. History was taught from the ancient to the modern era. Russian literature was taught thoroughly, embracing a wide range of writers and poets, but we were also made briefly acquainted with great foreign writers such as Shakespeare, Milton and Chaucer — in Russian, of course. The emphasis was obviously on spread rather than detail. One session a week was devoted to special lessons when the Jewish pupils, in a separate classroom, were taught Jewish history by a secular teacher, not a rabbi, and the Christian pupils were taught religious knowledge by a Russian Orthodox priest.

---

3. In Russian schools marks are generally given from 1 to 5: 1 is seldom used, 2 being the mark of the lowest degree of competence. Occasionally 2 minus and 5 plus are given for exceptionally bad or good performances.

4. Tatars (sometimes wrongly spelled "tartars") was the name used in Russia for the remnants of the Mongol invaders who conquered and ruled Russia between the 13th and 15th centuries CE. Tatars, though fully Russianized, still adhere to Islam. Their names, such as Ahmedov or Sultanov, although with Russian endings, betray their origin.

We would see the two teachers leaving the school after lessons, usually walking together and chatting like old friends; perhaps they were. The Tatar pupils, being few in number, received no special instruction; presumably they were taught religion and traditions at home.

Misbehaviour at school was punished by reports to parents, suspension, or, in rare cases, expulsion from the school. Physical punishment, even in the mildest form, was unthinkable: if such happened, one could imagine a procession of irate mothers marching on the school, demanding, and probably succeeding in, the discharge of the guilty teacher. There was no elite group of senior students with authority over other students, such as the prefects in British schools. As in most Russian schools, boys wore a military style uniform: black trousers and shirts with brass buttons, belts with brass buckles, and stiff peak caps. The badge, the same on the cap and the buckle, depicted the "caduceus" — the winged staff with two serpents, which is carried by Mercury, the Roman god of commerce, as befits a commercial school. The girls wore neat dark dresses with green pinafores.

I gradually came to like my school, made many friends, and was doing well in my studies, being among the top ten or so. I enjoyed the easy, comfortable classroom atmosphere and the good mature relationship with teachers. Most were very good at their work. By the third or fourth year, my favourite subjects became history, especially ancient and medieval, and literature. Science was fascinating, but frightening because of the ever-present, mysterious mathematics. I never felt comfortable with mathematics; unlike some pupils, I saw no beauty in it. I am amazed at the wide gap which has developed between advanced science and the subjects taught at schools, between the elite group of theoretical physicists and ordinary educated people: Einstein's theory of relativity, although a hundred years old and accepted by the entire scientific world, is not taught at schools and is still understood only by a few. In literature, I was totally awed by Dostoevsky and his powerful writing. I recall crying at Alexei's description of the little boy's funeral in *The Brothers Karamazov*. With a friend who was also entranced by literature, we revelled in the beauty of Russian poetry and searched for new recently published poets. These were such exciting times of discovery.

The one unfortunate thing about my school was the lack of a good playground. Apart from infrequent physical exercise classes, there were no games or sporting activities at the school. Unlike my brother Leo, who seemed uninterested in games or sport and never participated in any, throughout my life I have been keen on sport and games, though I never excelled in any. In the restricted space owned by the school, we still managed to play volley-ball and a ball-and-bat game not unlike baseball. However, during winter most of us spent a good deal of time ice-skating. We never skated on the frozen river as the ice there was very uneven, but in an excellent open air skating-rink. It was great fun, especially on Sundays when a brass band played a selection of Russian waltzes. In summer I swam in the river and became very good at paddling a canoe.

At Home

Our family managed reasonably well in a shared flat. We were on good terms with the other family though I found their little boy, I think he was called Grinia, not an interesting companion. His parents engaged a Russian governess to look after him, who also taught him to play the piano. Sometimes I listened to their lessons. It did not take me long to figure out where the notes on the piano were, and I began surreptitiously to experiment with the instrument. Perhaps this was the early awakening of a desire for music which was soon to play an important role in my life. If my parents were aware of this, they neither said nor did anything.

In the winter of 1925–26 two unpleasant events occurred: first, all four of us were accidentally poisoned with carbon monoxide, having left the fireplace burning at night. We all woke up with the most excruciating headache. Father took us on a horse-sleigh ride in the fresh air to get rid of the poison in our blood. Carbon monoxide poisoning was common in winter time, often with fatal results. We were lucky to be alive. The second unfortunate event was little Grinia contracting scarlatina (scarlet fever), at that time a very severe and dangerous disease which killed many children and adults.[5] Because of its infectious nature, we all moved out temporarily into a nearby hotel where we stayed for about three weeks. Though very ill, Grinia recovered, and none of us caught the infection.

Uncle David

In the spring of 1926, shortly before my tenth birthday, my uncle David, mother's younger brother, arrived from the Middle East to live with us. In 1918, during the civil war in Russia, he escaped from Sevastopol, in the Crimea, on a Greek destroyer and found his way to the Middle East where he earned his living as a violinist. My mother, a woman of strong character, decided that

---

5. Scarlet fever, or scarlatina, a bacterial infection which tends to occur in long-range cycles varying between high and low virulence. In the 1920s it was very virulent resulting in many deaths.

playing the violin in the sleazy cafes of Aleppo and Beirut was not a suitable life for her younger brother, a bachelor. His arrival enlivened our ordinary lives. We listened with undisguised wonder to the tales of his adventures in that exotic land among the Bedouins in the desert, coloured now and then by a few phrases in Arabic. On the wall, in his room, hung a photograph which showed only sand and palms; the caption underneath read, in Hebrew, "Eretz Israel" (Land of Israel). I would sometimes steal into his room to look again at this photograph, with awe and admiration. It was probably responsible for the first stirring in me of a feeling for Jewish nationalism, or Zionism, for shortly afterwards I joined the Jewish Youth organization Hashomer Hatzair (The Young Guardian).

Music School

A day or two after his arrival, uncle David took out his violin and began to practise, and my life changed from that moment. I could barely contain my excitement as I begged my parents to allow me to learn the violin. They consented after my uncle had offered to teach me. A half-sized violin was bought from "Kantilena", a well-known local music shop, and my lessons began at once. I progressed rapidly and recall enjoying my lessons very much. Uncle David settled well into Harbin life and soon found a job with the orchestra employed by the Hotel Moderne — a popular place for "wining and dining". After I had studied the violin for two years, my uncle announced that while he was satisfied with my progress, I should now be enrolled in the Glazunoff Music School (named after the Russian composer) to receive a broader musical education. My parents demurred at first but were persuaded to agree.

The School was located in an ornate, Oriental-style building, formerly occupied by a Jewish school. Music classes were held in the afternoons so that high school students could combine them with their normal school attendance. I was auditioned by the staff of the School, who tested my musical ear and my violin playing, and was admitted to start in the 1928–29 academic year. I immersed myself in my new musical environment with enthusiasm: the instrumental classes, the lessons in harmony and theory, the recitals by the staff and senior students, the school orchestra, and the constant contact with fellow-students, all added a new dimension to my perception of music. The violin lessons were given by the director of the School, a strict, demanding, but understanding teacher. Piano lessons were compulsory for two years; they proved a great asset to me in later years. The demands on my time during the first year were not heavy, but they gradually increased with added subjects, such as Harmony and Theory of Music.

More about Home

At home, life went on pleasantly. In 1927 father acquired a half-share in an optical business on the main street of our district. It was clear that our financial situation had improved, and also that father had abandoned his earlier profession of watch repairing to become an optician. He must have taught himself, for it remained a mystery to me when and how he acquired his new calling. He still liked to tinker with watches and occasionally repair them for close friends. But from then on and for the rest of his life he worked in an optical business. Since sharing a flat was no longer convenient, especially with uncle David joining the household, we rented a spacious flat on the first floor of a two-storey building.

The ground floor was occupied by a bicycle shop owned by a German by the name of Fischer. The sign-board on the shop read (in Russian) "Buying a bicycle? ask Fischer". Indeed, a bicycle was bought for me from Fischer next year on my twelfth birthday. The flat was near father's shop, so he was able to come home for lunch every day. After lunch he would lie down on a settee always with a book in his hand. After a minute or two the book would drop on the floor and he would fall asleep, but would wake up exactly twenty minutes later, get up and walk back to the shop.

Mother was an excellent cook. I now recall with much regret that at the time I did not appreciate sufficiently her culinary skills, nor did I like some of the Jewish dishes that she cooked. To add to this, I had an intense dislike of onions in any form (an aversion which had persisted throughout my life). Leo, on the other hand, made no fuss. Often did I hear that reproachful remark from mother: "You see? Leo likes everything". To be fair, there were mother's dishes which I could never forget: her Passover dishes, like Marcel Proust's "petites madeleines", still invoke memories of exquisite pleasure.[6] Sometime after we had moved into our new flat, we employed a Russian (non-Jewish) woman called Masha as a cook. She was an illiterate, ignorant, but good-natured woman and a good cook. She indulged me, against mother's instructions, by sometimes omitting onions from my meals. She believed that the earth was flat and once told me that her brother had walked to the edge and fallen over. How could such ignorance still exist? I asked myself, but did not try to correct her.

---

6. Marcel Proust, in his novel *Remembrance of Things Past*, wrote of his fondness for the plump little cakes called "petites madeleines" (reputedly called after a girl called Madeleine who made them).

My brother Leo finished school in May 1927. It seems to have been assumed in the family, and accepted by Leo, that he would follow in father's footsteps. Father imported optical goods from Germany and now arranged for Leo to study optometry in Munich and Berlin. While waiting for arrangements to be finalized, Leo helped father in the shop. In 1928 Leo left for Germany. As far as I recall, he did not know the language, not even Yiddish — a corruption of the German — which our parents sometimes used, but which Leo and I never bothered to pick up. That he achieved successfully his goal in Germany was a credit to his diligence and determination. My quiet, complacent brother was made of much sterner stuff than I had imagined. Although six years older than I, Leo was so much part of my world that I missed him terribly. He was away for three years.

Grandfather

A month or two before Leo left for Germany, my grandfather, mother's father, arrived from the Crimea to live with us (another successful effort on my mother's part to gather her folk together). His wife, ill with diabetes for some years, had died a few months earlier and he succeeded in obtaining an exit visa at a time when hardly anyone was allowed to leave Soviet Russia. I had met my grandparents five years earlier when mother and I travelled from Chita to Sevastopol to visit them. On that occasion grandfather spent a great deal of time with me and we had become very close. I was overjoyed to have him with us. A modest gentle man, he was religious but not excessively. He soon discovered that Leo had not had a bar mitzvah ceremony, and that no steps were being made to prepare me for a bar mitzvah due the next year when I would turn thirteen. Bar mitzvah (in Hebrew, literally "son of the commandment") is an initiation of a Jewish boy into adulthood which takes place at the age of thirteen. During the ceremony the boy reads a designated passage from the Torah in the synagogue on the Sabbath. Bar mitzvah is regarded so important that even Jewish families with little religious adherence usually follow this ancient religious tradition. Our family had always been very secular and only the annual high holidays were observed to any extent, when we all went to the synagogue. We did not keep kosher kitchen and never observed the Sabbath. But not to arrange for a bar mitzvah for their two sons was, I believe, very remiss of them. My grandfather certainly thought so and decided to restore the tradition, at least for me. Not wishing to appear as interfering in family matters, he went about it in a quiet, unobtrusive way. He found in me a ready pupil. Within a short time he taught me to read Hebrew,

though like he, I only understood a portion of the text. I learned to read a
prayer book without learning the language.[7] My preparation for the bar mitzvah,
due in 1929, was sketchy but adequate, watched with a mixture of scepticism
and approval by my father. On the appointed day I read the necessary passage
from the Torah and officially became an adult member of my community. I
did not feel like an adult. I looked upon the ceremony as part of a tradition
rather than a religious ceremony. By this time, although not fully formed, my
religious convictions were already leaning towards agnosticism. To reward me
for my diligence during the bar mitzvah preparation, grandfather now made
good his promise — given to me years before in Sevastopol — to teach me
to play the flute. He had played the flute many years before while serving in
the Tsar's army, and now amused himself occasionally by playing little tunes.
I learned quickly and was soon fairly familiar with my new instrument. My
parents were less enthusiastic. After enduring my early violin practices when
the sounds tended to be scratchy and unpleasant, they were now subjected
to a new, but equally disagreeable, sound of a learner-flautist. Thanks to the
reassuring efforts of uncle David, I was allowed to continue with my lessons.
He, himself, also played the clarinet and the saxophone. Familiarity with
another instrument would be useful for my musical education.

At the Music School

My progress was not impressive. There were too many distractions: after
ice-skating for three hours or spending time on the river, it was difficult to
put in an hour or two of hard practice on the violin, and there was still the
homework to be done for high school. The latter was sometimes finished
early in the morning before going to school. How could I possibly blame my
father for complaining, however mildly, that instead of practising the violin
in the afternoon, after school, when he was away at the shop, I practised
in the evening after dinner when he wanted to have a quiet time reading
his book. On several occasions my violin teacher was less than satisfied. At
the end of my second year, to my embarrassment I scored better marks on
the piano than on the violin. Still, I was enjoying my music lessons and the
musical milieu of the school. I met many fine young musicians with whom I
played in small ensembles. Together we explored pathways in music new to

---

7. Hebrew has an alphabet similar to Greek, though its vowels, expressed as dots
and dashes, are placed under the consonants. It is possible to read Hebrew without
knowing the words.

us and listened enraptured and sometimes confused to the strange harmony of Debussy and Ravel, and even stranger, of Stravinsky. In my third year I took a course in orchestration and conducting, though opportunities for the latter were few. The ability to play the flute was now an asset as the Music School encouraged students taking up conducting to learn a second instrument in a different category from their major instrument. I found myself strongly attracted to orchestral playing, and attended as many symphony concerts as time permitted; this interest was to play a decisive role in my later musical life. Sometime early in 1929 I attempted to form a small orchestra. I borrowed music from uncle David and we rehearsed in my home a few times (Rossini's *Barber of Seville* overture and Bizet's selections from *Carmen*), but the orchestra soon discontinued. I do not remember why. At about the same time, my high school had started an orchestra of plucked strings — the Balalaika Orchestra — after a popular Russian folk instrument, the balalaika. Some of my friends at school joined it but I did not, although as a violinist I would have made a passable mandolin player, the two instruments being similar. Foolishly, in my arrogance and ignorance, I treated it with disdain, regarding mandolins and balalaikas unworthy of my attention. I have since learned to like and appreciate plucked strings, amongst which the harp, lute and harpsichord have a tone of unmatched beauty, while years later, the Chinese pipa gave me moments of pure delight.

Summer Holidays

From 1927, mother, Leo (except when he was away in Germany) and I spent summers in one of the stations on the CER, or on the opposite shore of the Sungari River; both offered summer accommodation for rent. Other families did the same and there were always boys and girls to have fun with, to cycle, to hike, to have picnic parties. Father usually joined us on weekends. I loved those weekends, when father was relaxed, and we often walked together discussing my work at school and other subjects. He particularly liked to talk about Russian literature. Father was proud of the fact that he was virtually self-taught, having got no further than primary school: there were too many siblings and too little money in his family. He was very fond of quoting from the Russian classics. Gogol was his special favourite and he would quote long passages from *Dead Souls*, emphasizing some aspect of the novel. In music, however, we had little common ground. Both my parents' taste went only as far as the light operettas of Lehar: I often heard them humming tunes from the *Merry Widow*. Curiously, with mother, although I always felt her closeness and love, I recall no serious discussions between us. I felt her warmth and love especially strongly when I was unwell. At thirteen I was very ill with measles: high fever brought on nightmarish delirium, when mother's touch, as she sat by my side holding my hand and mopping my forehead, was immensely comforting.

One especially memorable summer was spent at a station called Azhihe in 1928. On a preliminary visit, to look for accommodation, mother and I walked past a splendid-looking mansion inside spacious grounds with a large garden. It was obviously the residence of an important person, I thought, and one not likely to offer a room for rent. But with surprising audacity, mother rang the gate bell determined to ask. I was even more surprised when the lady who opened the gate, after a brief exchange of pleasantries, offered to rent us a room for the summer. It appeared that the lady's husband was a very senior officer of the CER and the house was their official residence. The husband was away most of the time attending to his duties and it is possible that his wife was lonely and saw my mother as an agreeable companion. The family had two daughters, aged seven and eight. The girls were closely guarded and cherished and were seldom allowed outside the estate. Perhaps the parents also thought that an older boy like myself might be a suitable playmate-cum-guardian for the girls. Indeed, I proved to be one: the girls were delightful, and I, four years their senior, felt like their wise counsellor. The estate was fabulous, we were made to feel welcome and were very comfortable. Mother and our hostess formed a warm and affectionate friendship.

Her husband we saw but rarely. He was a small kindly-looking man with a trim beard who wore a military style uniform; he was still of the old pre-Soviet staff. On our first meeting after we settled in, he took me to the library and told me I could make full use of it at all times. The library had many books. I was ecstatic; reading was always one of my favourite pastimes. This was the time when I discovered and became virtually obsessed with the novels of Alexandre Dumas (père). The obsession lasted for some two years and only subsided when I had read all his novels. Curiously, I never wondered until much later why my heroes were called musketeers when they seemed to do all their fighting with swords. I still do not know the answer. In the library there were also books by Kipling and Dickens which I also enjoyed (in Russian translations, of course). In June, for my twelfth birthday, I was given a bicycle (Fischer was asked), and with friends I cycled all over Azhihe and in the countryside around. It was a great summer. When mother enquired the next year, she was told that our hosts of the previous year had gone (probably replaced by Soviet staff, we thought) and the rooms were no longer rented.

At High School

My advance from class to class was smooth and uneventful. End of year examinations were generally easy, consisting of one written and one oral session in each subject. Few pupils failed and were required to repeat the year. I made friends among boys and girls, some close ones; together we spent many hours discussing a wide range of subjects. Marcel Proust (in *Remembrance of Things Past*) wrote: "In later life we look at things in a more practical way, in full conformity with the rest of society, but adolescence is the only period in which we learn anything." We were experiencing the truth of this statement. We felt passionately about topics which really mattered. Our young minds were full of wonderful plans for utopian societies, for a united world free of wars, for humanity free of prejudice and injustice. We failed to realize that at the same time the world around us was moving in the opposite direction. Germany was rearming, Italy was also belligerent, dreaming of restoring the might of ancient Rome, in Spain fascism was gaining the upper hand, and nearer to us, Japan, emboldened by the success of its wars against China and Russia, was planning further conquests in Asia.[8] Ideals had little chance against the rise of nationalist forces, and soon we too were swept along by the overpowering influence of nationalism.

I do not wish to give the impression that we were solely occupied with noble impulses and lofty thoughts. We were young, adventurous, and fond of mischief. Like schoolboys all over the world, we were prone at times to play truant, smoke in the toilets, cheat at tests, invent cruel nicknames for our teachers, and engage in other pranks. We were all, boys and girls, also experiencing that exciting awakening of sexuality which brings romance, and the early feelings of love and jealousy, acceptance and rejection. The pleasure of physical contact was intense even if it went no further than gentle fondling and kissing. There was a wonderful sense of anticipation at every new sensation, every new romance. Strong friendships between same and opposite sexes were still valued, but the newly discovered romantic intimacy with the opposite sex gave us a new dimension in our relationships. Although it was uncommon for a boy and a girl in the same class at school to start dating, there were exceptions, and occasionally very lasting relationships developed: a boy and a girl, both classmates of mine, became school sweethearts, pursued the same profession after school, married and spent their lifetime together. My first romantic encounter was not crowned with success: I was thirteen

---

8. Against China in 1894; against Russia in 1904–05.

when I became strongly attracted to a girl my age who lived in the same street (but went to a different school). I recall how I tried to catch sight of her at every opportunity and the thrill I felt when it happened. After we met, she preferred a classmate of mine though she wanted to remain friends with me. The pain of unrequited love lasted for several months, but finally I stepped aside and gallantly accepted the role of a friend. My second venture into romance was more successful, though the initiative came from the girl who was in my class; we were both fifteen, in the 6th Form. She was pretty and popular in the class, but I paid little attention to her initially. It was clear that she developed a sort of a "crush" on me, and soon I found it easy to respond. Although both our work loads were heavy, we managed to spend many happy hours together in a platonic Elysium.[9] To the cynics I would say: "If you have never been in this domain, you have not fully lived."

Touched by Zionism

I have already mentioned that I joined a Jewish youth group, sometime in 1927, I think. It was a benign, wholesome, boy scout–like organization, vaguely associated with the synagogue. I remember little of its activities, probably because I spent little time with the group. It seems that the older Jewish boys, mostly students of the only local tertiary institution, the Harbin Polytechnic, took an interest in it and quietly changed it into Betar, an organization with strongly nationalist Zionist ideology. Betar was a youth movement, founded in 1923 by the Russian-Jewish Zionist Jabotinsky, which split off from mainstream Zionism and advocated a militant approach in the struggle for a Jewish state in Palestine.[10] By 1929 I found myself a keen member of Betar along with many of my Jewish friends, boys and girls. As for our lofty ideals of one world, one people, free of poverty and suffering, the world was clearly not ready for utopia. We followed the trend. Part of Betar's success in recruiting many of us lay in its emphasis on physical fitness. The organization provided a small but adequate sports ground and arranged for training in athletics and games — a popular move among its members. But a bigger factor was probably the ugly aspect of anti-Semitism which tended to alienate the Jewish youths from the Christian, and resulted in many street ambushes and fights between the two. During my childhood, in Chita, I had not been aware of anti-Semitism;

---

9. Elysium or Elysian Fields: in classical mythology a paradise for those favoured by the gods.
10. The name Betar stands for "Brit Yosef Trumpeldor", after the Jewish Zionist hero, Joseph Trumpeldor, who was killed in Palestine in 1920 during fighting with Arabs.

perhaps I was too young to recognize it, or it may have been less pronounced in Siberia. In Harbin, it was too obvious to be ignored, and it tended to reinforce Betar's message that, although Russian in language and cultural background, our true home and future lay in a Jewish state in Palestine. At the same time, by the early 1930s, some of the older Christian boys were attracted to the German Nazi movement, which further increased the enmity between the Jewish and Christian youths. Young men in brown uniform with the swastika on their arm-bands were beginning to appear on the streets of Harbin. It must be said, however, that girls on either side seldom, if ever, expressed or showed signs of intolerance. Also, the Jewish and Christian boys from the same school coexisted well and made friends easily. Familiarity does not always breed contempt!

Events in 1931

Leo came back from Germany just in time for our parents' 25th (silver) wedding anniversary, celebrated by a large dinner party on 6 June 1931. Our new cook, a Chinese man who had replaced Masha, excelled himself by preparing a marvellous menu for some thirty guests.

Leo, now a fully qualified optometrist, began working in father's shop while considering his future. Three years in Europe had done wonders for him: from a shy, quiet, hesitant teenager, he had become a self-assured, outgoing young man, and an excellent ballroom dancer. It was wonderful to have him back and the family listened with great interest to his "exploits" in Germany. For me the year marked a difficult period in my life. I was fifteen, I had just entered my final year at high school, the work load was heavy and it had become difficult, if not impossible to continue at the Music School. I left it with a heavy heart, thankful for the three marvellous rewarding years I had spent there, and knowing that I should cherish the happy memory of those years for the rest of my life.

In July 1931, a large family — my father's relatives — arrived in Harbin from Soviet Russia on their way to Argentina. They crossed the border into Manchuria illegally at considerable risk. They had entry visas into Argentina sent to them by relatives living there. During their two weeks' stay in Harbin, we saw a great deal of them, and for father it was a happy experience as he had not been in touch with them for many years. Before leaving for Argentina, they told father they would write to him about conditions there and that perhaps he should think about that country as a possible future place of residence. In fact, my parents had been concerned, as yet in a mild detached way, about our local conditions, as disturbing signs of instability were beginning to appear.

In Manchuria the political situation was worsening. The Japanese, who already had control of South Manchuria, began to make plans for the occupation of the rest of the province. As a preliminary move, to establish a pretext for intervention, they began to destabilize the area by introducing drugs and encouraging gang activities. In Harbin, crime, kidnapping, and general lawlessness were on the increase. The Soviets, unwilling or unable to oppose the Japanese, were preparing to negotiate the sale of their half-share of the Railway. Some of the Soviet citizens began going home and business was suffering.

The Symphony Orchestra

The summer of 1931 had yet another important and, for me, happy development. As the Soviet financial support of cultural activities ceased, a cultural vacuum developed. Then, in a surprising show of solidarity, almost the entire Harbin musical fraternity formed a self-supporting symphony orchestra with an experienced and popular conductor at the head. The violin section contained some of the best violinists in Harbin, uncle David among them. He advised me to apply to join the orchestra for the summer season when I would be on vacation. This I did and was accepted. The Orchestra opened its summer season of 1931 with a magnificent concert and continued with a highly successful series of performances held in the Railway Club Building, either in the indoor concert hall or in the garden. It was for me a memorable summer vacation. At fifteen I was playing in a professional symphony orchestra among Harbin's finest musicians, and gaining experience in orchestral playing beyond my wildest dreams. I left the Orchestra at the end of the summer when school resumed — my final year. Alas, any hopes we might have had that the Symphony Orchestra, conceived in such noble spirit, might continue to flourish, were not fulfilled. By the end of the year, dissensions, petty jealousies, and back-room intrigues had caused the Orchestra to disband.

Although I left the Music School, my musical training had by no means stopped. I continued violin lessons privately with my violin teacher, the director of the Music School, though at a slower rate than before. Then, in the autumn of 1931, a new opportunity opened for my flute-playing which I could not resist: a small semi-professional orchestra, formed at the Railway Club by the Soviet members, invited me to join as the principal flute. The rehearsals, although held once a week in the evenings, put a good deal of strain on me, and even more so on my parents who at one point threatened to confiscate my flute. Only the intervention of uncle David saved me from the very embarrassing situation of letting down the orchestra at its concert. Playing first flute was for me a tremendous experience, though I was aware that my violin-playing suffered as a result. I was the only non-Soviet, stateless person in the orchestra, and it must have been uncomfortable for the orchestra's management to address their rehearsal reminders to me as "Mister" instead of "Comrade", as they did to their own members.

Harbin, however, was not content to remain without a symphony orchestra, and in 1932 a freshly revived symphony orchestra arose from the "ashes" of the previous one, and another summer season was about to start. I enrolled at once. My violin teacher, the Music School's director was the new conductor and uncle David was made the concertmaster. The Orchestra opened the new summer season with Glazunoff's Triumphant Overture and Tchaikovsky's 5th Symphony, performing again at the Railway Club. I was placed as assistant principal of the second violins, but my enjoyment was somewhat marred by the principal sitting next to me, an elderly experienced professional musician, but a morose unhappy man who grumbled continuously. Rescue came unexpectedly when a third flute was needed (there are normally two) for the performance of Tchaikovsky's "Nutcracker Suite" and I was temporarily transferred to the flute section. Then, after a bizarre accident in which the second flautist, an innocent bystander, was wounded by a stray bullet in a street shooting, I was told to take his place and finished the season in that position. My flute playing benefited enormously from the help and advice I received from the first flautist, an excellent professional musician.

The Flood

The year 1932 proved to be eventful for Harbin and for Manchuria in general. In February the Japanese marched into North Manchuria and occupied Harbin. There was little fighting, but the adverse impact on life in Harbin was considerable. Shortly afterwards, Japan proclaimed the establishment in Manchuria of the Empire of Manchukuo and installed the last emperor of China, Pu Yi, as the emperor of Manchukuo. The new "empire" was, of course, nothing but a puppet state of Japan. There were some feeble protests from the Western powers, and a futile discussion at the League of Nations, but no action was taken. It was the beginning of the policy of appeasement, which was to guide the Western powers for the next several years and which would inevitably lead, in 1939, to the Second World War.

In July 1932, the Sungari River broke its banks and flooded Pristan, our district, to a metre or more in some places. The higher-lying districts, like New Town, were spared. Floods in Harbin had happened in the past, but not in the past decade. Our flat was on the first floor (second storey) and therefore unaffected, but we were effectively marooned unless one was prepared to wade in waist-deep water. Most of the shops had to be closed including father's and so he stayed at home. Now my skill with a canoe came in very handy. With commendable foresight, at the very beginning of flooding, I managed to hire a canoe (later unavailable as the flood progressed) and was now able, alone in my family, to paddle around freely and buy provisions for us at the few shops, in less affected areas, which were still open. In the current gloomy confinement, I must have secretly enjoyed my relative freedom of movement and my position as family provider. By the end of August the waters had gradually receded and life slowly returned to reasonably normal.

Crossroads

In May 1932 I graduated from high school and in the ensuing parties and other forms of celebration thought little of what lay ahead. But soon, when the excitement of graduation had subsided, I and many of my classmates knew we stood at the crossroads of important decisions. We were out of high school and had to make plans for the future. Some of my friends, in a newly found enthusiasm for communism, went back to Soviet Russia. It was a disastrous decision: most of them, as we learned later, were imprisoned or shot, or vanished without trace; one, a close friend of mine, committed suicide. Others, members of the Betar, went to Palestine as soon as visas, which were on a strict quota basis, were available. There is no doubt that Betar's avowed aim was to enthuse young Jews to migrate to Palestine as pioneers to work on the land. In that it was successful to a considerable degree. I certainly did not wish to go back to Russia, and I was partly disillusioned with Betar. I remained a Zionist at heart, but could not embrace entirely Betar's ideology. At home we discussed my future at several lengthy sessions. I was naturally inclined towards music as a profession. Predictably, my parents were against it. In this attitude they were no different from other Jewish parents whose concern that their children should embark on a good and secure profession is proverbial.[11] They could afford to send me to university, they argued, where I could choose a more rewarding occupation. This time uncle David, my mentor and friend who always supported me, was firmly on their side. Although I was competent on two instruments (piano did not count), he pointed out, I was

---

11. From the vast store of Jewish jokes, there comes one about a mother with two little boys who meet a friend in the street. The friend makes a complimentary remark about the boys and asks their age. "The doctor is three and the lawyer is four," replies the mother.

not good enough to pursue a career as a soloist; as a rank-and-file musician I should find life difficult and insecure. It would be foolish and imprudent to refuse an opportunity for a profession with a university education. I knew that David was correct in his assessment of my musical ability and, after some soul-searching, I agreed to follow my parents' advice. I was, however, unsure as to what that "good and secure" profession might be. In the final short list, of medicine and engineering, I was inclined, but by no means strongly, towards medicine. I tried to reassure myself that I was not abandoning music altogether, that it would remain my constant companion, a source of challenge and enjoyment, and that I would return to it wherever and whenever possible. I believe that this promise was largely fulfilled.

In the worsening political and economic climate in Harbin, my parents were clearly becoming worried. At the same time the letters from relatives in Argentina were very optimistic. They were doing well, they wrote, and if father and mother decided to move they could arrange for entry visas without any difficulty. I am sure that my father, and perhaps my mother as well, were beginning to realize that the good days of Harbin, as far as we were concerned, were numbered and that migration again had become a possibility. When medicine was first discussed as my possible choice of a profession, Edinburgh was mentioned as I had discovered that it had a famous school of medicine, but as time went on, it was decided that we should look for a nearer place and Hong Kong University, in which the medical faculty had earned a good reputation, became the preferred choice. By October 1932 our plans were made. Leo and I would travel to Shanghai — Leo to explore the possibility of starting an optical business there, and I to enter an English school to prepare for entry examinations into Hong Kong University. My parents' plan was to stay in Harbin for another year or two and then migrate to Argentina. Uncle David left for Shanghai in September. In October Leo and I followed and a new chapter in my life began.

Postscript

In May 1978, I visited China with a friend. The Cultural Revolution was over and there ensued a period of thaw in Chinese-foreign relations. The trip was organized by the New China News Agency and, responding to a special request by me, we were allowed to visit Harbin, which was out of bounds to foreigners. It was a nostalgic return to a place where I spent the formative years of my life, but I felt no sadness. The streets were thronged with Chinese people, who mostly looked healthy, happy and cheerful; no foreign faces were to be seen anywhere. Wherever we went, people were excited at seeing foreigners and many followed us, clapping their hands and wanting to shake hands with us. We were overcome by goodwill and friendliness. In Pristan, there was little change except that the buildings were more dilapidated than I could remember. All the former familiar landmarks were still there — the main buildings, the former shops, the houses where we lived, and the schools, music and high school, which I attended. As I stood in front of our house, where Mr Fischer once sold bicycles, and took a photo of the house, a young man approached me and asked, in Chinese of course, why I was interested in this old undistinguished house. I replied in my halting Mandarin that I used to live in this house forty-five years ago. He was astounded as he had no idea that foreigners once lived in Harbin.

The Harbin I once knew, that once was my home, was no longer there, but instead there seemed to be a new, vibrant place with a new community, looking towards their future.

3

ETON IN CHINA

"That's the reason they're called lessons,"
the Gryphon remarked:
"because they lessen from day to day."

Lewis Carroll (1832–1898), *Alice in Wonderland*

Destination Shanghai

In October of 1932, my brother Leo and I left our home in Harbin, North China, where I had graduated from high school and where I had concurrently attended a music school for three years, studying violin, piano and conducting. I was sixteen, Leo twenty-two. Our destination was Shanghai, on the eastern coast of Central China's Jiangsu (Kiangsu) Province. The circumstances and reasons for our departure are described in my essay "Manchurian Adolescence".

My main, indeed, my sole, purpose of coming to Shanghai was to enroll in an English school where I would learn English and prepare myself for the matriculation examinations for entry to the University of Hong Kong to study medicine.[1] In the summer of 1932, I met Ben who had been a year ahead of me at high school and was then on vacation from Shanghai where he was studying in an English school, the Public and Thomas Hanbury School for Boys, and was preparing for matriculation examinations to the University of Hong Kong. At high school Ben was a brilliant student especially in maths and science. He came from a poor Russian/Jewish family and had obtained a

---

1. The University of Hong Kong was established in 1911, its medical faculty stemming directly from the Hong Kong College of Medicine founded in 1887. Acknowledged as the foremost bearer of Western culture and science in the Orient, its medical degrees are recognized throughout the British Commonwealth.

scholarship to the University of Hong Kong established by a rich Sephardi Jew with widespread business interests in the Far East. What Ben told me about his school planted an idea in my mind to follow in his path and try to enroll there as well. In the meantime I began to attend English language classes at the YMCA college. Although I had had some English lessons at my high school, I retained little of that, but the YMCA was a different matter. After two months of concentrated and very productive teaching, I made significant progress. By the time I left Harbin for Shanghai, I could communicate and make myself understood in English, even if somewhat hesitantly.

Since by this time my parents were already making tentative plans to emigrate to Argentina, it might seem strange that I was not going with them. I was only sixteen and it would have been natural for me to follow them. Yet I recall no such thoughts: it seemed as if I had already firmly resolved to enter a British university. Even stranger was the fact that my parents voiced no objection to my plan and had accepted my decision, which would very likely take me on a different course in life from the rest of my family. Could it be that, faced with their own uncertain future, they decided to let me pursue my own destiny?

Leo and I travelled by train to Dairen, the southern port of Manchuria, where we embarked on a Japanese passenger ship operating between Dairen and Shanghai, with a short stopover at Tsingtao, a former German possession. The ship journey took two days. The whole of southern Manchuria was under Japanese control since the Russo-Japanese War of 1904–05, and was now incorporated into the newly created Manchukuo Empire, effectively a Japanese protectorate. Several seaside resorts around Dairen, scrupulously maintained by the Japanese, were very popular with summer holiday-makers from around the region. I recall our sea journey to Shanghai as enjoyable; we found several old friends on board and made some new ones. In Shanghai we were met by uncle David who had arrived in Shanghai a month before us. A room was reserved for Leo and me at a boarding house, run by a Russian family, in the French Concession.

Shanghai

Shanghai was exciting. The size of the city, the traffic comprising vehicles of every possible type, the streets teeming with people, European and Chinese, and the large imposing buildings, some in grand neo-classical style, lining the waterfront — the famous Bund — these were all beyond anything I had imagined. It was a new world opening before my eyes. To understand how a

Chinese city had become a great modern metropolis, one has to look at its history, especially during the preceding one hundred years.

Shanghai means "upon the sea" but in fact it is not. It stands on the banks of the muddy Huangpu River which opens into the mouth of the mighty Jiang (Yangtze) River some twenty kilometres from the East China Sea. Like many Chinese cities, Shanghai has an early history going back many centuries, but its real importance dates from the time it was opened to foreign trade in circumstances particularly humiliating to the Chinese. Britain and China engaged in armed conflict between 1839 and 1842 in what became known as the First Opium War, in which the Chinese, with their antiquated methods of warfare and ineffective weapons, were defeated on land and at sea. This phase of what became a protracted conflict ended with the Treaty of Nanking (Nanjing), 1843, by the terms of which China opened to foreign trade the five ports of Canton (Guangzhou), Amoy (Xiamen), Foochow (Fuzhou), Ningpo (Ningbo) and Shanghai, known as the Treaty Ports, where foreigners might reside and trade.[2] Among the five, Shanghai had a phenomenal rise, growing within the next fifty years into a great commercial centre.

Gradually foreign traders developed small autonomous settlements, usually referred to as Concessions, dominated by the British, American and French, in which they were not subject to Chinese law — a political status usually described as "extraterritoriality". In 1863 the British and American concessions amalgamated into the Shanghai International Settlement, soon to be joined by several other nations. The French remained separate as the French Concession. The International Settlement was managed by the Shanghai Municipal Council which was almost entirely British in character. It was an anomalous situation in which a Chinese city with an overwhelmingly Chinese population was ruled by foreigners subject to their own law. The Municipal Council continued to function until December 1941 when the Japanese occupied Shanghai at the outbreak of the war in the Pacific. It was also effectively the end of the International Settlement and foreign extraterritoriality.

Shanghai, sometimes referred to as the "Paris of the East" because of its exotic nightlife, gambling and racing, as well as its rich cultural life, was certainly a successful enterprise in which foreign expatriates enjoyed a comfortable life and prosperity while the Chinese provided the backbone of the labour force. Behind its exterior of glamour and glitter, however, lay the ugly side of exploitation and poverty. I can do no better than quote Robin

---

2. By the same treaty Hong Kong Island was ceded to Britain as a permanent possession.

Hutcheon: "The Europeans in that city [Shanghai] for the most part lived a detached existence, performing useful services and making big profits. Except for occasional emergencies, however, they were largely untouched by events. Not for them the grinding poverty of the masses who endured the hardship of civil war, unemployment, disease, squalor, crime and later, the all-out Japanese attack on the city. There were two worlds side by side: the world within the international settlement and the world outside. While the foreigners lived a comfortable and largely trouble-free existence, China played out its tragic search for nationhood and national identity."[3] Not all the foreigners, however, were rich and happy: there were scores of Russian refugees, mostly stateless, and although some had managed to make a success of their lives, many lived on the edge of poverty. China, with its lax immigration rules, proved a haven to refugees, initially to Russians fleeing from the Revolution since the early 1900s, and later, in the 1930s, to German/Jewish refugees from Nazi Germany.

Years later, I sometimes wondered whether, as a young teenager at the time, I was aware of that aspect of Shanghai identity. I was, of course, preoccupied with my immediate problems of learning English and getting admission to a university, but I do recall reflecting upon stories I had heard of the city's opium and vice dens, of child labour, and of the appalling treatment to which the Chinese were subjected in their own city.[4] I was also aware that many Russian refugees who had settled in Shanghai were poor, earning meagre wages, their daughters working as dance hostesses in cabarets of doubtful reputation. When later I heard the "old China hands" reminiscing nostalgically about the "good old days in Shanghai", I thought their perceptions of that period insensitive and shallow.

After a year's sojourn in Shanghai, I came to dislike its climate. Unlike Chita and Harbin, where I grew up, and where the seasons were well defined, Shanghai, being a coastal city, had a winter which was neither cold nor hot, the rare snowfall soon turned into mud and slush; summers were hot and humid, and the other seasons were not noted for pleasant weather or temperature. Although the city boasted fine buildings in a variety of architectural styles, it had few parks and, in my view, insufficient greenery adorning its streets.

---

3. *Shanghai Customs* by Robin Hutcheon, p. 4. Galisea Publications, Australia, 2000.

4. It was reputed that initially segregation was enforced on public transport in the International Settlement, but certainly there was no evidence of this during my stay in Shanghai.

It could never be a city of my choice to live in, I thought, but at the time it served my purpose well — to learn English and to prepare for university entrance examinations.

Search for a Guardian

A week after our arrival in Shanghai, Leo and I presented ourselves at the Public and Thomas Hanbury School and said that we wished to enquire about my admission to the School. We were ushered into the headmaster's office. Mr Crow, the headmaster, was a tall handsome middle-aged man with a kindly face. He had recently arrived from England to take over from the previous headmaster who had retired. I explained that I had already graduated from a Russian high school in Harbin, but wished to enroll in his school in order to learn English and to take entry examinations to Hong Kong University. Mr Crow enquired about my residence and family, and it soon became clear that to be admitted into the school I had to have either a parent or a legal guardian who was a ratepayer and of adequate residential record in the International Settlement. Neither my brother nor my uncle had either of these qualifications. It was not merely a matter of fees, but also of responsibility for the health and behaviour of a student. Leo and I were incredibly naïve to have imagined that I should be admitted simply on our word.

Crestfallen we left the school. We had no close friends or relatives in Shanghai; in short, we knew no one in Shanghai who could possibly act as my guardian. The new academic year at the school was due to start in January (1933), only two months away, and I could see no solution to my problem. Coaching by private study was a possibility, but I felt strongly that I needed full-time exposure to the English language and the benefits of a curriculum designed for the matriculation examinations which only an English school could offer. Feeling desperate, I wrote to my parents in Harbin describing my dilemma. In the meantime, uncle David made a useful practical suggestion, unrelated to my immediate concern: he had recently secured a job — leading a small orchestra in a Russian-owned cabaret called "Kavkaz" (Caucasus). Why not join as a second violin in his band and earn a little money while waiting for a solution to my problem? It seemed a sensible idea. Dressed in a hired dinner jacket, I joined his orchestra playing light music during dinner time, from 8 to 10 p.m., after which the place was turned into a dance-hall and I was packed off home. I enjoyed the attention of the young, pretty dance-hostesses who made quite a fuss over a sixteen-year-old lad in the orchestra. The rest of my time was now spent working on my English, mostly with a grammar book and a dictionary, and practising the violin. In November

Leo went back to Harbin. He had gathered the necessary information about starting a business in Shanghai and now wanted to discuss the matter with father. I contacted my friend Ben and one or two other boys whom I had known before, and felt less lonely.

When there seemed to be no solution to my predicament, a letter arrived from mother which offered a ray of hope. Three years ago (1929), she wrote, during a brief holiday with a friend in Dairen spent mostly shopping, a man rushed up to her and said he recognized her. He then revealed himself as the escaped prisoner-of-war whom she had sheltered and then helped on his way in Chita in 1918.[5] He told mother that when he reached Shanghai, he saw great opportunities there and settled down. A pharmacist by profession, he now had a well-established, successful pharmacy in Shanghai. Professing eternal gratitude, he said that if he could ever repay her the kindness and compassion she had showed him, it would make him very happy. "Find this pharmacist," mother wrote, "and I am sure he will help you." Unfortunately she remembered neither his name nor the name of his pharmacy.

There was no time to lose. I decided to start my search in the popular shopping area of the main artery of the International Settlement — the Bubbling Well Road. The first pharmacy I chose, if I recall correctly, was called "Regal". I entered and asked the girl at the counter if I could see the owner, and added that it was a personal matter. She went inside and a minute or two later a short portly man came out. He looked not unkindly at me with a questioning expression on his face. Not knowing his background, I spoke in English. My opening gambit was first to apologize for disturbing him, then asking whether he was on holiday in Dairen in 1929. Looking surprised, he answered that he was. I could feel my heart beating faster; could I have been so lucky as to find the right man on my first try? He had a similar accent to mine, but I decided to continue in English. "Then you must know my mother, Madam Bard, whom, I believe, you met on that occasion"; I do not know why I called her "Madam" and not "Mrs". Then came surprise and shock. He did not meet anyone by that name and the name was totally unfamiliar to him. I was taken aback. The man looked pleasant, agreeable. Why did he deny it? I muttered some excuse and started for the door, confused and a little angry. Then I heard him call back. He said he suddenly remembered that there was another pharmacist in Dairen that summer ("A summer of pharmacists!" I thought). And then he added: "His pharmacy is two blocks

5. Described in "Siberian Childhood".

away on the opposite side of the street — the Cathay Pharmacy — perhaps he is your man." Then, obviously overcome by curiosity, he asked me what it was all about, and when I explained briefly — the matter of a guardian — he said, "If things do not work out, come back and we will talk about it." This from a total stranger. "There are good people in this world!" I thought.[6]

Things did work out. Inside the Cathay Pharmacy a large corpulent man stood behind the counter. He had a double chin and a very kind benevolent face, which for some strange reason reminded me of Santa Claus. At the first mention of my mother's name he rushed out from behind the counter and nearly knocked me off my feet as he gathered me in a huge bear hug and kept repeating how happy he was to meet me. He was Mr Baruksen. Two days later I was back at school, this time accompanied by Mrs Baruksen who introduced herself as my guardian. Everything was arranged swiftly and efficiently. Mr Crow called a senior master into his office and after a brief discussion with him, informed me that since I had already graduated from a high school, they were placing me into the 6th Form (final year), provisionally for three weeks to find out if I could cope at that level. If not, the 5th Form might be more suitable for me. This both delighted and worried me: delighted because, if I managed to stay in the 6th Form, I should be able to sit for the matriculation examinations in November 1933 (by this time I had found out that the Hong Kong University intended to shift the start of the academic year in 1935 from January to September, which would mean an extra nine months of waiting). Worried, because I had only eleven months to prepare for the examinations in a foreign language.

I now had not only a guardian, but a family where I was welcomed like one of its members. Mr and Mrs Baruksen were warmhearted wonderful people. They had two boys, the younger about my age, but both boys went to a French school. Although both spoke English well enough, the language at home was either Czech or French. The new academic year at school was due to start in January, just three weeks away, and I threw myself into work even harder than before, determined to try to stay in the 6th Form. My friend Ben started school the previous year in the 5th Form and now we would be together in the 6th Form. Just before Christmas I finished my evening work at "Kavkaz" with a small party and was kissed goodbye by the friendly hostesses who professed to be saddened by my departure.

---

6. I never saw him again. By coincidence he turned out later to be a distant relative of my wife.

Public and Thomas Hanbury School for Boys

Thomas (later Sir Thomas) Hanbury (1832–1907) hailed from a prominent English Quaker family involved in a variety of mercantile and philanthropic activities. As a young man of twenty-one, he set up as a silk merchant in Shanghai and soon built up a prosperous business. He also became an ardent horticulturist and retired in northern Italy, where his gardens at La Mortola became renowned throughout the country.

Less known were Hanbury's efforts in promoting education. Around 1870, a few years after the establishment of the Shanghai Municipal Council, Thomas Hanbury was responsible for establishing a School for Eurasian Children which a few years later received grants from the Council. In 1890 the School was taken over by the Council to become The Public and Thomas Hanbury School for Boys, the first municipal school for the sons of foreign, i.e. non-Chinese, nationals. Located in Hongkew, a northern district of Shanghai, the School was housed in a splendid building with ample grounds and was well equipped. It had a boarders' section, an Officers' Training Corps, the Scouts, and laid strong emphasis on sport. The teachers were mainly from Britain. Over the years the School became increasingly cosmopolitan, but in all other respects was a typical English public school.

As is generally known, the so-called public schools in England are in fact private, fee-paying, independent schools. Some like Eton and Harrow have become famous as the breeding grounds of England's statesmen and leaders. There is little doubt that the Public and Thomas Hanbury School, far removed from its home soil, strove to emulate what was best in a typical English public school.

Back at School

In the first week of January 1933 I became a schoolboy again. It felt strange. Only six months before I had finished high school in Harbin. I was happy. I thought I was through with school. We celebrated, threw our school caps in the air. And there I was — back at school, sitting behind a desk. Unlike my first day at school in Harbin, I do not remember what happened on the first day at this school. During the first few days I observed my classmates, as they surely must have observed me — the new boy. They were a polyglot bunch, among them an Italian, a Spaniard, a Greek, a Latvian, two Chinese (both American subjects), a Japanese, a German, several Sephardi Jews, a few English and Scottish boys; some, I discovered later, were Eurasian. All spoke one common language — English, in which they seemed completely fluent. They were mostly friendly and within days I began to feel at home.

Not surprisingly I found many features of the school strange and very different from my old Russian school in Harbin. Classes started at 8.30 a.m. with a parade on the school ground commanded by the school captain — the most senior boy in the school. We then marched into our respective classes. Relations with teachers were strict and formal, unlike the liberal, mature atmosphere in Harbin. The boys called each other by surnames, which I found very odd. The system of prefects was altogether abhorrent to me, while punishment such as caning, or slapping hands with a ruler, seemed to me outlandish, cruel and primitive. It must be added, however, that Mr Crow, the newly appointed headmaster, had abolished caning for 6th formers, at the same time making uniforms for 6th formers optional. There were also many positive features of the school which I liked: the variety of activities offered, the excellent laboratories which made science so interesting, and the strong emphasis on sport. The School was divided into four Houses: Clare, Hertford, Lincoln and Pembroke, which encouraged a healthy competition within the School in areas such as chess, debate and sports. In spite of the unfamiliar features of the English school system and its more authoritarian rules than the ones I had previously experienced, I found myself liking my new school more and more. Was it, I wondered, that at some stage in our life we all like a certain amount of strict discipline over us? What was certain is that I was gradually embracing this atmosphere and liking it.

I was in the 6th Form on probation and I became worried when a test in geometry was announced just three days after I had started school. The subject was still fresh in my mind from my high school in Harbin, but I had no idea how the solutions were presented in English. My friend Ben, who was now in the same class with me, came to my rescue: he spent an hour with me explaining the format of a theorem solution used in an English school. I passed the test, but my status in the 6th Form was still in doubt, as two weeks later the class was given an essay to write. I struggled hard over my essay, but I knew that I was not yet good enough for this task. When Mr Rood, the English master, handed back the corrected essays, I did not receive mine, but was told to see him after the class. Dear, kind Mr Rood informed me gently that my essay was uncorrectable and that he would give me extra coaching after school during the next two or three weeks. He did not report me to the headmaster and to my great relief I was allowed to continue in the 6th Form. The extra coaching bore fruit, as two months later my first corrected essay earned me five marks out of ten.

Living on My Own

I continued to live in my rented room on Rue Bourgeat, in a dreary part of the French Concession. I remember nothing of my landlord, or was it a landlady? I hardly ever saw them. But I do remember lonely dinners at a nearby restaurant, and the long evenings spent alone in my room studying. If my social life was limited, it was not entirely absent. I visited my guardians regularly; the Baruksen boys sometimes took me to the YMCA for a swim in an indoor pool. Ben remained a close friend and I also made several good friends among my classmates, who invited me to their homes. On Sundays I sometimes went to Jessfield Park, in the western part of the International Settlement, to look at the beautiful display of flowers or simply sit on a bench with a book.

Of course, I saw my uncle David, though not as frequently as I would have liked. He was still working in the "Kavkaz" cabaret, but found time occasionally to supervise my violin practice. Then, just before the summer of 1933, by a stroke of luck, he obtained a position in a viola section of the Shanghai Municipal Orchestra — a steady, well-paid job with regular hours of rehearsals and concerts — and so much more preferable to playing in a cabaret. After starting his new job, once or twice a month he would take me to a concert, through the stage door, and I was able to hear some of the greatest musicians in the world who came to perform with the Orchestra. I missed playing in a full symphony orchestra and recalled nostalgically my two summer seasons with the Harbin Symphony Orchestra.[7] Leo was still in Harbin and I missed him very much.

The School

My lodgings were a good six or seven miles from the school. I had my bicycle sent from Harbin and rode to school, skilfully threading my way through the heavy morning traffic of rickshaws, cars, trolley buses and trams. The lunch break at the School was from 12 to 2. I usually spent it either in the school library or in the cafeteria opposite the school, where usually the same bunch of boys from the School would gather. The cafeteria was owned by a short and very fat Greek of genial disposition, who was passionately fond of opera. He did not mind us spending much time but little money at his establishment; I think he rather liked our company. The gramophone was continuously playing records of famous singers. Galli-Curci and Gigli were his special favourites. The atmosphere was pleasant. We ate our sandwiches and sometimes did our

---

7. Described in "Manchurian Adolescence".

homework, while listening to the marvellous arias, often accompanied by the gentle humming of our Greek host. I must confess that in my previous musical education I paid little attention to voice, and those midday breaks at the cafeteria, with operatic accompaniment, awakened in me a taste for singing which eventually developed into a deep admiration of voice as a great musical instrument. Classes resumed in the afternoon at 2 p.m. and went till 4 p.m. Wednesdays were half-days, while Saturdays were devoted mainly to sport.

My progress at school, I felt, was satisfactory. I had no problems with maths and science. My essays were improving and within six months I was getting 7 and 8, and once, a triumph, received 9; no one in my class, as far as I know, ever gained 10. But English literature was still difficult, especially since my vocabulary was far from adequate. On one occasion, during an English class, I stood up and asked "What is a beetle?" The whole class erupted into laughter, to my intense embarrassment. Mr Rood raised his hand and the class became quiet. He calmly explained what "a beetle" was. After this episode, I resolved never again to reveal openly my lexigraphic deficiency. If I encountered an unfamiliar word, the simple and obvious course was to look it up in a dictionary. We were studying Shakespeare's *Macbeth* and Milton's *Paradise Lost*. In spite of the difficulties encountered, I enjoyed the rich language which was a revelation to me. I knew about Shakespeare from my Russian school, and it was exciting to be reading his work in the original.

I was adjusting well to the School's system, accepting features of the school which were initially so foreign to me, and enjoying the class atmosphere and the new friendships, the fine facilities of the school and especially the multiple sporting activities. There was one feature, however, I could not come to terms with — the prefect system. As a result, a confrontation was inevitable. It came one day when I was making my way to the library. I was stopped by a prefect, a Japanese boy from my class called Doi, in a corridor which was apparently out of bounds to pupils at that particular time. He promptly ordered me to write five hundred lines "I must not, etc". Politely but firmly I refused, saying that I had no way of reaching the library except through this corridor, and that anyway I had no time for writing such nonsense. The same afternoon I was brought before the headmaster. Mr Crow, a sympathetic man with a reputation for fairness and progressive ideas, listened to me but declared that the authority of a prefect must be observed. I then suggested a compromise: I would write five hundred lines from our set book *Macbeth*. Doi agreed, Mr Crow approved, and the matter was settled. As far as I know, my tactic did not create a precedent.

Sports, Games and Music

Saturday was sports day and I enjoyed and participated in games and athletics, though with little success. At rugby, I was probably the only player who never learned the rules, and I recall one game in which I ran a lot, was in a scrum every few minutes it seemed, but never had a ball passed to me. Mr Tingle, our sports master, was an Australian, short and strongly built. He used to be a lightweight boxing champion. His nose was flat and slightly crooked, no doubt from countless boxing bouts. He tried to impart to me the intricacies of cricket, but without success; I could not see the purpose of so many ways of hitting or stopping the ball. In Harbin I played, and was good at, a Russian bat and ball game, a fast game which resembled baseball more than it did cricket, but I found the latter too slow and uninteresting.[8] I had some talent for long-distance running and basketball, but my only real achievement in school sports was in tennis. I was elected captain of the Pembroke House tennis team and we won the inter-house competition. On one occasion when I arrived at school I was informed by Mr Tingle that I was to run a cross-country race. Surprised, since it was not Saturday, I was not allowed to refuse. It was still cold, in March I think, and the ground very slushy. It was not an enjoyable run, but I managed to place twelfth out of more than forty runners, which was not bad at all.

The music master, Mr Kane, was a strict, somewhat unpredictable and generally feared man. He was, however, pleasantly disposed to me after he discovered that my violin playing and general knowledge of music was far in advance of the other boys. At the same time, I discovered to my delight that the Italian boy in my class called Puppo, a member of my tennis team, also played the violin; his father was a professional violinist and the principal of the second violins in the Shanghai Municipal Orchestra. Moreover, we both could play the piano. Thereupon Puppo and I devised a musical number which delighted Mr Kane immensely. Puppo and I would come out on stage, myself carrying the violin. We would perform a couple of pieces with myself on the violin and Puppo accompanying me on the piano. We would then retire and reappear on the stage, this time Puppo with the violin and I at the piano. This would usually bring the house down. So popular was this that Mr Kane took us to several schools to perform this act. Puppo and I also played in the school's small band, which, however, was of poor quality.

---

8. After the war Mr Tingle turned up in Hong Kong where he opened a private sports school teaching young children a whole range of sporting activities. My children went to him for training, thus becoming his second generation pupils.

Summer Vacations

July and August brought the long summer vacations. Ben and I went back to Harbin, travelling from Dairen to Harbin on a goods train to save money. I arrived home unannounced and unexpected, just for the lark of it I think, and it was something to see the expression of utter surprise on mother's face when she opened the door. It was wonderful to see my family again, to be surrounded by the familiar loving faces. Having spoken very little Russian in the preceding months, I found it a little strange to revert to it now. I brought with me my Shakespeare and Milton and read parts of them every day. When I was invited to play tennis with some English staff members of the Harbin branch of the Hong Kong and Shanghai Bank, I was surprised to find that I lapsed back into English quickly and easily.

Some of my old friends were still around and with them I again enjoyed some of Harbin's summer pleasures – swimming and canoeing on the river. I was also in time to attend my old school's Graduates' Ball to which all alumni were invited. It was a most enjoyable occasion. It was exciting to see the familiar classrooms, to feel again the old atmosphere. How different it was, I reflected, from my English school.

By 1932 conditions in Harbin were deteriorating, and many people were leaving. The city was slowly dying. Father was trying to liquidate his share in the optical business, while Leo was making plans to return to Shanghai to open one. Father and mother were still waiting for entry visas to Argentina which was proving more difficult than originally envisaged. In the autumn of 1935, after my last summer visit home, my parents left Harbin for permanent settlement in Buenos Aires. Amid the changing fortunes and turbulent events around us, they had given my brother and me a loving, happy home during the vital formative years of our childhood and adolescence. From the age of sixteen I no longer shared with them a home, a city or a country, going along a separate path of my own, but the memory of that happy childhood has remained fresh in my mind. The family link was never severed nor ever grew weak.

Examinations

When Ben and I returned to Shanghai, we decided to live together, which was both economical and convenient as we were preparing for the same examinations. We rented two rooms, a shared bedroom and a study, with a nice, friendly family in whose company we sometimes spent the evening, and who, by the way, had a very pretty young daughter. It is interesting to recall that by this time Ben and I no longer used Russian, our mother tongue, but spoke to each other in English.

Most of the boys in my class were preparing for the Cambridge Senior (C.S.) examinations to be held in December. The C.S. was equivalent to the present-day High School Certificate. A few were sitting for the London matriculation.[9] By the middle of the academic year, Ben and I had to make a choice of subjects to sit for the Hong Kong University (HKU) matriculation. The requirement was a pass in at least five subjects, with Maths and English compulsory. For me, as an entrant to the medical faculty, a second modern language was also required; I naturally chose Russian. The other subjects I chose were chemistry, physics, trigonometry, history and art.[10] Hong Kong matriculation examinations were regarded as tough: the pass mark was 50% compared with 33% in the C.S. Maths and science were regarded as more difficult than the C.S., but English was fortunately easier, only one set book required instead of three for the C.S. It was then that we discovered that the HKU matriculation set book for that year was Shakespeare's *Julius Caesar*. It was clearly unrealistic for the school to prepare its only two candidates, Ben and I, in *Julius Caesar* while its own set book was *Macbeth*. A letter was dispatched to HKU requesting it to set for us specially papers on *Macbeth*, and a prompt reply was received agreeing to this. During the classes which we were not taking, such as geography and French, we were allowed to leave the classroom and study in the library.

As the date of our examinations approached Ben and I worked harder and harder. It was crucial for us to pass. In Ben's case, who was embarking on a three-year engineering course, there was a scholarship at stake. I, although still only seventeen, was facing a six-year-long medical course. We sat for our Hong Kong University matriculation in November 1933. The examinations took place in a Chinese school, I do not recall its name. We were slightly apprehensive when opening our English Literature papers: did HKU remember to set the paper on *Macbeth*? They did. All was well. The results did not reach us until five weeks later. We passed. There was a hitch with our visas to Hong Kong (described in my essay "Mr Healey"), so that we were three weeks late for the start of the academic year in Hong Kong.

I left the School in December 1933. Although I was keen to get on with the next phase of my life, I could not help feeling a little sad. In just one year, I developed a strong affection for the School. The teachers were kind

---

9. I believe five credits in the Cambridge Senior gained a student the London matriculation.

10. Because maths consisted of arithmetic, algebra and geometry, trigonometry counted as an extra subject.

and helpful, and I made many friends among my classmates with whom I stayed in touch for many years. At the end-of-the-year ceremony I received a school leaving certificate and a handsome inscribed volume of Shakespeare as a prize. I still have it.

The Public and Thomas Hanbury School for Boys no longer exists. In December 1941, on Japan's entry into the war, the Japanese occupied the International Settlement, the Shanghai Municipal Council was abolished, never to be restored, and the School was closed. I know that the few of us, the old boys of the School, who may still be alive today, cherish the memory of this splendid school.

Postscript

What of my old classmates, the 6th formers of 1933? There have been no class reunions to keep us in touch. With the end of Shanghai we knew, most of us, I suspect, have scattered over many lands and continents. I know what befell some, can speculate about a few, and know nothing of the rest. Willis (Canadian) stayed two more years in the 6th Form just to become school captain. He appeared in Hong Kong after the war as the Canadian medical examiner for prospective migrants to Canada; we resumed our friendship until his return to Canada some years later. Baker, Knox and McCormick were with me in the battle of Hong Kong in December 1941; McCormick was killed. Baker and I both later migrated to Australia where we kept up our friendship until his death a few years ago. Drake joined the RAF and was killed in the battle of Britain. Thompson, I heard, was killed in North Africa fighting the Germans. I sometimes wonder if Ohrenberger, Doi, and Puppo went back to Germany, Japan and Italy (the Axis), respectively, and fought on the opposite side to us. Wolnizer settled down in New Zealand and died there. Moore qualified in England as an aeronautical engineer. Lipkowsky built up a successful business but died when only in his fifties of a heart attack in the Philippines. Litvin (my friend Ben) had a very successful career in South America as an inventor and businessman, and retired in Israel; we stayed in touch sporadically.

4

MR HEALEY

I am inclined to call this sketch a reflection on the British character. Before I introduce Mr Healey,* I have to explain how he came, though briefly, into my life. December 1933: I had spent one year in a British school in Shanghai and had just completed my matriculation examinations for entry into the medical faculty of Hong Kong University. I was seventeen years old. With my friend Ben, who also sat for the same examinations, but who was planning to study engineering, we waited anxiously for the results. None had arrived at our school, but a local newspaper published the results with our names on the "pass" list.

We were both stateless, possessing no passports except the so-called "Nansen Passport" — an identity document devised by the famous Norwegian explorer and diplomat, Dr Nansen, after the First World War and authorized by the League of Nations for issue to stateless people, mostly refugees. Useful though it was, it did not entitle the holder to enter any country which required an entry visa. "Visa" was a magic device sought by countless refugees who wished to settle permanently in some country of haven. Knowing full well that Hong Kong was a British Colony and that we needed a visa for entry there, we appeared at the British Consulate, armed with nothing more than a newspaper cutting with the results of the examinations, to request a visa for Hong Kong. The British Consulate in Shanghai was located inside attractive garden grounds on the famous waterfront called the Bund. It was an imposing building of stone and brick, its entrance flanked with two large neo-Greek columns. The British flag flew from a long staff next to the building. As we crossed the grounds and ascended the few steps of the main building, I felt very apprehensive. It was January (1934) and we were already two weeks late for the beginning of the term. The sea passage to Hong Kong would take three

---

* The name has been changed.

days and there was no daily service. Inside the building we found a large hall with many partially divided cubicles in which clerks, mostly Chinese, were working. For a while no one paid any attention to us; we stood waiting.

At last, one clerk who was nearest to us raised his head and enquired our business. We were seeking a visa to Hong Kong, we explained. He pointed to one of the rooms on the side of the hall and told us to see a Mr Healey. A small wooden board on the door proclaimed "J. C. M. Healey". We knocked on the door and waited. A voice from inside called "come in" and we entered.

A man sat at the desk writing. He did not look up and continued writing. Finally, after what seemed like a very long time, he looked up and asked "Yes?" We looked at a narrow face with a thin mustache, neatly groomed hair, and cold, steel-gray eyes which seemed to regard us with a mixture of curiosity and contempt. We explained our problem: we needed a visa to proceed to Hong Kong to study at the University there. We then showed our newspaper cutting as proof of our entitlement to the visas. Mr Healey barely glanced at the paper, but began to talk in slow measured sentences emphasizing every word as if talking to a child or a retarded person.

We must have a confirmation from the University about our admission. The University must then inform the Hong Kong Police of our admission and ask the Police, which also deals with immigration matters, to inform the Shanghai Consulate to issue visas to us. "But..." I began. "Good morning," said Mr. Healey and turned back to his papers. The interview was clearly over. We turned and left his office. In the hall again no one paid any attention to us.

Back at our school the headmaster and the housemaster were very sympathetic. A cable was sent to Hong Kong University requesting admission for us to the medical and engineering faculties and accommodation in the University hostels of residence. After some delay a positive reply arrived which cheered us somewhat. Another cable from our school requested the University to inform the Hong Kong Police of our admission and to ask for entry visas. Naively believing that the visas would be sent quickly, the following day we were back at the British Consulate.

Mr Healey was again brusque and unfriendly, telling us that we could not expect a communication from the Hong Kong Police so soon and that he could not tell when a message might arrive. We were to telephone daily to enquire.

For the next four days we telephoned the Consulate daily only to be told that no instructions on issuing visas were received from Hong Kong. We were now three weeks late for the start of the teaching term at the University. In despair and hope we booked passages on a Norwegian freighter due to sail for Hong Kong shortly. On the fifth day, Friday, we telephoned as usual in the morning and were told again: no message from Hong Kong. Desperate, as the ship was due to sail on Sunday, we telephoned again in the afternoon and were put through to Mr Healey; the message from Hong Kong had arrived authorizing the issue of visas but, warned Mr Healey, we must hurry as the Consulate closes at 4 p.m. and would remain closed for the weekend.

It was 3 p.m. in the afternoon. We lived in the French Concession, miles away from the Consulate. Everything seemed to conspire against us. We could not find a taxi and when at last we had, heavy traffic slowed us down at times to a crawl. We reached the Consulate at 4.30 p.m., dispirited and certain that we should find it empty. To our total astonishment, Mr Healey was waiting on the steps of the Consulate building. If we expected signs of irritation or annoyance, there were none. Mr Healey regarded us with a not unkindly expression on his face and a slightly whimsical smile on his lips. He led us inside the building which was empty — all the clerks had gone off work — picked up several chops from a table and stamped our papers with visas. Once outside, he smiled again, said "Good luck, boys", and hurried away. We caught our ship and arrived in Hong Kong in due course.

What caused Mr Healey's change in demeanour, from a cold, insensitive bureaucrat to a warm, sympathetic human being? I suppose the simplest explanation is that beneath that external veneer of coldness and indifference there were, though seldom displayed, a warm and friendly disposition and a strong sense of fair play. The latter is often cited as an example of the typical British character.

5

HONG KONG'S EPIDEMICS AND TYPHOONS

"It turned out that the typhoon was indeed a blessing
clearing up the sky and blowing away the epidemic."

Illustrated Chronicle of Hong Kong, Vol. 1, 1959, p. 213

Background

The quotation above brings into focus a particular summer of 1937 when an epidemic and a typhoon occurred concurrently and I, a medical student at the time, was a close witness. In this essay I aim to describe briefly the history of epidemics and typhoons in Hong Kong and give a personal account of a severe epidemic coinciding with one of the worst typhoons in the recorded history of Hong Kong.

It is well known that Hong Kong's recorded history as a city has been punctuated by natural disasters such as typhoons and epidemics. When first occupied and administered by Britain in 1841, as a trophy of the First Opium War (1839–42), it showed little promise, largely because of its unhealthy climate and a position exposed to periodic tropical storms, known locally as typhoons. Indeed, within months of Hong Kong being occupied by the British, it was struck by a severe typhoon which destroyed most of the buildings only recently erected in this fledgling colony; all this in a climate where fevers, dysentery and all manner of virulent epidemics took an alarming toll.

Hong Kong's progress as an entrepôt and a commercial and financial centre was, it is generally recognized, little short of phenomenal, but its success in coping with natural disasters was less spectacular. Of course, nothing could stop typhoons, though an improved warning system did in time reduce their devastating effects. Sanitation too had improved substantially with the years, but in the 1930s, nearly a century after Hong Kong's cession to Britain, disease in sporadic and epidemic form was still widespread.

Epidemics

Much of Hong Kong's early recorded history describes it as an unhealthy place. The hot humid climate with swampy marshy valleys contributed much to this picture. Military dispatches reporting sickness in the garrison make sad reading. In 1842 Lieutenant-General Gough wrote of the "destruction of the 98th Regiment [of Foot] by disease", mortality among the troops due to "malignant fevers" had reached 39%.[1] In 1844 it was described as "the melancholy return of death, when 373 died out of the garrison of 1800, which is one death for every five men![2] Nor were the civilians spared, 10% of whom were estimated to have died in 1843. An excellent pamphlet recently published by the Hong Kong Museum of History[3] traces the march of epidemics, reporting the first recorded cases of cholera in 1858, the incidence of dysentery, the prevalence of "remittent fevers" (undoubtedly malaria), smallpox and rabies, the establishment of a hospital for infectious diseases in 1867 (rather late!), and the first outbreak of plague in 1894. The last, significant if unfortunate event, propelled Hong Kong onto the world stage, for it was in its own Bacteriological Institute[4] that Drs Yersin, of French Indochina, and Kitasato, of Japan, made the milestone discovery of the cause of plague — a microorganism called *Bacillus pestis* — an important step in the control of the disease. Epidemics continued to affect Hong Kong, smallpox in winter, cholera in summer, with occasional returns of the plague, while dysentery, malaria, typhoid fever and cerebro-spinal meningitis had become endemic, that is, regularly found. Tuberculosis occupied a special place in this unsavoury list, recording the highest incidence in the world. Of lesser incidence were leprosy, rabies and diphtheria. Not a pretty picture! Why, it may be asked, would people, especially the expatriates from faraway and healthier lands, come to live and work in Hong Kong? Was it the lure of the East? The answer is probably far more practical: quick profits, higher-paid jobs, a comfortable life with servants, and probably a higher social position than at home. At the same time it must be said that for medical students Hong Kong's health situation offered a unique opportunity to learn about diseases which had been largely eliminated or had become rare in most Western countries.

1. Dispatches from Hong Kong Government to the Colonial Office, London, 18 December 1842.
2. *Friend of China & Hong Kong Gazette*, 16 April 1845.
3. "We Shall Overcome: Plagues in Hong Kong", published by the Hong Kong Museum of History, June 2003.
4. The modest red-brick building, in Mid-Levels, Hong Kong Island, was rebuilt in 1905. It has since been protected as a historic building.

Medical Studies

In January 1934 I began my medical studies at the University of Hong Kong. The first three years were pre-clinical. We read science subjects, such as biochemistry and physiology, and in the anatomy room dissected formalin-pickled cadavers. In January 1937, after passing the prescribed examinations, I was promoted to 4th year and at last entered the world of clinical medicine, attending lectures in hospital and learning medicine at the patients' bedside. There was no mistaking the excitement and pride which all of us — novice clinical students — felt in taking our first steps as medics, wearing white gowns and stethoscopes dangling around our necks. The hospital where we attended classes and walked rounds with doctors was the Government Civil Hospital (GCH), located at Sai Ying Pun, on Hong Kong Island. The building was old and dilapidated and poorly equipped, but already a larger and much more modern hospital was nearing completion at Pokfulam, on the southern side of Hong Kong Island, to be known as the Queen Mary Hospital. In June 1937 our lectures and all clinical training were transferred there.

During my clinical years I became very friendly with a classmate called Vsevolod, Seva for short, also Russian from Harbin, but several years older than I. We studied together a good deal and shared some of our textbooks. We were not, however, totally absorbed in our medical studies. The number of Russian students at the University by this time swelled to some thirty or forty, and there were parties, games of volleyball and "lapta" (a Russian game resembling baseball) in which Seva and I participated. We were also keen on sports. Seva, who was big and strong, held for a while the University shot-put record, until he was defeated by another Russian (bigger and stronger). I might have done well in long-distance running but for one phenomenal miler, a student in the Arts faculty, whom no one could rival. Being a fairly competent musician, I also took part in a number of Hong Kong's musical events, and practised my violin in my room at the hostel whenever I could spare the time.

With the advent of the clinical years also came a drastic shortening of summer vacations for medical students. Instead of three months, we had three weeks. Normally I resided in Lugard Hall, one of the University hostels. All University hostels were shut during summer vacations, but one or two non-University hostels, run by religious foundations, were kept open. In June 1937 I moved to Ricci Hall, a Catholic hostel and was delighted to find that my friend Seva had also moved there. During the day we attended lectures and ward rounds at the hospital. I recall it was my friend's idea to spend some evenings in the hospital casualty room watching the doctor-on-duty treat emergencies. The latter was only too happy to have unscheduled company and was generous with explanations and advice. Some evenings the casualty room was quiet and there was nothing to do, but on other occasions there might be an emergency operation at which we were sometimes allowed to assist. For the very green 4th year medical students, only at the start of their clinical work, this was an out-of-the-ordinary experience. We were keen, inquisitive, and impatient to learn more. When the three-week-long vacation came in August, it was too short a period to go away and in any case there was nowhere for me to go: my parents were no longer in Harbin, having migrated to Argentina in 1935, while Shanghai, where my brother had his optical business, was temporarily cut off due to the Japanese invasion of China, of which the fighting had now reached Shanghai. I missed my family, but the new experience of clinical work and a good deal of extra-curricular activity had softened any feeling of isolation I might have had.

In the meantime Hong Kong was struck by a cholera epidemic of exceptional virulence. By the time it had abated, out of the reported 1690 cases, 1082 died, giving it an appalling mortality rate of 64%. The year 1937 was certainly a bad year for Hong Kong. In a population which had just slightly exceeded 1 million (of whom 98% were Chinese), the Government Medical Department's report for that year lists 696 deaths from malaria, 1884 from smallpox out of 2,327 cases (almost an 80% mortality!), 316 from dysentery out of 576 cases, and 176 from typhoid out of 464 cases. Diphtheria, leprosy and meningitis are also mentioned, while tuberculosis had resulted in an awesome 3,061 deaths. It may be interesting to note, though outside the subject of this essay, that 11,620 Chinese and 30 non-Chinese deaths of infants under one year of age were registered in 1937; "the infant mortality rates showed some improvement over the previous year" adds the report somewhat wryly. It also adds that no case of plague had been reported during the preceding eight years — one bright spot in the report. The report comments that the apparent serious set-back in public health in 1937, as compared with the previous year, may be better appreciated when the severe cholera epidemic and a severe typhoon that year are taken into consideration. My friend and I experienced both that year.

I cannot recall whose idea it was first, Seva's or mine. At any rate we decided that it might be a good idea to spend our vacation working in a cholera hospital and to learn first-hand about the disease. We were joined in this worthwhile venture by Mark, a fellow-medical student from our class. Mark also came from Harbin, where he was a classmate of mine in high school. Some of the wards in the old GCH, we heard, had been converted into a cholera wing to cope with the epidemic, and this is where the three of us reported offering our services. Our offer was accepted but we were told to report to Dr Shaw at Lai Chi Kok, in Kowloon, where the upper floors of a prison on Butterfly Valley Road were also converted into cholera wards. Three large halls were used, each holding about seventy patients. I fear I may not be able to describe adequately the appalling conditions in the hospital. The epidemic began very suddenly and grew rapidly. There was clearly insufficient time to make adequate arrangements. Dr Shaw was assisted by only one part-time doctor, and there was a dire shortage of nurses. Very few beds were available. Patients were brought in a continuous stream and placed on straw mats. The poor overworked nurses were rushing about trying to cope with the inrush of patients. There was filth and human excreta everywhere, as cleaners were unable to scrub the floor in time. The predominant symptoms of cholera are vomiting and diarrhoea resulting in severe dehydration. Treatment requires prompt rehydration by intravenous saline infusion, but for many it was not prompt enough. We were first asked to watch the infusions and replace the saline containers when they were empty, but the hospital was so short of staff that soon we were shown how to administer the saline by inserting needles into the patients' veins. Sometimes it was necessary to expose the vein by a small skin incision before a needle could be inserted, a task normally performed by a doctor or a trained nurse. Now it was entrusted to us — junior medical students. All around us were cholera victims with sunken eyes and hollow cheeks lying on the floor. I recall on several occasions, as I knelt over a new case brought in, I could not tell whether the person was alive or dead, as I could not detect breathing or reaction of any sort; the vital signs seemed so utterly depressed. Then suddenly there would be a tiny twitch of an eyelid or some other part of the body and we would swing into action, thrusting a needle into a vein and getting the saline to flow in. Many patients died and it was obvious that there was a high mortality rate, but among these were many destitute people picked up on the streets already in a moribund state. There were also recoveries, especially among the cases brought early in their disease. Each was regarded as a triumph; they were moved to a smaller ward and received a little extra attention.

About a week after we started work, Dr Shaw suggested that we should improvise a test for measuring the density of the blood which would serve as a guide to the amount of saline to be infused. After some experimenting, we produced a mixture of two liquids, one of which was kerosene (I do not remember the other), in which a drop of blood retained its shape and did not diffuse. Taken from a patient and dropped into this mixture, the density of the blood could be roughly estimated from the position of the floating drop. It proved to be a quick and useful guide to the amount of intravenous drip needed.

My friends and I worked hard from early morning till six o'clock in the evening, with only a short break for lunch. It was an amazing experience and, we had no doubt, useful for us medical students. It was also very gratifying to know that one was giving much needed help in a sudden and terrifying calamity. But the emotional strain of witnessing so many die, of not being able to save more, was, for me, often almost unbearable.

I do not recall being worried about catching the disease. Cholera is a transmissible disease, but only by ingestion of infected food or water. In hospital the pressure of work was so great that no special precautions were enforced. We all had anti-cholera injections, which do not afford full protection, and it was assumed that sensible attention to personal hygiene, such as washing hands, wearing gowns and disinfecting our clothing, including shoes, on leaving hospital, were sufficient to protect us. Obviously, no food was consumed near the cholera wards.

Generally, those who embark on a medical profession accept the fact that as part of their training they will at times be exposed to infections. They accept this risk. As medical students we also learn that while observing basic and commonsense precautions, gradual exposure to infections induces some degree of immunity and in the long run is a better protection than excessive avoidance. I believe it is generally true that people in the medical profession are less vulnerable to infections. I do not remember, among my fellow students, anyone being frightened of, or making special efforts to avoid contact with, infectious diseases.

2 September 1937

Our three weeks' vacation was at an end. The first of September was to be our last day at the hospital. We left Ricci Hall in the morning, crossed by ferry to Kowloon and arrived at the hospital around 9 a.m. The early morning weather was fine, but by noon the day grew humid and the sky cloudy. We had no inkling of anything unpleasant in store, although we learned later that the No. 1 typhoon signal had been hoisted that morning. We worked until 5 p.m. and then had a short farewell ceremony at which Dr Shaw and the staff thanked us for our work and wished us all the best. We had earlier decided that after our hard and dedicated work of the past three weeks, we earned a good Russian meal with vodka. We therefore made our way to Tkachenko's Russian restaurant, at the corner of Hankow and Middle Roads in Tsim Sha Tsui, close to the cross-harbour Star Ferry. As we left the hospital, around 6 p.m., I noticed that it was becoming quite windy and I think there was a slight drizzle, but we still had no suspicion of anything sinister to come. Mr Tkachenko was a short, roly-poly man with a small brush moustache and a cheerful face. His restaurant was deservedly popular especially with the Russian community of Hong Kong, and certainly with the Russian university students. Mr Tkachenko greeted us with the friendly familiarity afforded to regular customers. The meal was excellent, starting with borsch, and accompanied with liberal amounts of vodka. During the meal we could hear the wind outside rising, and I was beginning to feel uncomfortable. I suggested to Seva that perhaps a typhoon was in the offing, in which case perhaps we should cross over to Hong Kong Island soon, and make our way home. When the sea gets very rough the ferries stop running. We crossed over around 10 p.m. The wind was now strong and the harbour very choppy; it was raining, but not heavily.

By the time we reached Ricci Hall, there was no longer any doubt in my mind that Hong Kong was about to be hit by a typhoon. Strong gusts of wind were whistling outside. The window shutters were all battened down but were rattling loudly. The hostel was dark since the lights were always switched off at 10.00 p.m. except for a couple of study rooms for students working late. I went to bed almost immediately, then woke up around midnight. It was blowing very hard outside and the shutters were still banging loudly, but what woke me up was a feeling of acute nausea. I tried to open the door into the corridor but the pressure of air was so strong that it took me awhile before I could force the door open. I rushed to the toilet and was violently sick with diarrhoea at the same time. During the next two hours I would return to my room exhausted, only to rush back to the toilet for another bout of vomiting and diarrhoea. Naturally, I thought, with these symptoms there could only be one diagnosis: I was infected with cholera, which was not surprising working as we had been in less than perfect hygienic conditions. I recall no fear, as I made my diagnosis. Statistics were going through my mind, and my recent experience taught me, that with proper and timely treatment, the mortality rate of cholera was under 10%, though "timely" treatment at that moment was problematic.

Outside the storm was raging and trying to reach a hospital seemed dangerous if not impossible. While occupied with these thoughts, I became aware after a while that the sick feeling and diarrhoea had abated somewhat, but at the same time the skin all over my body began to itch and felt as if it was stretched. In the darkness, by the light of a torch I looked at myself in the mirror: my face and neck were grossly swollen, so that I thought I resembled the man in the Michelin tyres advertisement. It was not cholera after all, but a severe allergic reaction, no doubt caused by something I ate at Tkachenko's; I never discovered what it was. Still feeling very weak, I managed to stagger to Seva's room and woke him up. When he looked at me he burst out laughing — somewhat disconcerting to me, but no doubt justified by my appearance. There was still no question of going to a hospital although the Queen Mary Hospital was only a ten-minute walk from Ricci Hall. The typhoon was now in full force and any venture outside would have been hazardous. Amazingly, like a magician who pulls out a rabbit from a hat, Seva produced, heaven knows from where, a syringe and an ampoule of adrenalin, and injected me with it. Within half an hour I was resuming a more or less normal shape. I recall looking at my watch: it was 3 a.m. Back in my room, I went to bed and fell asleep almost at once.

When I woke up in the morning, it was strangely quiet. Had the typhoon passed away? I felt tired but otherwise fine. I opened the shutters and looked out. A scene of utter devastation met my eyes. The street was littered with broken branches and debris, many trees were uprooted and all stripped bare of leaves. Looking towards the harbour I saw several masts of sunken ships or junks sticking out of the water. On the beach at Green Island a ship was resting on the ground as if a giant had lifted it from the water and placed it on the beach. The typhoon had lasted only six to eight hours over Hong Kong early on 2 September, but the damage inflicted was enormous. Later when I visited the Central District, I saw the same scene of devastation everywhere with several ships driven aground.

To quote from the Hong Kong Annual Report for 1937: "On the 2nd of September the most disastrous typhoon in local history passed over the Colony. At the height of the storm the barometer fell to 28.298 inches and it is estimated that a wind velocity of 167 m.p.h. was reached. Vast damage was done to property in all parts of the Colony, but by far the greatest sufferers were the Chinese fishing community. Information was received of 1,361 native boats being sunk and it can only be presumed that many thousands of seafaring people were drowned. No fewer than 27 steamers of various sizes were sunk or driven ashore." In fact it was estimated that there were about eleven thousand deaths, or 1% of a population of just over a million. Two large ocean-going liners, the *Osama Maru* and the *Conte Verde*, were grounded.

Hong Kong's climate is sub-tropical, without extremes of temperature. The onset of summer, in June, brings rains and the beginning of the typhoon season. Typhoon is a term used mainly in South-East Asia for a tropical cyclone, and is believed to be derived from the Chinese (Cantonese) *dai fung* — big wind. Each year, between June and October, typhoons form in the western part of the North Pacific, then move towards the land. Not all tropical cyclones develop into fully fledged typhoons: many pass bringing much rain but causing little damage. The few which strike full-on cause great devastation and loss of life. As a coastal area, Hong Kong has always been subject to threats of typhoons. It is therefore something of a surprise that not until 1883 was the Royal Observatory set up to deal with meteorological matters and to devise a typhoon warning system.

In terms of loss of life and property, three typhoons were regarded by the Royal Observatory as the worst: those of 1874, 1906 and 1937. The first of these struck Hong Kong on 22 September 1874 causing much damage and loss of life. Among the buildings destroyed were the Government Civil Hospital, St. Joseph's Church and the governor's house on the Peak. The *Hong Kong Daily Press* wrote, four days later, "...it was ascertained that not a single ship in port escaped undamaged and the loss of life was estimated at 2000 souls". Hardly less disastrous was the typhoon which struck Hong Kong on 18 September 1906. Described by the *Hong Kong Telegraph* as the "Holocaust", in the short space of two hours it "laid a great part of the city in ruins". Over ten thousand people lost their lives, among them five French sailors when their gunboat "Fronde" was involved in a collision.

Typhoons, of course, continued to affect Hong Kong; the one in 1962, called Wanda (after 1947 typhoons were given names) was severe enough but, with a death toll of 183, could in no way be compared to the one in 1937.

Cholera continued its annual visitation until the Japanese invasion and occupation in 1941, but seemed to have stopped during the occupation, probably due to strict quarantine regulations, reduction of the population by forcible repatriation of the Chinese from Hong Kong to the mainland, and the vigorous anti-cholera inoculation campaign. A friend, who was in Hong Kong during the Japanese occupation and not interned, told me that the Japanese took draconian measures to stamp out cholera. They set up small stations with a nurse and a clerk, and probably a soldier not far away, at street corners, and anyone who could not produce an anti-cholera vaccination card with a record of an inoculation not older than three months was forcibly given a jab. The Japanese succeeded in stamping out cholera, but it is inconceivable that the British Hong Kong government could have ever adopted such drastic measures. Cholera reappeared in Hong Kong in the 1960s and thereafter appeared only in sporadic form.

Postscript

I sat for my final examinations in December 1939. By a happy coincidence one of the questions in the paper on medicine was on cholera. The scenes from my spell in the cholera hospital came flooding into my mind. I recall writing with almost feverish excitement, so much so that I had to stop myself to allow time for other questions in the paper. Later I wondered if it helped me to win the Anderson Gold Medal; I shall never know.[5]

My friend Seva, after graduation and a couple of internships, went into general medical practice, building up a large and successful practice focusing almost exclusively on Chinese patients. During the Japanese occupation, being a stateless Russian, he was not interned and continued with his medical practice, treating many poor Chinese, as I heard later, free of charge and even supplying them with medicines. In 1961 Seva, now with a family, migrated to Australia and settled comfortably in a beautiful house at Castlecove in Sydney. Four years later he died suddenly of a heart attack, only fifty-five years of age.

Mark, after graduation and internships, worked for the government. During the Japanese occupation, he was interned in the civilian camp where, working as a doctor, he was highly regarded, earning the lasting gratitude of his fellow-internees. After the liberation, he was repatriated to England where he settled permanently, working for the National Health Service as a chest specialist. He retired in Luton, Bedfordshire; we have maintained contact over the years.

---

5. After Dr John Anderson, first professor of medicine at Hong Kong University, 1922 to 1929. The medal was established upon his death in 1931 with a fund bequeathed by him. It is awarded annually to a medical graduate with the highest aggregate of marks for the entire course.

1.1 Chita, c. 1908. Post-card: Amurskaya Street, the main thoroughfare of Chita. In spite of general drabness, the two buildings on the right are of fine architectural style. My parents' shop "Renaissance" is in one of them, seen on the extreme right with signboard showing a large clock. This post-card was sent by my mother to her parents in Sevastopol with a short message on the back.

1.2 My brothers Leo (left) and David aged five and seven, Chita, 1915. Photograph taken indoors (against a painted canvas of a winter scene) but wearing usual winter clothes. Note the felt boots known in Russian as "katanki".

1.3 Myself aged three (1919) dressed for a lark by the White officers in their uniform, sword in my left hand, a rifle in my right, and a cheeky expression on my face.

1.5 Myself with mother (left) and aunt Sonia. Sevastopol, Crimea, 1923.

1.4 Father, mother, Leo and I. Chita, 1921.

2.1 Harbin, 1920s (post-card). It shows Pristan's main street, Kitaiskaya (Chinese) Street. The large building on the left side is a Japanese department store. On the right, a signboard of the well-known German firm of Siemens.

2.3 Myself in school uniform, aged 11 (1927).

2.2 My first lesson on the violin, aged 10 (1926).

2.4 Harbin Symphony Orchestra's summer season, 1932 (written in Russian on the photograph). Taken during a rehearsal in the magnificent concert shell of the Railway Club garden. The conductor (principal of the Music School) is on the podium. Uncle David is in the concertmaster's seat, front desk, on the conductor's left. The manager of the Orchestra is sitting on the edge of the shell, extreme left. Next on the left are the principal flautist and myself, the second flautist.

2.5 Grandfather and I, in our flat, Harbin, 1932.

2.6 The flood, Harbin, summer 1932. Pristan's Kitaiskaya Street (see Photograph 2.1), now a thoroughfare for small boats. The large building on the right is Hotel Moderne.

2.7 The flood, Harbin, summer 1932. I am in my canoe outside a butcher's shop; this one, however, is shut.

2.8 High school graduation class, Form 7, Harbin, 1932. Taken in the school hall. Seated in the centre, with girls on either side, is the Russian literature teacher who is also the class master. I am in the centre of the back row. Some of us, including myself, are wearing ties: some flexibility in uniform was allowed in Form 7.

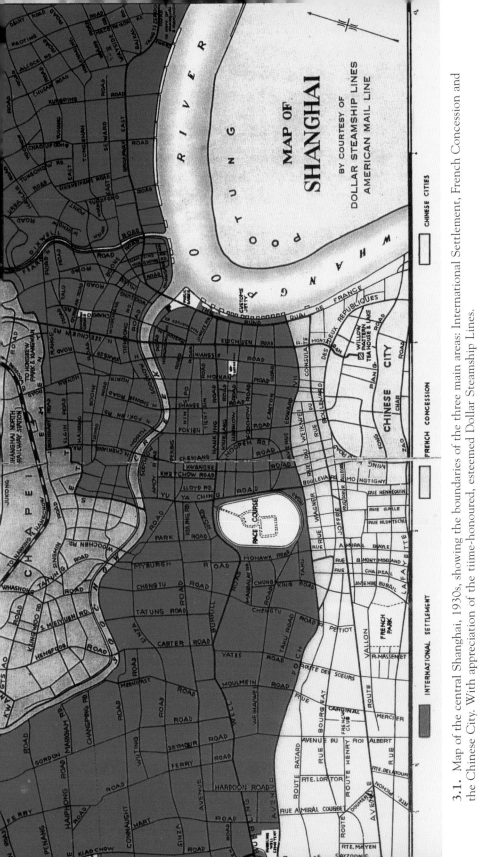

3.1. Map of the central Shanghai, 1930s, showing the boundaries of the three main areas: International Settlement, French Concession and the Chinese City. With appreciation of the time-honoured, esteemed Dollar Steamship Lines.

3.2 Shanghai waterfront, 1932–33. Splendid western-style buildings line the famous Waterfront — the Bund. Prominent among them are the Cathay Hotel with the conical top and, further on the left the Chinese Maritime Customs with the clock tower. Still further on the left is the domed Hong Kong & Shanghai Bank. (Photograph courtesy of Hong Kong Museum of History).

3.3 The façade of the Main Building of the Public and Thomas Hanbury School for Boys, Shanghai, 1933.

3.4 The 6th Form, Shanghai, 1933. Prefects are wearing badges on their lapels. I am in the second row, second from right.

3.5 My tennis team, Pembroke House. From left to right: Baker, Wolnizer, Puppo, myself. Shanghai, 1933.

3.6 Ben and I in the chemistry laboratory. Shanghai, 1933.

3.7 In the School Library. From left to right: myself, Murray, Welwig, Litvin (Ben), Kew. Shanghai, 1933.

5.1 Hong Kong Island, 23 February 1936. I am standing on Conduit Path, Pokfulam. In the background is the Queen Mary Hospital during construction. It was completed in 1937 and became the largest and most modern hospital in Hong Kong. It also replaced the Government Civil Hospital as the teaching hospital for the University's Medical Faculty.

5.2 Hong Kong Harbour after the typhoon of September 1874. The picture shows damaged piers and sunken vessels. One of the worst typhoons in Hong Kong's history, it struck Hong Kong suddenly and with little warning, on 22 September, and in six terrible hours 2000 lives were lost, mostly fisher-folk at sea, many ships were lost and extensive damage done to property. (Photograph courtesy of the Hong Kong Museum of History).

5.3 Hong Kong Island's waterfront, c. 1937. This view would be unfamiliar to most people in the present-day Hong Kong since, except for the domed former Supreme Court (now Legislative Council) Building, second from the left, none of the other buildings are extant. Dominating the scene is the magnificent new Hong Kong & Shanghai Bank (completed in 1935). On the extreme left is the Hong Kong Club. On the right of the Bank are Queen's, St. George's and King's Buildings. On the extreme right is Blake Pier. (Photograph courtesy of the Hong Kong Museum of History).

5.4 Hong Kong Harbour during the typhoon, 18 September 1906. A remarkable photograph showing the ferocity of the storm as it caused havoc and destruction in the harbour. It struck Hong Kong with little warning and, although it raged over Hong Kong for only two hours, it caused heavy loss of life and enormous damage to ships and property. (Photograph courtesy of the Hong Kong Museum of History).

5.5 Hong Kong waterfront after the typhoon of 2 September 1937. A ship is blown ashore by the force of the gale. The worst typhoon in Hong Kong's recorded history, it struck Hong Kong with tremendous force causing immense damage to ships, property and great loss of life among the fisher-folk at sea. (Photograph courtesy of the Hong Kong Museum of History).

7.1 Myself, shortly after being commissioned as lieutenant in the HKVDC, 1940. Pith helmets were still considered essential in sub-tropical Hong Kong. (Photograph from the author's military ID Card).

7.2 HKVDC Camp at Fanling, New Territories, 1939. Members of the Field Ambulance practising their medical skills. (Photograph courtesy of the late Lady May Ride).

7.3 Japanese invasion of Hong Kong, December 1941: a detachment of Japanese troops and vehicles advancing towards the Star Ferry Pier at Tsim Sha Tsui, Kowloon. (Photograph courtesy of Mr Tim Ko).

7.4 Japanese invasion of Hong Kong, December 1941: Japanese troops in action at North Point, Hong Kong Island. (Photograph courtesy of Mr Tim Ko).

7.5 Japanese Victory Parade, Hong Kong, 28 December 1941: riding in front is Lieutenant-General Sakai, who was in overall command of the Japanese forces in the battle for Hong Kong. Riding on his right is Vice-Admiral Niimi. It was reported that while the Chinese population was encouraged to come out and cheer, the few foreigners remaining in Hong Kong were forbidden to watch the parade. (Photograph courtesy of Mr Tim Ko).

7.6 *The Lasting Honour* was painted in 1982 by A. C. ("Andy") Neilson, former captain and adjutant of the Royal Hong Kong Regiment (The Volunteers). It depicts a scene from the battle at Stanley, Hong Kong Island, in which No. 2 ("Scottish") Company of the HKVDC and the men of the Middlesex Regiment put up a heroic stand against a greatly superior Japanese force. Andy Neilson, himself a Scot, created a dramatic moment in what was undoubtedly one of the defenders' proudest and most gallant episodes of the Hong Kong War.

8.1 This photograph, taken by the Japanese interpreter Tsutada in 1943, was one of the very few taken inside Sham Shui Po Camp. It shows three HKVDC medical officers, standing from left to right: Solomon Bard, Albert Rodrigues and Geofrrey Balean. Kneeling in front are their "batmen", from left to right: Leo Silva, "Nobby" Clark and Carlos Basto.

6

MYSELF A RELUCTANT MIDWIFE*

Hong Kong, Early January 1941

In Europe the "phoney war" was over.[1] France and the Low Countries were overrun and England, bombed mercilessly from the air, was fighting for her life. In Hong Kong, it was widely expected that Japan would soon join the war on Germany's side. Preparations for war were in full swing: women, not in essential services, and children were evacuated to Australia, air-raid shelters were built, and food stores were established for a long siege.[2] In spite of this, life continued as before, seemingly normal, oblivious of the impending calamity.

Although I was a lieutenant in the Field Ambulance of the local territorial unit, the Hong Kong Volunteer Defence Corps, I was allowed to continue with my medical work. However, I was required to attend military training and all field exercises. I had just completed two six-months' internships, in clinical medicine and pathology. Both were stimulating and rewarding, but also very arduous, allowing no time for leisure or recreation. I felt that I deserved a couple of weeks' rest before taking up my next residency as a house-surgeon. A trip to Shanghai to visit my brother Leo, whom I had not seen since 1936, seemed an attractive proposition. It would also give me an opportunity to meet the parents of Sophie Patushinsky, a medical student at Hong Kong University whom I hoped to, and later that year did, marry. Leave from the Army was secured and I set about to arrange my trip.

---

* In homage to Austin Coates.

1. "Phoney war" referred to a period in the Second World War, around October 1939–April 1940, when, following the conquest of Poland, there was little fighting on land.

2. This was gross over-estimation. Against vastly superior Japanese forces, Hong Kong fought bravely, but only lasted eighteen days. Described in "The Battle for Hong Kong, December 1941" essay.

The Journey

The Indo-China Steam Navigation Company, a subsidiary of Jardine, Matheson & Co. ran a passenger service between Hong Kong and Shanghai, a three-day journey. I obtained a passage on the SS *Wing Sang*, a small but comfortable passenger ship of some three and half thousand tonnes. We sailed in the first week of January. I was hoping for a peaceful and enjoyable sea trip.

The weather was sunny and cool, the sea calm, and a mild refreshing breeze made it a perfect combination. The ship had only two widely contrasting classes: the upper deck with cabins and the lower deck, or steerage. The former accommodated about twenty passengers in comfortable cabins, mostly two to a cabin. The latter, an open deck, covered above only by a stretched canvas, seemed densely crowded with, I reckoned roughly, two hundred or more passengers, all as far as I could tell Chinese and obviously poor. It was not a pleasant sight.

The first day passed pleasantly enough. The weather continued fine, the sea calm and I found the time very relaxing. I met and exchanged casual remarks with other upper deck passengers. A friendly middle-aged Englishman, with whom I shared a cabin, asked me if I played bridge, and on being told that I did, suggested a game if we could find two more players. We did and had an enjoyable game after dinner. I went to bed pleased with the journey so far.

At night the weather worsened and the ship was rolling and pitching a lot. When I came down for breakfast the next morning only about half of the passengers were up and about. The sky was overcast, the sea rough, and the ship was still rolling a good deal. I was glad that I did not seem to be prone to sea-sickness. When I looked down at the deck passengers below, some were huddled together, many were seasick and looked miserable. I felt sorry for them, but there was nothing I could do. At lunch the second officer approached me and introduced himself (I cannot recall his name). He explained that his duties included basic medical care and taking charge of the sick-bay. On learning that I was a doctor, he wanted to meet me. He had some duties to attend to presently, but would appreciate it if I could join him for dinner that evening. I said that it would be a pleasure. In the afternoon the weather improved, the sea became calmer, and there were occasional sunny periods. Most of my fellow passengers came out on deck and everyone was clearly enjoying the fresh air and the smell of the sea.

At dinner time I sat with the second officer. A young man, perhaps in his late twenties, he turned out to be a very pleasant companion. We chatted about a variety of things, but the conversation inevitably turned to the subject of medical facilities on board the ship. He confessed that apart from simple first aid he did not have any expertise to deal with medical problems. I expressed my surprise that the ship did not carry a ship's surgeon. "It's only a three-day run. The Company saw no need for a ship's surgeon," he said. "But you have some two hundred steerage passengers who had not been medically examined prior to boarding the ship. Something may happen to anyone of them, perhaps an emergency which may be beyond your medical skills," I said. "We have been on this route for some time, and nothing much happens," he replied. That seemed to be the end of the matter. We switched to other topics after dinner and spent a very pleasant evening chatting and drinking wine until nearly midnight.

"Nothing Much Happens"
That night I was awakened by a knock on the door of my cabin. I looked at my watch; it was 2 a.m. I opened the door and there stood my friend the second officer looking very distraught. "You'd better come," he pleaded. "I think a woman in the lower deck is going to have a baby. I have moved her to the sick-bay." "Heavens," I thought, "did I bring this on by talking last night about emergencies?" I dressed quickly and quietly, trying not to disturb my cabin-mate. The sea was very rough and the ship was rolling heavily as we staggered towards the sick-bay which was at the ship's stern. Inside, a young Chinese woman, obviously pregnant, was lying on the couch groaning loudly. I examined her; there was no doubt that she was in labour. I did not relish the role of midwife now thrust upon me. As a student I had fulfilled my quota of thirty normal deliveries and assisted in a few difficult ones, but that was two years ago. I had done no obstetrics since then and it was certainly not my field of interest. I now tried to recall all the steps to follow in correct sequence, hoping silently that this would be a normal case. The sick-bay was very well equipped, with plenty of dressings, medical materials and instruments, though not for a difficult labour. On examination, I found that the head of the baby was well down, "engaged" in the language of obstetrics; it seemed to promise a normal birth. I spent the next half-hour or so coaxing the woman to "push" and holding the head back to make the baby's passage slow and gentle. All the while, the second officer was watching anxiously and, I hoped, learning the "art of delivery" from a very inexperienced midwife. Finally, to my great relief, and I am sure to the mother's, the baby slipped out easily and effortlessly. I tied and cut the cord, and soon the baby started to cry. It was a girl; she was very small, which no doubt accounted for the easy delivery, but otherwise seemed perfectly normal.

The second officer washed the baby, then gave it to the mother to hold. The three of us were very happy, though I am not sure about the fourth who was still making loud noises. I advised the second officer to leave the young mother and child in the sick-bay under regular observation. Having satisfied myself that there was no excessive bleeding and all was normal, I went back to my cabin and to bed. The whole operation took about two-and-a-half hours.

When I got up the next morning, the weather was fine and the sea much calmer than the previous night. I went to see my patient in the sick-bay and found the excited second officer sitting with the mother; he was obviously taking his new role seriously. She was feeding the baby. All seemed well. The captain also came to the sick-bay and thanked me for my help. The news of the birth on the ship spread quickly, and there was much interest among the upper deck passengers. A hat was passed around and soon a tidy sum of money was collected for the young mother and child. I became the centre of attention, plied with questions and feted as a hero, while I, somewhat embarrassed, tried to pass some of the credit onto the second officer. There was also visible excitement among the passengers on the lower deck.

Another Emergency

Early next morning, the ship entered Huangpu River; we were just two hours away from docking in Shanghai. If I thought this was the end of my adventure, it was not to be. An agitated captain rushed into my cabin accompanied by the second officer. Looking extremely distressed, he informed me that a dead body was discovered among the steerage passengers. This could spell disaster. Shanghai, although ostensibly under Chinese administration, was controlled by the Japanese through their puppet government of Wang Ching Wei. The Japanese were notoriously nervous about cholera. Even though it was winter, when cholera epidemics are rare, the captain explained that unless it could be certified that the person had not died of cholera, the ship with all on board could be placed in quarantine for a week or even longer. This was bad news indeed. Could I, as a qualified doctor, possibly certify in writing that the death was not caused by cholera, the captain asked. This may not be possible without an autopsy, I replied, and I could not see how I could conduct one in the circumstances. Clearly the captain had hoped that I would readily agree to avoid the unpleasant prospect of a quarantine, and was disappointed at my reply. However, I assured him that I would examine the body and then consider the situation.

The body was of an emaciated Chinese man around forty to fifty years of age. There was a great deal of blood around him and in his mouth. He had no family, but by questioning people who were near him, I elicited the information that he was coughing a lot throughout the journey. No one actually saw him cough or vomit blood or witnessed his death; it probably occurred during the night when people around him were asleep. There were no signs pointing to cholera or any other intestinal condition as the cause of death. I felt confident enough to tell the captain that I would certify that the man had died from a massive lung haemorrhage due either to tuberculosis or lung cancer, and that he most certainly did not die of cholera. Greatly relieved, the captain cabled my findings to the port authorities. There was no certainty, I thought, that the port health officials would accept this statement, but I kept these thoughts to myself. The news of our precarious situation reached my fellow passengers and they were waiting anxiously in the lounge for the outcome. I was again the centre of attention, all hopes pinned on my declaration. So much was at stake: Will we be allowed to disembark and proceed to our destinations, perhaps to our families or important meetings, or languish for so many days in quarantine? It was a most anxious wait which seemed to last a long time, but in fact was probably no longer than an hour. Then suddenly, the captain burst into the room and announced that we were cleared for landing! I shall never forget the loud cheer with which this announcement was greeted. I was surrounded by the crew and passengers, everyone thanking me; I certainly felt like a hero then.

We docked without any incidents. Before disembarking, I visited my patient and her baby and saw that both were fine. She clasped my hand in silent thanks and I was very touched. The captain and the second officer came to say goodbye and thanked me again warmly. When I returned to Hong Kong two weeks later, after an enjoyable holiday in Shanghai and an uneventful, if a little dull, journey, there was a letter waiting for me from Jardines thanking me for my help. As far as I know, the Company did not change their policy regarding a ship's surgeon.

7

THE BATTLE FOR HONG KONG, DECEMBER 1941

"To delight in conquest is to delight in slaughter."

Laozi (6th century BCE)

Preamble

The region of South China which we call Hong Kong and the New Territories, or politically, Special Administrative Region of the People's Republic of China, boasts of some six thousand years of human activity within its territory. Local archaeological and historical research indicates that during the initial two-thirds of this period the region was inhabited by stone-age, seafaring aborigines of non-Chinese origin; then invaded, annexed, and later settled by the Han Chinese; ceded to and administered by Britain from 1841 to 1997, returning afterwards to China.

Prior to the British occupation, the territory was essentially rural with fishing and farming as its main occupations. Under the British, Hong Kong became an important trading and shipping centre, the settlement of Victoria on the Island of Hong Kong expanding rapidly into a major city. From 1841 the development of Hong Kong and its environs was a story of almost uninterrupted growth and success. Almost! The major setback was the Second World War when Japan invaded, occupied and governed Hong Kong from 1941 to 1945. Against the background of Hong Kong's long history it was but a short eclipse. Nevertheless, being very traumatic and relatively recent, it has left a deep scar, if not on Hong Kong's ultimate prosperity, at least on the collective memory of its people, some of whom are still alive.

As a medical officer in the Field Ambulance of the Hong Kong Volunteer Defence Force (HKVDC),[1] I was an active participant in the Battle for Hong

---

1. The Hong Kong Volunteer Corps was first formed in 1854 when the Crimean War led to a reduction of British military presence in Hong Kong, and ninety-nine citizens volunteered to defend the Colony.

Kong. This is my story and the story of the people who were with me during those violent days of combat; it is also the story of Hong Kong's agony as its forces fought a hopeless battle against a deadly and merciless enemy.

A Record of the Actions of The Hong Kong Volunteer Defence Corps in the Battle for Hong Kong, December 1941 is a little red book familiar to most members of that Corps. Published in 1953, its author is anonymous.[2] It is written factually without exaggeration or a sense of drama, but throughout its pages there are examples of remarkable heroism and gallantry by the Volunteer Corps defenders and their British, Canadian, and Indian fellow soldiers. I am filled with profound sadness as I read the familiar names of friends, schoolmates, and fellow volunteers, many of whom fell in the battle; many more would die later in the prisoner-of-war camps. Their gallant fight received but scant attention in the history books.

Hong Kong in the 1930s
Almost a century of British administration saw Hong Kong grow from a small naval and trading base into a commercial centre of international importance. One of the world's greatest harbours was built in Hong Kong's enclosed waters and freedom of the port has been maintained. Banking and shipping flourished, and by 1935 the population exceeded a million. But for those of us accustomed to the appearance of Hong Kong in the 21st century with its skyscrapers, heavy traffic, fly-overs and bustling commercial activity, the Hong Kong of the 1930s would seem like a scene from an old picture post-card. In Central Hong Kong hardly a single modern landmark would be recognizable. Apart from the Hong Kong & Shanghai Bank, there were no buildings of more than four storeys along the entire waterfront. Few cars but many rickshaws would be seen on the roads. At the bottom of Wyndham Street, sedan-chair coolies would be waiting to carry customers to Mid-Levels. Some of the buildings carried names familiar today — Prince's, St. George's, Alexandra — but all were massive, colonial-style structures bearing no resemblance to their present namesakes. If one chanced to walk in Central on a Saturday afternoon, one might observe a leisurely game of cricket being played on the ground next to Statue Square, the latter actually ringed with royal statues!

---

2. The author, who modestly chose to remain anonymous, was an HKVDC officer, a teacher in private life. After the war he was decorated for bravery in action.

This was Hong Kong as I first saw it when I arrived in January 1934 to spend the next six years as a medical student at the University of Hong Kong: an outwardly charming, tranquil colonial place where life moved at a slow leisurely pace. During those years I gradually perceived another side to this picture: while a small number of expatriates and wealthy Chinese lived in comfortable houses surrounded by servants, a large segment of the local population experienced overcrowding, poverty and malnutrition. Periodic epidemics of cholera, meningitis, and smallpox ravished the Colony; tuberculosis was widespread, and typhoid, malaria and dysentery were endemic. At the University, life was enjoyable enough as work and fun went alongside. There was little academic pressure and some students stayed on for years hardly bothering to attend lectures. While the majority of students were Hong Kong Chinese, there was a substantial number from North China, India, Ceylon, Malaya and Singapore; there were Russian students from Shanghai and Harbin and a small number of offsprings of British expatriates. The variety made student life interesting.

The War Clouds

The world seemed at peace, but already menacing events were taking place, foreboding disaster and conflict. By the middle of the 1930s Nazi Germany was rearming and on the warpath while Europe deluded itself that Hitler could be appeased. In the Far East, Japan too was on the march. In 1932 it had established in Manchuria a puppet state of Manchukuo totally under its control, and in 1937 invaded China, plunging the region into a long and brutal war.

In October 1938 several divisions of Japanese troops landed at Bias Bay, only thirty miles from Hong Kong, and occupied Canton. They were thus on the very threshold of the Hong Kong territory. It was a threat Hong Kong could no longer ignore. In June 1939 conscription was introduced for all male British subjects, who were mostly allocated to the local territorial force — the Hong Kong Volunteer Defence Corps (HKVDC) or its naval counterpart, the Hong Kong Royal Naval Volunteer Reserve (HKRNVR). In the same months, evacuation of British expatriate women (those not engaged in essential work) and children was begun and nearly 3,500 were evacuated to Australia. Air-raid precautions were rigorously enforced and construction of air-raid shelters was speeded up.

War in Europe

In Europe in the meantime appeasement had ended; in 1939 Britain and Germany were at war. On 3 September 1939, the day Britain declared war on Germany, although still three months away from my final medical degree and hard at work, I entered the Headquarters of the HKVDC and enrolled as a private in the Corps' Field Ambulance, soon to be promoted to lance-corporal. It is difficult to describe my motivation without appearing self-righteous; suffice to say that I felt I could not remain indifferent to the events unfolding around me, plus a strong conviction that the Japanese would sooner or later attack Hong Kong. The Field Ambulance was a unit of about 100–120 men of varying age, nationality and aptitude. Its commanding officer, Major Lindsay Ride, was professor of physiology at Hong Kong University, in which capacity he was able, it seemed, to persuade a number of medical students to join his unit. Our part-time training included both military and medical skills: the treatment of wounds, fractures, and medical emergencies as well as the handling of weapons; the Geneva Convention allowed non-combatant medical personnel to carry weapons for self-defence and protection of wounded in their charge. In retrospect, I do not think our training prepared us adequately for the sort of casualties we would soon be called upon to treat in battle, nor for the grim reality of war. The latter, I believe, can only be learned under fire.

In the summer of 1940 I became a naturalized British subject and at the same time commissioned as full lieutenant in the Field Ambulance, HKVDC.[3] I was twenty-four years old. Events now moved fast towards a global conflict. In September 1940 Germany, Italy and Japan concluded the Tripartite Pact, known as the "Axis", and Japan's relations with USA and Britain steadily deteriorated. When economic sanctions were imposed on Japan, in July 1941, war in the Pacific became inevitable. It certainly seemed so to me as I well recall. It seems inexplicable that with this conviction firmly in my mind, I travelled to Shanghai in September 1941 to marry Sophie Patushinsky, a fellow medical student at Hong Kong University.[4] Put it to the impetuosity of youth? With some anxiety lest I might be too late to rejoin my unit, we hurried back to Hong Kong; two and a half months later the "balloon went up".[5]

---

3. While in most British army units, officers are first commissioned as second lieutenants, medical officers (Royal Army Medical Corps) start as full lieutenants. The same applied to the HKVDC medical officers.
4. Sophie's and my parents were in Shanghai at the time.
5. The expression meaning "when the action starts" is said to date from the First World War.

The Battle Lines

It was estimated that the Japanese forces across the border, under the command of Lietenant-General Sakai, numbered three divisions (about 27,000 men) with plenty of reserves. They had sufficient artillery and aircraft, and a considerable naval blockade force. The troops were well-trained, experienced in fighting under all conditions and of high morale. The Japanese intelligence work was thorough and there was an extensive network of spies and Fifth Column[6] among the local population placed well in advance.

Hong Kong's position on the other hand was weak. The garrison, drawn from units of Middlesex, Royal Scots, two Indian regiments, HKVDC, and reinforced in the last three weeks by two battalions of Canadians, numbered barely twelve thousand.[7] It had no air power, little naval support and inadequate anti-aircraft defences. Strategically, Hong Kong was considered by many indefensible — "a hostage to fortune" as its General Officer Commanding (GOC), Major-General C. M. Maltby MC, described it. In tribute to the spirit of Hong Kong's defence, it must be stated that surrendering Hong Kong without a fight never entered the minds of those in command.

The Battle

Early in December 1941, as news of the Japanese troop concentrations on the border came in, the Hong Kong garrison was put on the alert and by 7 December most of the battle stations were manned. The HKVDC was mobilized on the same day and we were told that Japanese attack across the border was expected at any moment. The demolition of frontier bridges, in

---

6. "Fifth Column" means traitors, or those within a country working for the enemy. The term is said to have originated during the Spanish Civil War (1936–39), when General Mola had encircled Madrid with four columns while a fifth column was working for him inside the city.

7. Sending two Canadian battalions, The Royal Rifles of Canada and The Winnipeg Grenadiers, to reinforce what was deemed to be an indefensible outpost, was blamed on Britain and severely criticized in Canada after the war. It is true that the move could not alter the inevitable fall of Hong Kong. The Canadians, arriving in Hong Kong only three weeks before the Battle, were unfamiliar with the local terrain and poorly acclimatized. In the fighting they suffered heavy casualties, and many died in the prisoner-of-war camps. But in my opinion the criticism is unjustified. They fought bravely and with distinction, and did enhance the defenders' resistance to the enemy. As soldiers they were committed to the war; if sent to a different area, who could tell what difference this would have made to the war effort, and whether they would have fared better or worse than in Hong Kong?

84   Part 1

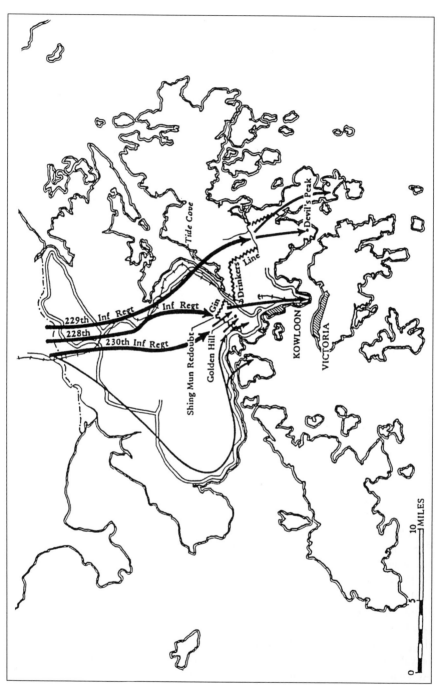

Route of Japanese attack on Hong Kong

which the sappers of the HKVDC played an active part, were mostly completed in time before the Japanese attacked.

I was ordered to report to the HKVDC Headquarters, in uniform and with kitbag packed, at eight o'clock on the morning of 8 December for deployment. As I was preparing to leave home, I could hear series of explosions in the distance and knew that an air-raid was on; the war in the Pacific had started. I said goodbye to my wife of two and a half months; I do not recall at the time a sense of foreboding that, apart from a few hours during a truce in the fighting, I would not see her again until three years and eight months later. At the headquarters, tension was palpable and there was a good deal of commotion as various units of Volunteers were dispatched to their positions. I was issued with a 38 mm revolver — a standard officers' issue — and twelve rounds of ammunition, and accompanied by six field ambulance men and medical equipment, proceeded to our assigned post — a concrete bunker by the Pok Fu Lam Reservoir, on the narrow road leading from Pok Fu Lam Road to Victoria Gap on the Peak. A strange position for an ADS (Advanced Dressing Station), I thought at the time, which should have been occupied by a combatant unit to guard the reservoir — an obvious target for saboteurs.

The Japanese troops crossed the border in force at Lo Wu in the early hours of 8 December 1941, and advanced swiftly using outflanking movements against our forward units. Simultaneously Kai Tak airport was bombed and the few planes, mostly reconnaissance type, were destroyed on the ground. Advancing by day and night and never-relaxing pressure, the Japanese reached the Gin Drinker's Line, Hong Kong's main defence line on the mainland, at dawn of 9 December. It seems that apart from a few minor skirmishes, they met with little resistance, though at least one ambush against them was effective. Clearly, the defenders had decided to put up a determined stand at the Gin Drinker's Line — an unfortunate name as it soon proved. On the night of 9/10 December, the Japanese in a brilliant assault captured the Shing Mun Redoubt, thus turning the left flank of the Line. Intended to hold up the Japanese advance for at least a week, the Gin Drinker's Line fell after only two days of fighting, exposing the rest of the New Territories to the Japanese advance.[8]

8. The Gin Drinker's Line, a ten-mile-long string of fortified pillboxes and bunkers, stretched from Gin Drinker's Bay (Tsuen Wan) in the west to Shelter Bay in the east. It relied heavily on the integrity of Shing Mun Redoubt, an underground fort guarding the most vulnerable part of the Line. The origin of its strange, obviously British, name is obscure.

At my ADS, at Pok Fu Lam Reservoir, I arranged duties and issued necessary precautionary instructions. Fifth columnists were reported to be active around our area. As I impressed on my men the importance of being alert and ready, although a complete novice, I felt in a strange way fully in control. We could hear sounds of distant gunfire, but the front was far away and our location was quiet except for a nearly tragic event on the very first day, when a medic from the neighbouring ADS, at Aberdeen, turned up asking for bandages which, in an oversight, were not issued to his unit. As he sat down inside the bunker, he dropped his rifle on the floor and the rifle fired. The sound inside was deafening as the bullet ricocheted from the walls but amazingly no one was hit: the 303 Enfield rifles had notoriously unreliable, often loose, safety catches.

At night occasional rifle shots were heard, probably nervous sentries alarmed by strange noises firing at unseen targets. We were told later that in the first few days of fighting a number of our men were killed by "trigger-happy" sentries. No casualties were reported at my ADS and the men spent their time practising bandaging and arms drill. The quiet was broken on 10 December when waves of Japanese planes bombed Mount Davis Fort, on the west side of Hong Kong Island, not far and easily seen from our ADS. The heavy bombing continued most of the day, and as I was reflecting on the relative safety of our position compared to Mount Davis, I saw a dispatch rider riding on his motorcycle towards our bunker. He brought orders for me to proceed immediately to Mount Davis Fort for attachment as the medical officer. Clearly the Field Ambulance Command anticipated casualties at the Fort. I ordered the sergeant in my unit to take charge of the ADS, then jumped on the pillion seat of the motorcycle and told the dispatch rider to take me forthwith to Mount Davis Fort. We managed to arrive safely at the Fort with the air raid still on, in the blaze of exploding bombs.

Located high on Mount Davis, Mount Davis Fort housed the 24th Coast Battery, Royal Artillery (RA), manned by some 120 British and Indian gunners under the command of Major L. Anderson — all regular soldiers. The Battery was armed with three large 9.2 inch guns, installed before the First World War, and a 3.7 inch anti-aircraft gun. The three heavy guns, placed at different levels on the mountain, were numbered 1, 2 and 3 from the lower to the upper. Only the topmost (No. 3) had a full circular range of fire; the others were pointing southwards towards the sea and so no threat to the Japanese on the mainland. There were also a number of machine-gun pillboxes scattered around the mountain. The Fort contained several buildings of various degrees of protection — storerooms, cookhouse, quarters, and a medical room. A well-protected complex of rooms contained the Battery Plotting Room shielded by thick steel and concrete — the battery nerve centre. I was welcomed by the Battery's Commanding Officer and was informed that the Battery's two medical orderlies would be placed at my disposal. Throughout the following days the Fort was heavily bombarded from the air and by the land-based enemy batteries in the now captured New Territories. After most of the buildings of the Fort had been either severely damaged or destroyed, the Battery Plotting Room complex offered the only real protection and most of the men who were not on duty took refuge there from the shelling.

During the first few days Major Anderson became convinced that the Japanese landing on the Island would take place at the west end, below Mount Davis, and as a result issued instructions for fighting a rearguard action down towards Pok Fu Lam Road, the assumption being that the Japanese would prevail and we would be forced to retreat. Major Anderson's prediction of the landing was not entirely unfounded, as concentrations of junks were seen off Lamma Island and even an attempted landing at Aberdeen had been reported, but not confirmed, all close enough to Mount Davis. My orders were to stay behind with the inevitable casualties relying on the Red Cross armband for protection. Having little faith in the protection offered by the latter, I did not relish the prospect, but neither did I believe that the landing would take place where the Commanding Officer had predicted — a bold opinion for a young and inexperienced subaltern.

When the landing did take place, it was at the logical place, at Lei Yue Mun, the narrowest strait between the mainland and the Island. In the meantime, on 11 December, the Battery was put on "stand-to", or state of alert, orders until further notice, and we had to endure the discomfort of sleeping with our boots on and encased in webbing equipment. The mood of despondency was evident. Without aerial observation the Battery could not pinpoint enemy positions. The Battery's topmost gun (No. 3) disabled by the bombing, we could fire only occasional salvos from the second gun at random targets.

After the loss of the Gin Drinker's Line, most of the Mainland Brigade was withdrawn to Hong Kong Island by 12 December. Only some Indian units (5/7th Rajput Regiment) remained on Devil's Peak Peninsula in Kowloon, but after a heavy enemy attack late on 12 December these too had to be withdrawn and were successfully evacuated by the much depleted Royal Navy. By the morning of 13 December the whole of the New Territories and Kowloon Peninsula were in Japanese hands.

As the Japanese consolidated their gains and brought more guns into position, the beleaguered Island came under heavy artillery and aerial bombardment. The defenders, besieged and with no hope of relief, the Japanese now had reason to expect them to give up. On 12 December, even before the last of the Rajputs had left the mainland, a launch with the Japanese under a flag of truce crossed the harbour with a letter addressed to the Governor of Hong Kong demanding an unconditional surrender. This was curtly rejected.

The truce which lasted several hours gave me an opportunity to walk to my home on Pok Fu Lam Road, not far from Mount Davis, and take a much needed shower, but I missed Sophie. She was working at St. Stephen's College, on Lyttleton Road, which had been converted into a hospital.[9] After being subjected to the nearly continuous noise of gunfire and explosions during the previous four days, the silence of the truce felt strange and unreal, even slightly unnerving. As I walked back to Mount Davis, it was getting dark. I walked openly in the middle of the road, making enough noise with my heavy boots — I was not going to be shot by some nervous sentry! Before I reached the top, gunfire started again: the truce was over.

On 13 December the enemy artillery fire was intensified. At Mount Davis we had been lucky so far, incurring only few casualties, none serious, mostly by shrapnel from exploding shells, but that afternoon an excited gunner rushed into the Battery Plotting Complex with the news that the anti-aircraft position received a direct hit and there were many casualties. I decided to reach the wounded men with emergency kit to treat the worst cases and assess the situation. I recall my feelings prior to this as being fear mixed with frustration from being powerless to respond, but now I felt roused into action. The men inside formed a corridor and some patted me on the shoulder in encouragement as I prepared to emerge outside where the bombardment was still going on. Then the steel door was opened and I rushed out and up the steps to the anti-aircraft position running so fast that it felt as if I had wings. At the site a horrible scene of carnage met my eyes. Four men were dead and ten were wounded, some very badly. Blood was everywhere.

I cannot remember how long I spent with the wounded, injecting morphia and stopping bleeding. During the next lull in the shelling, I organized a party to bring the dead and the wounded into my medical room, now damaged and

---

9. There were two St. Stephen's Colleges; the other one was at Stanley, where frightful atrocities were committed by the Japanese at the end of the Battle (see further in the text).

sandbagged, for more treatment; two small ambulances arrived at the Battery to take the dead and the wounded to hospital. Even as we were loading them into the ambulances, the shelling resumed, but fortunately no one was hurt and the ambulances got away safely. I never found out what happened to the wounded men.

The following day, Sunday 14 December, a large, 9.5-inch armour-piercing shell, fired possibly from a cruiser, penetrated our protected "sanctuary" in the Battery Plotting Complex but failed to explode. Some sixty men inside narrowly escaped being blown to bits. The shell's entry was accompanied by a loud crash and total darkness. When the emergency lights were switched on, we saw the monster shell with its nose imbedded in the floor — it was no more than five feet from where I was. The Commanding Officer ordered evacuation of the Complex since it was no longer safe; another shell exploding nearby could cause a "sympathetic" detonation of the unexploded one, he explained. As the shelling outside continued, small parties of three to four men rushed out through the back door timing their escape between explosions. I was instructed to stay until the last party, and I must confess that remaining in close proximity to an unexploded shell, which could go off "sympathetically" at any moment, was possibly the most unpleasant experience of my life. I cannot recall exactly how long I remained inside; it might have been thirty or forty minutes. By that time the air had become oppressive and thick with sulphurous smell, probably issuing from the shell, so much so that we had to put on our respirators. Ironically, during this critical period, I was able to observe men acting under stress. All were frightened, but most were able to function effectively, a few less so. I saw at least one, a sergeant, who broke down completely and had to be helped. When at last it was my turn to leave the Complex, I needed no reminder as I ran out, up the hill and then down the other side of the mountain, away from the shelling. Sliding down a steep slope, I propped myself against a tree and lit a cigarette.

It was a beautiful sunny afternoon. The war seemed far away. I felt happy and at peace. I do not remember how long I was in this state when I was awakened from my reverie by a voice: one of the men was reminding me that we were due to assemble at our new headquarters. The Battery Complex now abandoned, the Battery headquarters was transferred to the basement of Felix Villas, an old building on Mount Davis Road. There we were issued with new instructions. The Mount itself and all the undamaged posts would still be manned by the gunners. My medical room was to be moved to a concrete guard-room half-way up the road to the Fort; it soon proved to be an unsuitable location as it had no telephone.

Throughout 15 and 16 December heavy bombardment of the Island continued, the Japanese now concentrating on the defenders' pillboxes and shore batteries, clearly attempting to "soften" shore defences in preparation for the imminent landing. Their accurate fire destroyed many pillboxes. There were also numerous air-raids on Shek-O, Lei Yue Mun, and Aberdeen. Mount Davis was also heavily bombed, fortunately with only minimal casualties, and the No. 2 gun was rendered useless. The morale of the civilian population, already affected by heavy bombardment, "remained shaky, chiefly due to rice distribution difficulties", reported General Maltby in his dispatches. In fact, the civilian population suffered substantial casualties. Many people were displaced from their homes and there was heavy damage and destruction of property. On the night of 15 December, an apparent attempt by the enemy to land at Pak Sha Wan was beaten off by the prompt action of the 4th Battery manned by the Volunteers, for which they earned a commendation. The day of 17 December saw another spell of intense bombardment followed by the second Japanese party under a flag of truce with another demand for an unconditional surrender. This time, I made directly for St. Stephen's College where I was able to spend the few hours' respite with my wife. The demand for surrender was again rejected and the battle was resumed.

On 18 December the Japanese shelled heavily the north shore of the Island, but this time the defenders were able to hit back with their own batteries and it was reported that at least one enemy battery, on Devil's Peak, was silenced. After ten days of fighting, Hong Kong's garrison was reported as still in good spirits and fighting order, but the waiting for the inevitable landing on the Island was a severe strain. It was about this time that my medical room was transferred once more, this time into a flimsy, plywood hut that had once served as a signal station for ships using the western passage into the harbour. Although equipped with a telephone — the main reason for placing me there — it proved a singularly bad choice since it was close to the Battery's last, still undamaged, heavy gun — the No. 1 gun. The Japanese bombers now turned their attention to it, dive-bombing day upon day until the end of the Battle. They missed the gun, but many of the bombs fell uncomfortably close to the hut, and on one occasion, as I was attending to a wounded man outside, the enemy plane returned firing its machine-gun at us, none of the bullets, however, finding the target. It is difficult to convey to anyone who has not experienced dive-bombing the unnerving crescendo noise of a dive-bomber followed by the horrible piercing sound of a missile.

I shared the hut with two RA officers, both seasoned old soldiers, veterans of the First World War. Perhaps it was their *sang-froid* which passed on to me, for after the first two or three days of sheer terror, I was able to share their calmness and stop wondering whether the next bomb would yet again miss the target and hit us instead.

The night of 18/19 of December was unusually dark. With this and the tide running in their favour, the Japanese launched their assault that night, landing across the narrow strait between Lei Yue Mun and North Point. They advanced rapidly inland along the routes leading to commanding heights. It was unfortunate that after expecting the landing for several days and foiling the enemy's few attempts, the actual landing was undetected. Once recognized, the defenders launched counterattacks, and the Volunteers' 4th Battery, at Pak Sha Wan, opened fire at the enemy landings, but by then the Japanese had consolidated their positions and could not be dislodged. In fierce fighting which developed at and around North Point, the Rajputs tried desperately to stop the enemy's advance as also did the Canadians; both failed suffering heavy casualties. The attackers, fighting mostly uphill, were utterly ruthless, taking no prisoners and killing our wounded. The 5th anti-aircraft Battery at Sai Wan Hill, manned by the Volunteers, was overrun and the captured gunners bayoneted. A similar fate befell an ADS at the Salesian Convent where civilian and army medical personnel were massacred.

Large enemy reinforcements were seen ferried from the mainland to the Island throughout 19 December, and although our motor torpedo boats (MTB) tried to attack them, it was of no avail. Bitter fighting continued with defenders, often surrounded and always outnumbered, stubbornly holding their positions as long as possible before being overrun. By early on 20 December, the Japanese had driven a wedge between the East and the West Brigades. As they pressed on towards Wong Nai Chung Gap, they surrounded the Canadian (West) Brigade Headquarters and in the ensuing close fighting Brigadier Lawson and most of the Headquarters personnel were killed. On the same day, the Japanese reached Repulse Bay occupied by our forces. In the bitter fighting, the Japanese were repulsed and the Hotel held, at least until 22 December. But some Japanese units bypassed it and were advancing towards Aberdeen.

At Mount Davis, the situation was static. The Japanese landing having taken place at the opposite end of the Island, the "stand-to" was cancelled, but the various positions around the Fort were manned around the clock. The two officers and I remained on duty at the signal station while the Japanese bombers continued to attack the No. 1 gun but without success. The gun's crew had sustained some casualties, fortunately none major. There is little doubt that inability to respond effectively against the enemy was deeply

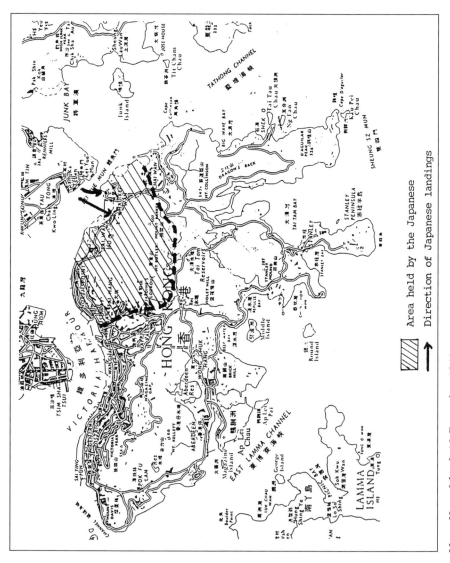

Hong Kong Island: 19 December 1941

frustrating for the Battery personnel. Japanese shelling was now directed periodically against low-positioned coastal batteries, among them the Jubilee Battery, at the foot of Mount Davis, although its three 6-inch guns, directed west and south, posed no threat to the Japanese positions. It was during one of these sporadic shellings that I had another brush with death, and in the process acquired a canine friend. It was either 21 or 22 December, when on my way to a meeting at the Fort's new headquarters, I found myself in the middle of shelling. An explosion some thirty or forty metres away sent me scurrying into the nearest house, which turned out to be empty. I was frightened and desolate when suddenly I felt something brushing against my leg. A dog shivering and obviously very frightened was snuggling up to me, a total stranger, and at that moment we each found comfort in the other's company. How terrifying it must be for the poor animal, I thought, to sense but not understand the horror around. And then a strange impulse, a strong urge, impelled me to leave the house immediately.

I seized the dog and ran with the speed I did not think I was capable of. As I ducked into the basement of the house which served as our Headquarters, I turned around and saw the house we were hiding in a few moments ago hit by a shell. To this day I cannot explain that sudden impulse which may have saved my life. Inside the safe, sandbagged Headquarters, the warmth, the sound of friendly voices, and the inevitable hot, sweet cup of British army tea brought a wonderful sense of relief and calm. The dog remained with us at the Headquarters till the end of the Hong Kong Battle.

On the Island, by 20 December, the Japanese had made substantial progress with a large eastern portion of the Island in their hands. At Stanley Gap, the Hong Kong Volunteers made a gallant stand but were overwhelmed, suffering heavy casualties. The little red book describes the heroism of Lieutenant Field who "was severely wounded on four separate occasions, and the wonderful determination he showed under the circumstances was beyond all praise".[10] Heavy fighting developed at Wong Nai Chung Gap, where the Canadians, the Middlesex and the HKVDC fought hard. Both sides suffered heavy casualties, but the Gap was lost to the enemy. The battle now shifted to the Ridge, the high ground between Repulse Bay in the south and Wong Nai Chung Gap in the north, where repeated attacks by the enemy were beaten off, but which was eventually lost, on 22 December, after a full-scale attack by the enemy.

---

10. *A Record of the Actions of the Hong Kong Volunteer Defence Corps in the Battle for Hong Kong December, 1941*, p. 29.

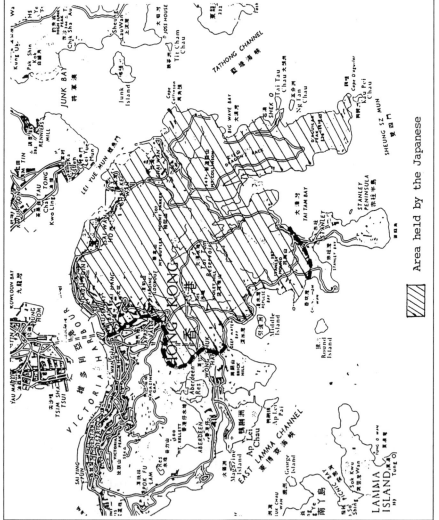

Area held by the Japanese

Hong Kong Island: 22 December 1941

The Japanese committed horrible atrocities, both at the Gap and the Ridge, where our captured men were "roped together ... and butchered".[11] Repulse Bay Hotel, which held out until 22 December, had to be evacuated leaving Stanley Peninsula isolated. Tytam Reservoir was captured, thus seriously reducing the Island's water supply.

On 23 December the Japanese attacked Mount Cameron (south of Jardine's Lookout) in force, capturing it. The Canadians, outnumbered ten to one, fought fiercely but were driven back. In Leighton Hill area (Happy Valley) the situation was becoming critical. The exhausted defenders, without any reserves and under continuous shelling, were falling back but still managed to hold out for two days. By 24 December the Japanese were on the very doorstep of the densely populated Wan Chai and Central District; both were heavily shelled and several large fires were started in Wan Chai. Stanley Peninsula, bypassed and isolated, still held out but the Japanese were bringing reinforcements to the Stanley area with the obvious intention of breaking through the defences at the narrow isthmus. When eventually they attacked, on 24 December, the fighting on both sides was as ferocious as any in the whole of the Battle for Hong Kong. The Battle of Stanley, in which the Middlesex and the HKVDC fought against a greatly superior Japanese force, was one of the defenders' proudest and most gallant episodes of the Hong Kong war. Casualties were very high on both sides. The No. 2 Company of the HKVDC (The Scottish Company) lost more than half of its men who were killed, wounded or missing. The Japanese lost hundreds, killed in the attack. It was all the more tragic as the men died just twenty-four hours before Hong Kong was forced to surrender.

At Mount Davis, apart from sporadic shelling and dive-bombing attacks on the No. 1 gun, there was little activity. We listened helplessly to the news of the fierce fighting on the Island and the hopeless plight of our comrades. A few units from our Battery were sent as reinforcements but we knew they could hardly alter the outcome of the fight. On Christmas Eve, units which could still be reached, including our Battery, received season's greetings from the governor and the general-in-command, probably the saddest Christmas they would ever experience.

---

11. *A Record of the Actions*, p. 37.

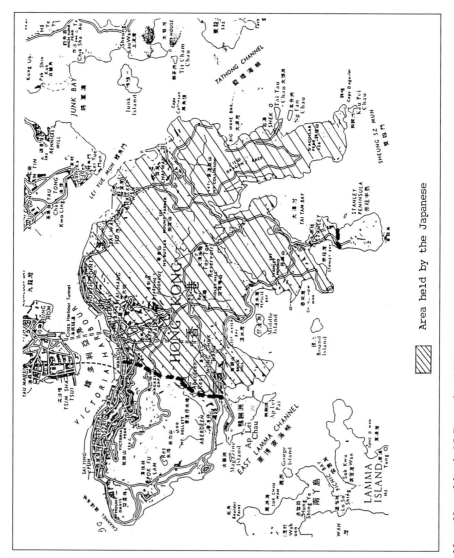

Hong Kong Island: 25 December 1941

On 25 December, Christmas Day, the situation on the Island was critical. Everywhere the defenders were giving ground. At Stanley the last desperate stand by the Middlesex and the HKVDC was made near Stanley Fort; having lost all their machine-guns, they were reduced to rifles. The Japanese, infuriated by the heavy casualties suffered, went on a rampage committing frightful atrocities on defenceless people. At St. Stephen's College, which was converted into a hospital, wounded men were bayoneted to death and nurses raped and killed. Two doctors who attempted to stop the massacre were shot on the spot.[12]

The Surrender

The garrison had fought for eighteen days with but two very brief pauses. Serious water shortage, lack of ammunition, and the risk of severe retaliation against the civilian population persuaded the governor and the general-in-command that no further resistance was possible and that the only way left was to lay down arms. At 3.15 p.m. on Christmas Day, Hong Kong capitulated to the Japanese.

At Mount Davis, we realized that the end of our resistance was near. When the order of surrender arrived on the afternoon of 25 December, it bore no instructions on the disposal of our weapons. Suspecting that the latter may follow shortly, our commanding officer ordered all weapons to be destroyed immediately. I buried my revolver which was never fired (will some future archaeologist perhaps come across it?). All around me, gunners were bashing their rifles against rocks and throwing away rifle bolts, while the plucky No. 1 gun, which had survived a whole week of bombing, was blown up with a tremendous bang. I believe we were the sole unit of the Hong Kong garrison to have destroyed our weapons.

However inevitable the surrender was, we felt stunned and depressed — a defeated army, facing long imprisonment, indeed with the slimmest chance of survival. I said goodbye to the gunners with a heavy feeling; we had shared many harrowing hours together in difficult conditions. The Royal Regiment of Artillery would always have a warm place in my heart. The day following the surrender, I reported to the nearest Volunteer collecting centre, at Hong Kong University, and we spent the next two days searching for our wounded and dead comrades; the Japanese were searching for theirs. I had no news of my wife and was not able to reach her, which made my despondency worse.

---

12. They were Lieut.-Colonel Black (HKVDC) and Captain Whitney (RAMC).

After two more days, 28 and 29 December at Murray Barracks on Garden Road, we marched to Sham Shui Po Camp — a sad and humiliated procession of bedraggled defeated warriors marching towards an uncertain future.

Conclusion

In summing up the Battle for Hong Kong, it may be conceded that the New Territories and Kowloon were lost too early and too easily. However, the Island was defended with courage and stubbornness which surprised the enemy and which, knowing that Hong Kong must ultimately fall, can only be described as heroic. In the subsequent analysis by the Army in 1961, the Volunteers were described as having fought bravely for every inch of the ground.[13] The casualties were heavy. Excluding HKVDC, the Hong Kong garrison, numbering about 9500, lost about 2100 killed or missing and 2300 wounded. The heaviest loss was sustained by the Rajputs who lost all their officers and nearly 65% of the men. The HKVDC suffered 36% killed and wounded.

Thirty-seven Volunteers were awarded decorations for bravery in action.

The Japanese losses were difficult to estimate. The true figure is probably close to the one given by General Maltby in his Dispatch, viz. three thousand killed and nine thousand wounded. The Japanese committed a number of particularly brutal atrocities, the worst at Stanley. There can be no excuse for that, but an explanation may be found in the very stubborn resistance of the defenders and the heavy Japanese casualties. The atrocities were mostly committed by other ranks, i.e. common soldiers, and on occasions might have been worse, had not a Japanese officer intervened and stopped them.

It has been asked: if Hong Kong's fate was sealed from the start, what was the point of resisting and subjecting both troops and civilians to the seemingly futile slaughter and the agony of war? The answer probably lies in the philosophy of war, which, abhorrent though it may be, still has its rules, its traditions, and its heroes. One such tradition is not to surrender until all means of resistance have been exhausted. It also has its military value — delaying enemy advance and inflicting upon it a maximum number of casualties. It was surely this tradition that the prime minister, Mr Winston Churchill, had in mind when on 23 December he sent a telegram to the governor, Sir Mark Young, exhorting the garrison to resist to the utmost.

---

13. This was a secret document containing the British Army's "post-mortem" analysis of Hong Kong's defence; unfortunately I am unable to give details of the document.

The telegram ended with the following words: "Every day that you are able to maintain your resistance you help the Allied cause all over the world, and by prolonged resistance you and your men can win the lasting honour which we are sure will be your due." Whatever military strategists may say about the defence of Hong Kong, it cannot be denied that its defenders fought as hard and as long as possible. Theirs was the Lasting Honour.

Thus, on 25 December 1941 the bloodshed and the fury of the Battle were over, and the long nightmare of occupation began.

> "To all nations War is a great matter.
> Upon the army death or life depend:
> It is the means of the existence
> Or destruction of the State."

Sunzi (5th century BCE)

Bibliography

Anonymous *A Record of the Actions of the Hong Kong Volunteer Defence Corps in the Battle for Hong Kong, December 1941*, Ye Olde Printerie, Hong Kong 1953.

Bard, S. M. *The Battle for Hong Kong and the Japanese Occupation of Hong Kong 1941–1945*; an unpublished research paper, May 1989.

Endacott, G. B. (ed. Birch, A.) *Hong Kong Eclipse*, Oxford University Press, Hong Kong 1978.

Hong Kong War Emergency Legislation, Hong Kong Government 1939 & 1941, Noronha & Co.

Lindsay, Oliver *The Lasting Honour*, Hamish Hamilton, London 1978.

Maltby, C. M. *Operations in Hong Kong, December 8–25, 1941*, London Gazette Supplement, 27 January 1948.

8

BEHIND BARBED WIRE: LIFE IN A JAPANESE PRISONER-OF-WAR CAMP

"I dream of that great day
On which the enemy will quit the land..."

Emile Cammaerts (1878–1953)

My essay "The Battle for Hong Kong, December 1941" ended with the words: "Thus, on 25 December 1941 the bloodshed and the fury of the Battle were over, and the long nightmare of occupation began." What follows is the sequel, the story of that long nightmare.

I did not keep a diary during my imprisonment, with the result that while the events are clear in my mind, some of the dates are not. I hope this will not lessen any interest which my story may contain.

Hong Kong Surrenders
The capitulation of Hong Kong was signed by the governor, Sir Mark Young, on 26 December 1941 at the Peninsula Hotel, and the conquering Japanese army entered the city in a ceremonial victory parade, on 28 December. After the noise of battle, an uneasy quiet fell on the shocked, expectant population. Several weeks of disorder followed, in which looting was widespread, before law and order were restored.

Sham Shui Po Prisoner-of-War (POW) Camp
Within a few days of the surrender, all combatants in uniform, previously assembled at various points, were marched off to POW camps. The main one was established at Sham Shui Po, in Kowloon, to house British, Canadian and Hong Kong Volunteer Defence Corps (HKVDC) troops. As we marched towards Sham Shui Po, dispirited and humiliated, we presented a sad and depressing picture, one which later became familiar in war documentaries:

a long procession of miserable, bedraggled soldiers, all their smartness gone, clutching their few belongings. Added to the bitter humiliation of defeat was the despair of an expected long imprisonment. There were not a few jeers from onlookers who gathered to watch our pathetic progress, but the Japanese sentries guarding us behaved with propriety. It was the most degrading experience of my life.

The camp, formerly British army barracks, occupied an area of approximately forty thousand square metres on the western shore of Kowloon Peninsula. It contained a parade ground and two large four-storey buildings, called the Jubilee Buildings; the rest were mostly wooden huts. This was to be my home for the next three years and eight months, though I did not know it at the time. Inside the camp chaos and confusion reigned. If we were not prepared for the camp, the camp was certainly not prepared for us. More than five thousand captured troops were placed in the limited confines of the Camp, built to accommodate between one and two thousand, resulting in gross overcrowding. With no idea of what was required, the Japanese had not bothered to outfit the camp. There were shortages of everything — accommodation, bedding and furniture, toilets and washing facilities.

Previous barracks amenities were mostly looted or damaged during the fighting. What was left was now quickly seized by the smart, quick-thinking among us; it was each man for himself.

It took two or three weeks for conditions to improve and for order slowly to emerge. Gradually the basic necessities were brought in, such as blankets, mattresses, soap and suchlike, and issued to all. Essential amenities, in particular the cookhouse, toilets and showers were organized.

Men were lodged in large communal huts, primitive and overcrowded, but a few smaller huts were assigned to officers. Because of overcrowding, lice and bugs became a problem, never really eradicated; weekly "delousing sessions", begun in the early phase, were eventually abandoned and we all learned to live with these pests.[1]

Nutrition and Health

It soon became clear that our food rations would be woefully inadequate, consisting mainly of rice and green vegetables with rare additions of a little

---

1. I found that bedbugs appeared to be discriminating in whom they bit: while some people were driven nearly mad from bites, others like myself were relatively unaffected.

meat or fish.[2] The daily calorie intake could not have been more than 1200–1500 per man (against an average daily adult requirement of around 3000). Fortunately, friends and relatives who were not interned were allowed to send in parcels. Although themselves often short of food, they selflessly brought what they could, relieving what I believe would have been a far worse situation in the camp; indeed, they were saving lives. Parcels were usually shared with others inside. Unfortunately, the Japanese often stopped parcels for varying periods of time as punishment for infringements of camp discipline. The Swiss Red Cross too had attempted to send parcels into the camp regularly, but in Sham Shui Po, to the best of my recollection, only three parcels per person were received — all near the end of our imprisonment.[3] A camp canteen, where food, cigarettes, and other minor consumer items could be purchased, was operated by the Japanese, but as with parcels was often closed as punishment; after the first year, it contained little of value. Men going out on working parties were paid small wages while officers were paid monthly salaries, both in Japanese military money (yen). The money could be used in the camp canteen, but the enormous devaluation of the yen, especially towards the end of the war, made the money almost worthless.[4]

These payments to officers and men may seem at first glance to be a surprising observance by the Japanese of the Geneva Convention,[5] knowing their general disregard and even contempt for it. But the money had, in fact, been paid by the British government, through the Swiss government, at a proper rate; in other words — good pounds sterling for worthless military yen. It is to the credit of the British government, that after the war these payments to prisoners at Sham Shui Po Camp (and perhaps at other camps in South-East Asia) were ignored and the released officers received their back pay in full.

---

2. Headline on 17 June 1942 in the *Hong Kong News*, the local English-language tabloid under Japanese control, read: "Hong Kong War Prisoners Thriving". It added: "each soldier received four ounces of meat daily plus a regular food allowance". It might have been four ounces per month!
3. It was widely believed that the Japanese had appropriated most of the Red Cross parcels for their own use, but allowed a few to get through near the end of the war when the tide turned against them.
4. The Japanese military yen did not even have serial numbers. I recall that by 1944, my monthly pay, of some 50 yen, could buy perhaps a box of matches.
5. Geneva Convention: An international agreement of 1864 regulating, among other things, treatment of prisoners-of-war.

On arrival at Sham Shui Po, there were some seven or eight Royal Army Medical Corps (RAMC) doctors, three HKVDC doctors, and three Canadian Army doctors. There were also two dentists, and a number of RAMC and HKVDC medical orderlies. Makeshift wards were urgently organized as there were still men who needed medical attention from wounds received during the fighting. The medical facilities, primitive at first, were gradually improved until we could boast a simple hospital with several inpatient wards staffed by the RAMC orderlies. An outpatient section was also established in which daily "sick parades" — an army term for men who reported sick — were attended to by the medical officers. HKVDC medics could not be used in these medical facilities as they had no experience in hospital care. The Officer Commanding (OC) the Field Ambulance, Major L. T. Ride, professor of physiology in peacetime, escaped during the first two weeks, but not before telling his medical officers that as he had no clinical experience he would be useless in camp but hoped that the rest of us would remain with the men. He made his way into China where he subsequently organized and commanded the British Army Aid Group (BAAG).[6]

Serious cases which could not be effectively treated in camp and those requiring major surgery were sent to Bowen Road Hospital, on Hong Kong Island, formerly a British army hospital which continued to be used for the prisoners-of-war and was staffed by British army and navy, and HKVDC doctors not interned at Sham Shui Po. There were nearly always long delays in sending patients there, and not a few died while waiting for the Japanese to arrange the transfer across the harbour. We seldom saw the senior Japanese army doctor, one Captain Saito, who was responsible for our medical "welfare". On the few occasions when we did, he showed no sympathy nor any sign of medical solidarity which might have been expected from a fellow member of a healing profession. When sickness and poor physical condition had reduced the number of men fit for working parties, he demanded the numbers be maintained irrespective of the men's condition, and I recall one confrontation with him when he angrily accused camp doctors of deliberately shielding men from work. He failed to provide an adequate supply of medicines and generally made no effort to help us in any way. Fortunately, his medical sergeant showed some sympathy. The latter visited our hospital at regular intervals: we could hear him approaching with shuffling gait, his sword bouncing on the

---

6. BAAG — British Army Aid Group — was a British Intelligence Unit which operated successfully in China and maintained contacts with its agents in Hong Kong. One of its objectives was to help POWs to escape.

ground. First, he would tell us of the great successes of the Japanese forces, which sank the whole American fleet (several times over) and were about to invade Australia, and that we would surely lose the war. He would then empty his pockets of tablets and capsules — some drugs desperately needed by us — which he had managed to scrounge secretly: he undoubtedly risked severe punishment if discovered. We could only be supremely grateful to this Japanese medic who had more humanity than his superior officer.

Around April 1942, the Japanese replaced the senior RAMC officer, initially in charge of our medical establishment, with Major Ashton-Rose of the Indian Medical Service (IMS). From his dark complexion and a slightly Indian accent, we assumed that he was Anglo-Indian. Rumours circulated that he assumed major's rank on his own when in fact he was a lieutenant.[7]

If by putting him in charge the Japanese expected a compliant, spineless man, they were completely mistaken, for Ashton-Rose from the start took a firm, even demanding, stand with the Japanese and got away with it. He also proved to be a very capable administrator, and our medical facilities in camp improved substantially; in due course he even managed to equip a small operating theatre where he personally operated on a number of occasions, especially when the Japanese were slow in arranging a transfer to Bowen Road Hospital. With us — medical officers under his authority — he behaved correctly and in a friendly manner.

Our medical provisions were grossly inadequate, consisting of what the medical officers managed to bring with them to camp and barely a trickle of items provided by the Japanese. It soon became clear that with such shortages and the insufficient and unbalanced food rations, we would be faced with malnutrition, deficiency diseases, and a difficult struggle against infectious diseases, many already endemic to Hong Kong. It turned out worse than we had expected. By the fourth month of our imprisonment, beri-beri, a disease due to deficiency of Vitamin B1, made its appearance accompanied by loss of weight. It was the type known as "wet beri-beri" characterized by the accumulation of fluid (dropsy) and affecting the heart. It also became clear that not everyone was affected to the same degree, adaptation presumably being an important factor in individual response. Food parcels from outside, even if shared, still did not reach many prisoners. Dysentery, diarrhoea and malaria became frequent and very troublesome, and there was never enough medicine to offer effective treatment. The year 1942 proved to be particularly

---

7. This was subsequently shown to be incorrect: he was in fact a bona fide acting major.

bad, for on top of malnutrition and infections, a sudden and severe epidemic of diphtheria[8] attacked the camp in late June. It spread like wildfire, picking and killing the more susceptible, and ceased just as suddenly some three months later. Mortality was high, nearly 30–40%, as no specific serum or antitoxin was made available until the end of the epidemic in September. Was this criminal negligence on the part of the Japanese or were they unable to ship or fly serum to Hong Kong? The fact that the Japanese had at first refused to admit that the disease was diphtheria points to negligence. The epidemic caused a state of panic among the prisoners who at the slightest sign of sore throat imagined the worst. The doctors and medical orderlies in the diphtheria ward worked hard, disregarding their own safety.

In 1943, a distressing deficiency condition appeared among many of the inmates, which caused very painful feet variously described, from the sensation it produced, as "burning" or "electric" feet. So intense were the pain and discomfort that the unfortunate victims had to be treated with morphia, one of the few drugs of which we had a reasonable supply.[9] I made special evening ward rounds to see my patients with "burning feet" to check who needed morphia for the night. They always lay with their feet sticking outside the blanket as the heat made the pain worse. It was heart-rending to see their anxious pleading faces and yet to remain firm for they were limited to no more than one dose every four days. This tormenting disease was probably related to malnutrition and was thought to be a type of vitamin deficiency, possibly of Vitamin B6. It was clearly a neurological condition affecting the nerves of the feet, and when after months of suffering the pain and distress subsided, the patient was left with an unsteady gait which persisted for many years.[10] As with other conditions, some men were less or not at all affected, even among those who were obviously undernourished. I was one of the lucky ones, although my weight had dropped from the usual 156 to 116 lbs by the end of the internment. I suffered several attacks of dysentery and malaria, but on the whole remained fairly fit.

---

8. Diphtheria: An infectious disease in which a membrane forms in the throat. Untreated, it may result in paralysis or death; it is preventable by immunization.
9. All field ambulance medical officers carried ample amounts of pellets of morphine for quick relief of pain in severe war injuries.
10. After the war, in 1946, I attended a clinical meeting at Queen's Square Hospital, London, when several patients with nervous diseases were demonstrated. One was a former prisoner-of-war, though not from Sham Shui Po Camp, whose disability was the result of old, burnt-out, "electric feet". The doctors discussing this case regarded it as a deficiency disease, but were still uncertain about the exact cause.

By the end of 1944, deaths and transportation to Japan had reduced the camp population from over 5000 to about 1500 and conditions seemed to have stabilized. The survivors were thin and weak, many walked unsteadily, but most seemed to have attained a kind of physiological balance — neither gaining nor losing — living and functioning on the minimum of food intake.

Discipline and Punishment
Overall Japanese treatment was harsh and punishment, both collective and individual, was swift and ruthless. Slapping the face on the spot for minor offences — for instance for failing to salute a Japanese officer — was so common that in time we became almost used to it; after all, the Japanese slapped their own men, often in our view. Certainly my pride was hurt, when I was slapped for the first time — for not saluting a sentry (I did not notice him) — but not unbearably so. I was slapped only once more, for an equally minor offence, throughout my time in camp. A list of major offences and corresponding punishments, promulgated by our captors, included possession of a radio, offensive or riotous behaviour, stealing, escape or planning an escape. All incurred heavy jail sentences, while the last was punishable by death. Although punishment such as beating was inflicted for the slightest infringement, I recall no cases of totally unprovoked cruelty. In a wider sense, the failure of the Japanese to provide prisoners-of-war with adequate food and medical supplies was their worst offence. There was certainly no excuse for keeping POWs on very low rations during the early years as there were ample stocks of food in Hong Kong at the time of the surrender: Hong Kong had prepared itself for a long siege. But by 1944, with the blockade of Hong Kong more effective, it may be conceded that perhaps the Japanese found it increasingly difficult to resupply Hong Kong. Obviously, feeding their own troops would have been their first priority. Charles G. Roland in his excellent book *Long Night's Journey into Day*, about prisoners of war in Hong Kong and Japan, refers to a Japanese supply officer virtually admitting that the POWs were short of food but that he could do nothing about it.[11]

Camp Administration
The camp was administered by a Japanese army officer acting as camp commandant and assisted by several Japanese interpreters. His house — a

---

11. *Long Night's Journey into Day*, by Charles G. Roland, Wilfrid Laurier University Press, Canada 2001, p. 129.

small two-storey building — was located on the waterfront, immediately outside the camp. He had under his command about twenty men, mostly Formosans recruited into the Japanese army,[12] who constantly patrolled and guarded the camp.

There were two roll-calls a day, in the morning and in the evening, called by our own bugler. They were conducted by the camp commandant accompanied by a couple of guards and an interpreter. After the morning roll-call, camp routine would resume: men assigned to working parties would be taken out of camp to work as labourers, mostly on the extension of Kai Tak airport; officers were not sent on working parties. Those remaining in camp would be occupied with various camp "fatigues",[13] such as cleaning, sanitary, or gardening tasks, or with their own chores. Cooks — all chosen from among the prisoners — would begin preparing food; although most of them were experienced army cooks, it took some time before they could cook a decent meal of rice — our staple diet. Some of the officers had duties to perform: doctors worked in makeshift hospital wards, Army Service Corps officers looked after the stores. Although the camp was managed by a succession of reasonably benign camp commandants, one of whom — warrant officer Honda — we all regarded as a good and fair man, physical punishments were frequent and often severe. It was generally believed, and with good reason, that the degree and type of punishment was decided at a higher level — by senior Japanese officers such as the chief of all camps, Colonel Tokunaga, who was not at all well disposed towards prisoners-of-war.[14]

Camp Liaison Office and Interpreters

The prisoners' liaison office, set up from the start by the Japanese, proved unfortunately to be one of the ugliest aspects of the camp. With exceptional cunning, or perception, the Japanese selected an effete, weak-kneed Royal Army Service Corps major to act as the liaison officer between them and the prisoners. As they no doubt planned, this man throughout the imprisonment did nothing to protect our interests but became, from fear or weakness, totally subservient to his Japanese masters. Surrounded by a bunch of despicable

---

12. Formosa (later Taiwan) at that time had been under Japanese occupation since 1894.
13. "Fatigue" in military jargon refers to a small party assigned some task.
14. After the war Colonel Tokunaga and Captain Saito were convicted as war criminals and sentenced to death, but the sentence was later commuted to life imprisonment. It is doubtful if they served more than a few years in prison.

minions, who were all too ready to carry out his orders, they were despised and hated by everyone in camp.

The Japanese used several English-speaking interpreters in their dealings with us. They wore military uniform and varied in seniority and rank. Some were sadistically inclined and took pleasure in slapping prisoners at the slightest provocation, but there were others who helped and tried to improve conditions in camp. Among the latter, one whom we fondly nicknamed "Holy Joe" became a legend. At great personal risk, he smuggled medicines and messages into camp, earning the prisoners' lasting gratitude.[15] Another, a young interpreter by the name of Tsutada, used to visit the doctors' quarters and showed some friendliness towards us. He made no effort to conceal his hatred of the British, which he disclosed was rooted in the bad treatment he received as a schoolboy in Singapore. However, he reasoned that since it was the policy of the Japanese authorities, however misguided, to maintain POW camps, it was his duty to ensure that the camps were properly maintained. He did his best to obtain materials such as bricks and cement for essential repairs in camp, and spent some of his off-duty hours taking prisoners' spectacles and dentures for repairs in town.[16]

Morale and Spiritual Needs

Men, defeated and deprived of freedom and of common necessities, are all too prone to become demoralized. I believed that our morale would be an important factor in our ultimate survival, that it would take a great effort not to succumb, not to lose hope. The year 1942 was especially bad not only because of the prevailing illnesses and many deaths, but also because of the consistently bad news about the progress of the war. Clearly our fate depended on what was happening in the other theatres of war, and the Allies appeared to be doing badly everywhere. Personally, I nurtured no happy illusions as to our ultimate fate, irrespective of the outcome of the war, and only a faint hope that I might be wrong. Most of the time I tried to be busy and not to think of the future.

---

15. His name was Watanabe. A protestant pastor in civilian life, he took enormous risks to help POWs and civilian internees at Stanley. Happily he was never discovered and survived the war. His life was written up after the war in the book *Small Man of Nanataki* by Liam Nolan.
16. Although convicted after the war of ill-treating POWs, he received a light sentence: two years' imprisonment.

At the beginning of our captivity, some talked about rumours of a "large Chinese army descending upon the Japanese in Hong Kong and liberating us", or of the "skies turning black with a massive British air armada bombing and driving the Japanese out of Hong Kong". These misbeliefs or wishful thinking were dispelled when Singapore, regarded as impregnable, fell to the Japanese on 15 February 1942. This event, not surprisingly, dipped low our morale as we realized that there would be no quick reprieve and that we were in it for a long time, facing a bleak future.

As a medical officer, I was shocked to observe how many men had simply given up, and I am convinced that it hastened the death of some. How did we get the news? Possession of a radio was strictly forbidden, but news did trickle in through the barbed wire. Chinese newspapers were smuggled into camp and, although prohibited, were tolerated; after all, they were only allowed to print news favourable to the Axis powers. There was also an English-language newspaper, the *Hong Kong News*, Japanese-controlled, which was allowed into camp and which regularly reported news from the German-Soviet eastern front. The news from that front was obviously crucial to the overall Allied effort. Although always couched in terms favourable to the Germans, it could not conceal the real situation, and while in 1942 it gave us no consolation, after the defeat of the Germans at Stalingrad, in January 1943, and the subsequent Russian advance, the news from the Russian front became a powerful morale booster. Some strategists in camp drew elaborate maps marking the situation on the Eastern Front with red and blue arrows. Letters, of course, were not permitted, but prisoners were allowed to send and receive post-cards once a month, when the camp was not under punishment. These had to be couched in brief, standard terms and were heavily censored. They contained little information, but did offer some comfort to the parties on either side of the fence.

Drinking and smoking habits were difficult to sustain in camp. Alcohol was totally unobtainable but proved to be an easier habit to break than smoking; I cannot recall any real suffering caused by alcohol deprivation. With smoking it was a different story: cigarettes were always in short supply and this was the age when nearly all adults smoked. Cigarettes became the chief currency in camp and traders inside took full advantage of this. The addiction was so strong that many men had traded their last belongings for a few puffs of smoke. It was disturbing to observe the degree of moral corrosion, when senior officers could be seen picking up cigarette butts thrown away by the Japanese guards. True, those of us who smoked saved our butts to be recycled and smoked again, but this is different from picking up someone else's butts.[17]

Although subjected to harsh treatment and semi-starvation, and aware of the early reverses on the war front, most of the men managed to retain a fair level of morale. This was in good measure due to the efforts of the officers and senior non-commissioned officers (NCOs) who strove to maintain in men a semblance of discipline and self-respect. They were encouraged to wear uniform, however tattered, except when engaged in hard manual tasks, maintain rank distinctions, salute their officers, and were thus made to feel that they were still soldiers, defeated but not broken. As a non-combatant medical officer, who never took military discipline seriously, I had to admit that in the POW camp environment it helped to maintain morale and sense of duty.

Many discovered a new need of religious comfort, not surprising in the circumstances. Church services, Roman Catholic and Anglican, were regularly conducted by the interned chaplains. Even the small Jewish group of prisoners managed to gather for Sabbath services using prayer books sent into camp by the YMCA (!), and duly passed by the Japanese censor. Incidentally, the Japanese made no effort to isolate or distinguish Jewish POWs; Nazi propaganda had either not reached Sham Shui Po or was ignored by the Japanese.

Leisure and Recreation

After working parties and camp fatigues, men in camp still had some spare time which they used as best they could. Sport and games were popular at the beginning but, as our physical condition declined, these gradually gave way to more sedentary pursuits like card games and chess. Some discovered in themselves surprising skills and aptitudes for activities they had never followed before, such as knitting, wood-carving, painting and other hobbies. Lectures were given by former teachers on a variety of subjects and always attracted a ready and eager audience. The Japanese encouraged these leisure activities believing that keeping prisoners occupied would prevent discontent and pose fewer problems for them. They allowed books in, after censoring them, and brought a number of musical instruments. Stage entertainment became very popular and several remarkably good plays and musicals were produced with men taking the parts of women. Among the latter, "Sonny" Castro, of HKVDC, was excellent at impersonating women: his portrayal of

---

17. The habit of saving cigarettes butts stayed with me for nearly three months after the war.

Carmen Miranda, a popular South American singer and dancer of the time, was amazing and usually brought the house down.

It was sometime in 1943, after several instruments had been brought into the camp, that I decided to form a small orchestra: I knew that several Canadian army bandsmen, as well as a few amateur musicians in the Hong Kong Volunteers, were among the prisoners. There were no orchestral music scores, but I was able to collect a number of pieces for the piano. My past musical training in conducting and orchestrating (arranging a musical composition for an orchestra) made it possible for me to arrange these pieces for an orchestra. There was an acute shortage of paper and certainly no special paper available for writing musical notation. When this problem was overcome with scraps of paper of varying type and consistency, I was able to gather my musicians, and a very strange ensemble it turned out to be: three guitars substituted for double-basses, a single clarinet played its own and flute's part, and a trombone pretended to be a cello. Later on, as I had been lamenting the lack of a cello, two Canadian prisoners constructed one from a petrol drum. It was so heavy that two men had to carry it onto the stage; it had a surprisingly good tone.

I was fortunate to find six violinists but no viola player. Orchestrating and rehearsing took a great deal of time and I was therefore able to stage only three "Bard Concerts"; they were all well received. Three single programmes, one for each concert, were written in ornate script and beautifully illuminated with coloured designs on, wonder of wonders, fine white paper, by the Hong Kong Volunteers' company sergeant-major Baptista; small wonder for he was a descendant of the famous Macao/Hong Kong artist Marciano Baptista (1826–1896). These programmes are at present kept in the Hong Kong Museum of History.

When advised of the camp orchestra, the Japanese informed us, through our liaison office, that we were forbidden to play three pieces of music: "God Save the King", "Rule Britannia" and "Home Sweet Home"! The first two were understandable, but the third? Could it be, I wondered, a concern however misguided, for our mental balance — to protect us from falling into a state of acute nostalgia? In a sudden flash of defiance I arranged for our second concert the overture "Plymouth Hoe" based on naval themes, which I discovered among the collected music sheets. At the end of this overture, amidst many grand and loud chords, the strains of "Rule Britannia" could be clearly heard. The camp commandant and two interpreters sat in the front row and applauded at the end of the performance. In retrospect, I think it was a foolish and dangerous act. I was risking not only punishment for myself — at least a severe beating — but also for the rest of the orchestra, and possibly for the whole camp. A surprising encounter occurred after one of the concerts, when a British officer, whom I had not met before in camp, came up to me to tell me how much he enjoyed the performance. He introduced himself as Captain Rossini. Jokingly I asked him if he was, by any chance, related to the famous composer Rossini. "As a matter of fact I am," he replied. He then told me that he was not a direct descendant; his parents settled down in England at the turn of the century and he was born there.

Daily Life in Camp

In spite of restrictions, punishments, a high sickness rate and frequent deaths, by the middle of 1943 the camp seemed to have settled into a smooth routine. Men went about their various tasks.

When time permitted, they played games, pursued old or newly acquired hobbies, read books if they could find any. One of my Canadian medical colleagues, Captain Martin Banfill, somehow acquired an old edition of Buchanan's *Textbook of Anatomy* and read it from cover to cover several times. It served him in good stead: he made a career in the academic field of anatomy after the war, becoming professor of anatomy, first at Hong Kong University and later in Canada. I tried to learn Spanish from a little book which I had bought for two cigarettes. Men talked about old times. In the medical officers' huts, when the day's work was done, we sat around and chatted well into the darkness of the night. I suppose the subjects of our talks were no different from the others: they were mainly food and home. Bacon and eggs or a juicy steak seemed as far away and unattainable as Mount Everest. My English colleagues talked continually and nostalgically about England and London. I, who had never been to England, could after a while visualize Piccadilly and Leicester Square perfectly and got to know most of the Lyons Corner Houses. There were also discussions about religion, philosophy, science, but hardly ever about our future.

Apart from a communal vegetable garden, the produce of which in a small degree augmented our daily rations, some cultivated their own little gardens where space permitted. The latrine fatigue parties were responsible for supplying the communal garden with ready-made fertilizer, but some was also made available for private gardens; none was wasted! In our lines, my room-mate and I successfully grew tomatoes and even a couple of papaya trees. Incidentally, an attempt was made to smoke dried papaya leaves in cigarettes. It proved so revolting that no one, even in the total absence of cigarettes, could tolerate it. There never has been, nor probably ever will be, a substitute for tobacco. It was while engaged in gardening, that we acquired a pet — a cat — which suddenly appeared and was furtively watching our activities. It stayed with us. We named the cat Louis after Louis Mountbatten, the uncle of Prince Philip (and supreme allied commander South-East Asia from 1943, though we did not know it at the time). There was no need to feed Louis the cat; it was extremely adept in catching sparrows.

Occasionally the camp was visited by the Red Cross representative who was a Swiss national resident in Hong Kong. He was always accompanied by several senior Japanese officers. I recall three or four visits, but there may have been more. The visits were farcical. All prisoners were strictly warned not to speak to the man, and the man never spoke to any of us or asked questions. No doubt he too was warned not to speak to us. Presumably he decided that a restricted visit was better than no visit at all. In the hospital wards silence was also strictly enforced and the patients in bed had blankets drawn up to their chins — so that their emaciated bodies could not be seen.

In total silence the Red Cross representative walked through the camp, but on one occasion a brave officer — actually of the HKVDC — said to him in French: "We are starving". There was no response from the visitor, but the officer was taken out of the camp immediately after the visit and severely beaten up. There were no discernible improvements in our food rations or in any of the camp amenities after these visits. This, however, should not be viewed as a poor reflection on the Red Cross in general, since it did good work, I learned later, in Hong Kong and Macao, providing families of the interned men with food and money.

Among happier occasions were the visits by relatives and friends bringing parcels. They were not allowed to come close to the fence but were kept a fair distance away. It was difficult to recognize our "guardian-angels" as we vainly peered into the distance. Sometimes the Japanese allowed children to come near the fence. A friend of mine, whose father was in Sham Shui Po Camp, told me recently that as a girl of twelve she saw her father and talked to him separated only by the barbed wire. I was among the lucky ones to receive parcels since my wife Sophie was not interned (she was British only by marriage). Our benefactors, we learned later, sold their possessions to buy food for POWs while short themselves. Some walked long distances to the camp, as there was no public transport, carrying parcels, sometimes not only their own but also for friends who could not make the journey. The parcels were taken and examined by the Japanese at the reception point. The recipients were then called to collect them. Sometimes the Japanese searched the parcels for hidden messages and found them, in spite of the ingenuity in the way the messages were hidden. The sending of messages stopped after several recipients (not the senders) were beaten as punishment.

Traders Within

As in many POW camps in other parts of the world, trading across the barbed wire developed early at Sham Shui Po camp. The traders on our side of the wire were those of our own inmates who were quick to see an opportunity to benefit themselves, to survive in better conditions than others: the smart types who in peacetime might have been "wheeler-dealers", the opportunists. They certainly looked fitter and healthier than the rest of the inmates and by camp standards were more prosperous. On the other side of the wire were the sentries or guards who were equally ready to engage in trade for whatever benefit they might gain. It is difficult to assess how many of our traders there were, but probably a mere handful. Trading was illicit, and the traders were taking risks, but I do not recall any being punished by the Japanese: perhaps because of the involvement of their own men. Gold in any form (tooth crowns, pen nibs), jewellery and watches went out and food and cigarettes came in. There is no doubt that this black market, sadly inevitable, created a repugnant situation in which the traders took advantage of the others' adversity to profit themselves. However, not all traders were unscrupulous dealers. I became friendly with one, a Hong Kong Volunteer, when I discovered that he had an understanding, humane side to his character: I happened to mention one day that I had a patient in hospital who would surely die soon unless I found some additional, nourishing food for him. The same evening my trader-friend came to my hut bringing eggs, milk and some meat for my patient. From then on, I could usually rely on him to supply me with some extra food for a needy patient. One day I discovered that my old fountain pen, which I somehow still retained, had a gold nib; it brought me, through my friend, ten pounds of beans! Incidentally, our friendship continued after the war.

Some Notable Events

There were several successful escapes from the camp, especially during the early period before security was strengthened. The escape, in April 1942, of four officers led to especially serious consequences in the camp. Shortly after the escape was discovered, the Japanese arrested about fifteen men, including the brother of one of the escapees, and took them out of the camp. All but one returned about a month later, after being subjected to beatings, torture and solitary confinements under appalling conditions; it was generally assumed that the one who did not come back had died under torture. The speed with which the arrests were made suggested that the Japanese had come across some information. Since I was among several who assisted in this escape, I wondered at the time why I was not taken away with the rest, but decided that I had been lucky. The painful truth was revealed to me some two years later, when a sergeant named Beard approached me and told me that he believed he was mistakenly taken out instead of me, the names Bard and Beard being similar. At the time of the arrest he did not know me, had no idea why he was taken, and although he repeatedly told the Japanese that he had nothing to do with the escape, they ignored his pleas. Long afterwards when he heard my name he realized how the mistake might have occurred. I felt wretched and helpless at this revelation, especially as there was nothing I could do to make amends except to say how sorry I was about this terrible mistake. But Sergeant Beard had no longer any resentment and certainly did not blame me. I asked myself a question: if the Japanese confused the names, had the escapees negligently left behind some notes with names, or was there an informer involved? I had no answer to it.

Following this escape, the canteen and parcels from outside were suspended for several months, the fence around the camp was electrified, leading to two prisoners being fatally electrocuted in two separate accidents, and most of the officers were transferred to another camp, at Argyle Street, Kowloon. About twenty officers, mainly Medical, Service Corps and Liaison Office remained with the men to take charge of various duties. My two Volunteer medical colleagues and I, as well as two RAMC and two Canadian medical officers, remained in Sham Shui Po.

Two or three weeks after the escape we were subjected to a very unpleasant experience. All the POWs were lined up on the parade ground, as for a roll-call, but instead several Japanese military lorries drove up and took positions in front of the lined-up men, the backs of the lorries facing us with the interiors ominously hidden by tarpaulins. As we stood there, it crossed my mind, and I am sure that of others around me, that perhaps hidden behind the tarpaulins were machine guns ready to open fire upon us. Happily this did not happen, and when the tarpaulins were raised, a number of Japanese soldiers jumped out and surrounded us. Then a Japanese officer appeared and declared through an interpreter that we would be ordered to sign an undertaking not to escape. Our senior officer, a colonel in the Royal Scots, went up to the Japanese officer and pointing to a book in his hand, declared that we would sign no such undertaking, and that his demand was against the Geneva Convention. The Japanese, in obvious rage, snatched the book, hit our officer with it on the face, then threw it on the ground and stamped on it with his feet. That much for the Geneva Convention! He then announced that we should all be called out individually and made to sign the paper. Since my name started with "B", I was called out shortly afterwards and led inside a building to a table with a Japanese officer seated behind. Without a word he pointed to the paper and where to sign; the paper was in English and Japanese. As calmly and politely as possible, I said that it was against our principles to sign such a paper as it was our duty as British officers to escape if possible. He became angry and shouted: "You have surrendered — you have no rights", but I still quietly insisted that I could not sign it. He signalled to a Japanese sentry who led me to a wall, my hands were roughly tied behind my back with a wire, and there I stood for perhaps three hours with the sentry next to me, not knowing what was going to happen. I could hear what sounded like raised voices but could not see anything. I recall that after an hour or so my fear or anxiety seemed to have subsided, and instead I felt tired and bored!

Then suddenly I heard a commotion and the adjutant of the HKVDC rushed past, shouting that a message was received from General Maltby (GOC[18] HK Forces) advising us to sign the paper; it was invalid because of duress. It appeared that faced with a wholesale refusal to sign, the Japanese had sent one of our officers to see the general. I have to admit that I signed the paper with some relief, as I am sure did all the others. Nearly all, for a small group of POWs, perhaps about twenty, adamantly refused, insisting that no general could absolve them from their duty. They were taken out of camp, but returned two weeks later apparently unhurt. They claimed that they did not give in. I believed them: we needed heroes even in camp.

Men who escaped risked their lives. The fate of unsuccessful escapees was a swift trial and execution. Such was the fate of Captain Douglas Ford, of the Royal Scots, and two other officers. The Japanese discovered the escape still in the planning stage. It was widely believed that they were betrayed by an informer from among the prisoners. The unfortunate men were sentenced to death and shot in December 1943.

From the middle of 1942, batches of POWs were shipped from Sham Shui Po to camps in Japan to work in various Japanese factories or mines. Conditions in Sham Shui Po were bad enough for many to volunteer for these drafts but, as they discovered later, conditions in camps in Japan were no better, and sometimes worse with regards to food and the treatment of prisoners. One ship, the *Lisbon Maru*, carrying some 1800 POWs to Japan,

18. GOC = General Officer Commanding.

was torpedoed and sunk, presumably by an American submarine. The POWs were callously battened down in the hold and left to drown. In a desperate effort, they managed to break out just before the ship went down, but were fired upon by the Japanese, and many perished. Among the survivors, a few managed to swim to the Chinese shore and to freedom, but the majority were rounded up and ended in a POW camp in Japan.

In September 1942, Chinese prisoners-of-war, around 120, mostly members of the HKVDC, were released from camp. This was in keeping with the Japanese propaganda that they had no quarrel with Asian people. Moreover, the Japanese claimed, the Chinese must have been forced by the British to fight the Japanese. As far as I recall, there was no resentment in camp at the release of the Chinese POWs, especially as most of them had families in Hong Kong or Macao. As we learned later, some of the released men managed to escape from Hong Kong and rejoin the Allied forces in China and India, mainly the British Army Aid Group (BAAG).

Towards the end of 1942, when American aircraft began regular bombing raids on Hong Kong and its harbour, we saw it as an encouraging sign that the Allies were far from being defeated. One particularly heavy bombardment, which occurred, I recall, in October 1943, lasted eight hours and we heard that many Japanese ships in the harbour were sunk. During another raid, oil installations at Lai Chi Kok, opposite the camp, were hit and continued burning for two days, wrapping the sky in thick smoke. We rejoiced in these air-raids and although we had strict orders to remain indoors during the bombing, many, risking instant face-slapping, ventured outside to watch and cheer. Kai Tak airport was a frequent target, and as our men were usually working there and the camp itself was not far from Kai Tak, there was some concern, but apart from a few very minor shrapnel injuries, there were no casualties among our men.[19]

Sometime about the end of 1943 I became involved in a strange situation which was also ironic given our status as prisoners: an interpreter arrived in our quarters with summons for me and an RAMC officer, Captain Lancaster, to come to the camp commandant's house. We had no idea why we were summoned and could only anticipate something unpleasant. We were therefore surprised to find on arrival there that we were to play bridge with the chief of all the camps, Colonel Tokunaga; his partner was another interpreter. In

---

19. The civilian internees at Stanley were not so lucky, as we learned after the war. In January 1945, during an air-raid, a bomb hit one of the huts killing several occupants.

fact, it turned out to be a teaching session rather than a straight game, as we were asked to point out our opponents' mistakes.

The atmosphere at first was formal and slightly tense, but gradually relaxed a little. There was no small talk, however, the conversation being confined to bridge language. The colonel either did not know English or chose not to use it; he spoke only through the interpreter. Lancaster and I were obviously ill at ease as the situation was so completely alien to us: playing bridge with our captors — the enemy. We were served tea but no food or refreshments. At the end of the session, which lasted about two hours, we were each given two packets of cigarettes and taken back to camp. As we walked back, we wondered how the Japanese found out about us for we seldom played bridge in camp; personally, I preferred cribbage, which I learned in camp and liked.[20]

They must have had good intelligence sources inside the camp. We also wondered briefly whether our behaviour was politically correct, but decided that playing bridge with the enemy could not in any way be regarded as aiding or abetting, and the two packets of cigarettes made it worthwhile. Back in camp, our colleagues, fearing that we were taken out for punishment, were happily reassured, and amused at our story. The cigarettes were immediately shared all around.

During the next twelve months Lancaster and I were "invited" to three more bridge session and then they stopped. Each time there was only tea and two packets of cigarettes for each of us. Although we had become more at ease, the general atmosphere remained formal and frosty.

If only outwardly, by the end of 1943 the camp seemed to have acquired a semblance of normality, even enjoying occasional entertainment. Underneath this appearance of peace, however, there lay constant anxiety, uncertainty, and fear. We were prisoners, our fate in the hands of our unpredictable captors. Men were still dying, though not at such an alarming rate as in 1942. We were deprived of freedom, that most precious state which people extol and glorify, but which we are all too apt to take for granted. Although we were not shut between four walls and the camp grounds gave us a fair amount of room to move about, the restriction was still painfully felt, so much so that the occasional venture outside the fence, for instance leading a burial party or accompanying a patient to Bowen Road hospital, produced an almost indescribable, exhilarating sensation of pleasure. Our burial party normally consisted of an army chaplain, another officer, and four men generally from

---

20. Cribbage, or "crib" as it is known for short, is a card game which is popular among British servicemen.

the same unit as the deceased. Several Japanese guards accompanied the party. The burial ground was an empty lot opposite the Argyle Street Camp for Officers. At the grave, previously prepared, the chaplain read a short service, the attending party saluted the departing comrade and the men filled the grave. After the bulk of officers were moved from Sham Shui Po Camp in April 1942, the twenty or so of us remaining agreed to take turns in going out with the burial party. I remember going twice and experiencing, even in the short spell outside the camp on a mission so sad, an acute sensation of pleasure.

On one of these occasions, I acted as chaplain to read the Jewish prayer for the dead for a deceased Jewish soldier — an unusual role for a medical officer.

Sometime in 1943 the medical officers conceived a plan of relieving men from working parties by requesting batmen (officers' servants), one for each officer. There was, of course, no intention of using them as servants; there would be a roster so that men would be attached to us on a rotation basis. To our surprise, the request was granted without even our liaison office questioning it; no doubt the Japanese took it as another sign of the British officer class decadence. The ruse worked and we continued to have batmen until the end of the war. To make sure that the ruse was not discovered, our batmen brought our food from the cookhouse, but did nothing else.

Liberation

By 1944, and especially after the Allied landing in France in June that year, there was no longer any doubt in our minds that the war was progressing in our favour. But most of us, including myself, did not believe that our liberation would occur peacefully and uneventfully. If and when the fighting reached our area, the retreating Japanese, we thought, would try to "liquidate" the prisoners-or-war in their custody.[21] When liberation finally came, in August 1945, it was to our utter disbelief peaceful and without any violence. In camp we had an inkling that something unusual was happening: a few days before the end our working parties returning to camp reported that the people outside, formerly keeping well away, were making "thumbs up" signs and other encouraging gestures. At the same time the *Hong Kong News* reported that the Americans had dropped an extremely powerful bomb on Japan causing very heavy casualties; this was, of course, the atom bomb dropped first on

---

21. It has been claimed that there was evidence of this intention by the Japanese, but I have not been able to confirm this.

Hiroshima and then on Nagasaki. On 15 August we saw all the camp sentries lined up outside the fence solemnly listening to a broadcast: it was, as we soon learned, the emperor's order to lay down arms. The following day, our senior officers took over the camp, ordering all the Japanese staff and sentries to leave the camp; they meekly complied.

A British flag, tattered and stained, produced from heaven knows what hiding place, was raised at a silent and moving ceremony in front of a visibly shaken crowd of emaciated prisoners-of-war. Recovering from my third, or fourth, attack of dysentery, I managed to struggle up to the ceremony; there were tears on many faces. What did I feel at that moment? A lump in my throat and singing in my head: our long ordeal was over, we were free at last. But not all POWs were rejoicing: the infamous liaison officer and his gang were immediately arrested by our senior staff and kept in custody until their trial in England several months later.[22]

Technically, we were not yet free. Allied planes flew over the camp dropping parcels with food and cigarettes, and leaflets advising us to stay in the camp until we were relieved. It took another two weeks before units of the Royal Navy steamed into Hong Kong harbour and we were truly free.[23] During these two weeks relatives and friends came to the camp and there were many happy reunions. However, it became increasingly more difficult to keep our men inside the camp, so our senior officer began to issue short-term passes. A few days after the passes were introduced, I used one to visit Sophie. As I walked along the street, I recalled the last time I walked on the same street, humiliated and downcast, towards the camp and an uncertain future. This time I held my head high, but it was not pride or arrogance I felt but the sheer joy of the newly found freedom.

The Japanese were still in control, still fully armed. I was in uniform, unarmed and completely alone, but I felt no fear. They looked dejected, beaten. As I walked on, a group of Japanese nurses stopped and bowed to me; I saluted back. Further on I came across a few soldiers. They saluted and I returned their salute. Suddenly I felt sorry for them. There was no reason for

---

22. At the trial the charge of collaboration with the enemy could not be sustained and he was acquitted. I never believed that he was a collaborator, but simply a weak man and a coward. A charge of behaviour unbecoming a British officer would have been more appropriate.

23. I recall vividly that the first man who strode into our camp on 30 August 1945, ahead of a relieving naval unit, was a Canadian war correspondent armed with a camera!

me to feel pity for them: the Japanese treated us cruelly, many of my comrades died because of their neglect. I tried to fight the feeling, but it stayed. Was it because I had gone through the same experience and knew how they felt, how defeated men felt? To this day, I am not sure.

Some General Reflections

Much has been written about POW camps in other parts of the world, especially with regards to changes in men's character and values under adverse conditions and stress. Sham Shui Po was no exception. It brought out the best and the worst in people. One saw firm bonds of solidarity and comradeship forged, people who had little to share yet shared what they had with others. There was a new sense of equality, when former employers and employees shared common privations.[24]

There were instances of remarkable courage and fortitude: heroes like the officer who spoke to the visiting Swiss Red Cross representative, or the Catholic chaplain who confronted the Japanese and demanded better conditions for the prisoners; both were severely beaten. Or the successful escapees who risked death if captured, and the unsuccessful ones who faced execution bravely on a lonely beach in Hong Kong. On the dark side, there were those who took advantage of their less smart comrades, the traders and "wheeler-dealers". Even worse — there were a few who became informers and collaborators, who sold themselves to their captors for a few privileges and favours. Their sorry work led to many severe beatings and several executions.

The Japanese were strict and often ruthless. They failed to provide some of the basic needs of the prisoners, especially in medical care. But there were also among them a few who were fair and who made gestures of kindness and compassion towards the prisoners. It was a complex situation where good and bad, cruelty and kindness, weakness and strength co-existed, a situation which no generalization can adequately describe.

Life in Hong Kong during the Occupation

It may perhaps be of interest to describe briefly the everyday life in Hong Kong during the Japanese occupation. My information about it, however, is not first-hand as throughout this period I was interned at Sham Shui Po Camp.

In general, the Japanese by word and deed made it clear that they were fully in control in Hong Kong, that Hong Kong's resources, limited though

---

24. Unfortunately these relationships did not outlast the war.

they might be in war time, were there to assist Japan in its war effort, and that henceforth Japanese influence was to be felt in all aspects of Hong Kong life.

Drastic reduction in population, mainly by deportation, or repatriation to China, as the Japanese preferred to call it, was carried out ruthlessly and was designed to facilitate control and defence of Hong Kong should it be attacked by the Allies. They succeeded in reducing the population from the initial two million to 700,000 by the end of the war.

The health measures introduced, even if not primarily for the benefit of the people of Hong Kong, were remarkably successful, and in the long run benefited the latter. Always, very conscious and fearful of infections, the Japanese forcibly inoculated everybody against cholera, and managed to stamp out the disease completely — something Hong Kong had not been able to achieve in the past. Food was scarce and although the main route of supply from China was never seriously threatened, stocks of meat, rice, fish and vegetables varied widely and were usually in short supply. It is not surprising that the people's main preoccupation was with securing food and other essential commodities like cooking oil and fuel.

Hong Kong was under military law and the Japanese gendarmerie in control of the local police. The activities of the dreaded Japanese secret police, the "Kempeitai", had reduced Hong Kong essentially to a police state. Because of the prevailing instability, rumours were plentiful and were strongly condemned by the Japanese. Spreading rumours, especially unfavourable to the Japanese, was a serious offence punishable by imprisonment or worse.

Although initially public utilities were restored, shortages soon developed resulting in curtailment and finally stoppage. Hong Kong was blockaded and supplies reaching it were often lost. Electricity for general consumption was stopped in April 1944. Public transport also gradually failed, and people grew accustomed to walking long distances and doing without electric lights. Air-raids by American bombers, with increasing frequency and intensity, further helped to disrupt Hong Kong's already failing utilities. Inflation was high and increased rapidly towards the end of the war, when confidence in the military yen became almost non-existent.

Hong Kong was described by some, with some truth, as a dying city. But in spite of the hardships and the uncertainties, there were glimpses of almost normal life as people tried to make the best of difficult circumstances. Cinemas and theatres continued to function, and, incredibly, horse racing went on at Happy Valley almost throughout the occupation and only stopped in April

1945, a testimony to the indomitable spirit, or was it gambling spirit, of the Hong Kong people!

Postscript

After the liberation, I remained in Hong Kong for several months, mainly looking after the released members of the HKVDC who were domiciled in Hong Kong and consequently not repatriated to the United Kingdom. In February 1946, Sophie and I were repatriated to the United Kingdom.

I was demobilized in July 1946 and remained in England, working as a doctor and catching up on medical developments which I missed during my imprisonment, while Sophie was completing her medical course interrupted by the war. I returned to Hong Kong at the end of 1947, Sophie following me in 1948 after finishing her studies.

PART 2

9

THE POST-WAR YEARS

"Home, Sweet Home"
Song by Henry Bishop, 1852

Hong Kong after the War
In the postscript to my essay "Behind Barbed Wire" I referred briefly to the post-war years. This essay deals with that period of my life in more detail.

The Second World War ended with the defeat of Japan on 15 August 1945. It was not, however, until 30 August that a naval force under Rear-Admiral Cecil Harcourt steamed into Hong Kong harbour and reoccupied Hong Kong; there was no resistance from the Japanese. We were finally free after three years and eight months of captivity, of uncertain fate and constant fear, to resume our lives. While in the POW camp, I had built a somewhat idealized mental picture of the reunion with my wife Sophie. When it happened, it was not as I had imagined. We did not fall into each others arms. We felt awkward, like strangers. Perhaps I should not have been surprised, as we had only been married for two and half months before the war separated us. It took several months of gradual adjustment before we felt comfortable again in our relationship.

I was still in the army and there was work to be done, looking after members of the Hong Kong Volunteer Defence Corps (HKVDC) whose health had been severely affected by the long imprisonment. Expatriates were repatriated to Britain, but locals in Hong Kong — mainly Chinese, Eurasian and local Portuguese — were not entitled to repatriation and were now being treated and rehabilitated locally.[1] An out-patient clinic was set up in

---

1. This was regarded at the time by those affected as discriminatory and was deeply resented.

the former HKVDC headquarters, where I attended daily to those requiring medical care.

Hong Kong was slowly recovering from the ravages of war and enemy occupation. The city was under military administration; even civil servants had to wear uniforms, some donning these for the first time after the war. The University presented a picture of desolation, its buildings looted and damaged. It would be several years before it returned to full function. My career in the University Medical Faculty, where I last occupied a post equivalent to a Junior Registrar, had come to a stop. Sophie's medical studies were interrupted only a year and half before graduation. There seemed no future for us in Hong Kong, at least for the present.

It was therefore with some eagerness that Sophie and I accepted the offer of repatriation to Britain; "repatriation" seemed hardly an appropriate term when referring to a country where we had never lived before. I asked our regimental adjutant if we could possibly visit our parents in Shanghai before proceeding to the United Kingdom, and he promised to arrange a passage on a military aircraft.[2] We then waited, with our bags packed, for the Americans, then in control of Shanghai, to give clearance for a British aircraft to land. Nothing happened. We were supposed to be allies, I thought wryly: some allies! After two weeks of fruitless waiting, the adjutant advised us to travel on a ship which was sailing to Shanghai to pick up some British civilians who had been interned there. We accepted and arrived in Shanghai three days later to a great welcome by our families.

Shanghai

It was an emotional reunion: we had not seen our families since our wedding in September 1941, and they were relieved to find that we had survived the war and the occupation. I thought I could detect a touch of pride in my father at the sight of me in uniform. Leo and his wife Luba were now the proud parents of two small children, a boy (Alik) and a girl (Becky).

As advised by the adjutant, I reported my arrival at the British Consulate. As I walked into the familiar building in the splendid spacious grounds on the Waterfront (the Bund), I could not help but recall my previous visit twelve years earlier when, as a stateless young boy, I came here seeking a visa, and

2. Sophie's parents lived in Shanghai. My parents, who had migrated to Argentina in 1935, were waiting for a sea passage back to Argentina. They had come for my brother Leo's and my weddings in 1941 and got stuck in Shanghai by the outbreak of the war in the Pacific.

was treated coldly if not with disdain (related in the essay "Mr Healey"). How different it was this time! I was welcomed enthusiastically. A British army captain was clearly a welcome sight as there was only a skeleton staff and a couple of liaison officers at the Consulate, and virtually no British military personnel in Shanghai. We sat and chatted and there were many questions and many cups of tea. It felt friendly and comfortable.

Shanghai streets were booming with life. There were uniformed American servicemen everywhere. My uniform, on the other hand, excited curiosity. It seemed that no one, including the Americans, was familiar with a British officer's uniform. I was frequently asked which army I belonged to!

Sophie and I were having a wonderful time, fussed over and indulged by our families in every possible way. I visited my old school, but found it shut and deserted. Then, just after Christmas, a message arrived from the British Consulate that a British plane was flying to Hong Kong in the next few days. We were advised to take passage as there was no certainty when the next opportunity would come. After hasty goodbyes, we were on our way back to Hong Kong. Two weeks later I left by air for England. Sophie was to follow a month later by sea on a converted aircraft carrier.[3]

England

There were a handful of us travelling. It took two weeks to reach England. First we were flown inside a huge Liberator bomber from which some inside machinery had been removed and canvas seats fitted. We huddled in our greatcoats in intense cold, having been warned not to push or pull anything as this could open a hatch and hurl us into space. Then we flew in a comfortable Sunderland flying boat. After the Liberator bomber this was like a delicious luxury. We stopped in transit camps in India, in Egypt and Marseilles. Everywhere we were met like heroes by kind solicitous young women in uniform who plied us with presents — sweaters, socks and chocolates. I was embarrassed as I did not feel at all like a hero, having only seen action for eighteen days before being locked up in a POW camp; still, it was very pleasant to be fussed over.

I arrived in England on a crisp cold evening, in early February 1946, and was taken to an officers' club in the old Marylebone Hotel in London. I was told I could stay in various officers' clubs until I found accommodation of my own. After unpacking, I walked out onto Baker Street. It was snowing. The

---

3. A war-time measure when a merchant ship was converted into an aircraft carrier by building an extra flat deck.

lights on the street, the people moving about, the crunching sound of snow under my feet — all seemed friendly, and suddenly I felt happy and at peace: so this was my new home; I knew I was going to love it. But that beautiful first evening in London was an exception. In the forthcoming weeks, the grim reality of the English winter revealed itself: dark at four o'clock in the afternoon, the thick, pea-soup fogs, the poorly heated "digs" (the winter of 1945/46 was especially bad, with low gas levels in heaters due to the fuel shortage).[4]

There was much to be done in the first few days. I reported at the War Office, received my back pay — a healthy sum of around a thousand pounds[5] — and was issued with vouchers for petrol, for one journey by rail, and one each for a bottle of whisky and gin, both virtually unobtainable at the time. London University had organized medical refresher courses and intern jobs quickly and efficiently. Then began months of studying and working at the British Postgraduate Medical School or at St. James's Hospital in Balham, interspersed with short *locum tenens* jobs. The latter, usually offered by doctors going on holiday, and lasting between two and three weeks, generally paid fourteen guineas a week with full board and lodging and were therefore highly sought after.[6] It was an exciting time in medicine. At the Postgraduate School, medical research of the highest quality was taking place. I was witnessing early experiments with cardiac catheterization and the first heart-lung machine which made open-heart surgery possible. Dr Willem Kolff, from Holland, demonstrated his invention, the kidney machine which allowed patients with advanced kidney disease to survive; he joked that the first patient to benefit from his machine happened to be a Nazi. The Postgraduate School was a whirlpool of exciting new theories, experiments and discoveries. On one occasion, while I was doing a short stint as a junior registrar at the Postgraduate School, a senior member of the ruling Labour Party was admitted with a serious heart condition. A new drug was being tried at the School for

---

4. "Digs" is a popular English name for a boarding house or lodgings.
5. In the POW camp officers received their pay from the Japanese in what seemed to be Japanese compliance with the Geneva Convention. In actual fact the money came from the British government via the Swiss Red Cross. The Japanese obtained good English pounds and paid us with Japanese military yen, which by the end of the war were worthless. After the war, the British government very generously disregarded the Japanese payout and gave us our back pay in full.
6. Guinea: An almost obsolete, somewhat pretentious, way of charging fees, and at the same time extracting an extra shilling, for while 1 pound = 20 shillings, 1 guinea = 21 shillings.

this condition, and it was my job to draw blood from his vein every day to determine the dose to be administered. I was nervous and did not relish the task, especially as the man was impatient and often brusque. While enjoying the stimulating environment at the School, I was constantly reminded of how much I had missed during the preceding four years, and how far behind I lagged in my medical knowledge. I found it difficult to concentrate on my studies.

Sophie arrived in March, her ship docking at a secret war-time dock called Faslane, north of Glasgow; even with the war over, it took me some time to discover its location. By that time, I had found accommodation in a boarding house at No. 20 Holland Park, W12 — a crescent, both ends of which connected with Holland Park Avenue. We had a large comfortable room overlooking the street. The cost was seven guineas per week with breakfast and dinner for the two of us. Nearly all the houses in Holland Park were large handsome Georgian-style three-storey buildings conveying the well-to-do "upstairs-downstairs" atmosphere. Most had been converted into boarding houses; there was a great demand for temporary accommodation by families who had lost their homes in the London blitz. With one or two exceptions, the lodgers in our boarding house were kindly, unsophisticated people with little knowledge of the outside world. One middle-aged couple who always sat at a table next to ours at meals, when told that we were from Hong Kong, asked innocently: "Are you Chinese?"

We had few friends in London, but our nearest pub, between Holland Park and Notting Hill, became in time our small social club where we met, talked to, and became friendly with several people. However, we never met them outside the pub. It took me some time to get used to the Cockney accent. On one occasion, in a pub near Kew Gardens, I ordered two beers for myself and a friend. The barmaid said what sounded like "it's two light". As I was fond of light ale, I said "Alright, two light", whereupon she repeated her remark, but impatiently raising her voice. Then it dawned on me: she was saying "it's too late"; it was 2 p.m. and the pub was closing for the afternoon.

When I had time to look around, I could see how much London had suffered in the war. There were many ruined buildings and many empty spaces where buildings had once stood. War-time rationing was still in force. Judging by the food in our "digs", meat and eggs were in short supply, though potatoes and cabbage were plentiful. There were shortages of many commodities: newspapers, cigarettes, even beer bottles.[7] Not surprisingly, after a war of

---

7. It was a strange situation: one could drink any amount of beer in a pub, but to buy bottled beer one had to produce empty beer bottles in exchange.

gigantic proportions and lasting six years, life was hard. In spite of this, I found the general atmosphere cheerful. Half of the people on the streets were still in uniform. Strangers found it easy to talk to each other. There was joy and hope in the air. The war was won and the greatest catastrophe facing us, and perhaps the world, had been avoided.

Sophie was anxious to resume her medical studies interrupted in Hong Kong by the war. Many enquiries and several applications proved fruitless. Incredibly, only two teaching hospitals in London admitted women — the Royal Free and the West London Hospitals. With many servicewomen returning after the war and seeking admission, the demand for places was very high. When hope was all but gone, a sympathetic professor at the Postgraduate School, with whom I became friendly, managed to secure a place for Sophie at the West London Hospital. A letter from Rear-Admiral Harcourt thanking Sophie for her efforts in bringing food parcels to prisoners-of-war and civilian internees in Hong Kong, which Sophie showed to the dean of the West London Hospital, also helped.

In June 1946 a victory parade was held in London. It was a grand occasion, and was accompanied by much public celebration. Large crowds of people gathered to watch the parade. Sophie and I made our way on foot to Marble Arch where we knew the procession would pass. All around us were people; we are both short and would not have had a good view of the parade, but a mounted policeman pushed his horse through the crowd and beckoned us to come to the front. I believe he saw the "Hong Kong" flashes on my uniform and decided to give the "colonials" a better view, which he certainly did. We were very touched by this gesture. The following month I was instructed by the Ministry of Defence to proceed to Guildford to be demobilized. In Guildford, signboards with arrows led to the Demobilization Centre. There I handed in my uniform and was conducted through stalls, picking a complete set of civilian clothing, from head (hat) to foot (shoes). Complete? Not quite. In a strange lapse in the otherwise efficient system, neither braces nor belt were supplied. At any rate, I walked out of the Centre (fortunately not clutching my trousers) a newly born civilian. The following month, I bought a second-hand car, took eight driving lessons, and armed with a provisional driving licence (there were no driving tests due to a lack of driving examiners), took Sophie and two friends to a small village called Aller, in Somerset, for a marvellous two-week holiday on a farm. On the way, we stopped briefly at the famous Stonehenge, on Salisbury Plain. There was not a soul around. The magnificent megalithic structure stood in splendid isolation: no fence, no shops, no parking enclosures.[8] Our hosts at the farm treated us royally. There was plenty of food, including fresh meat and eggs, a pleasant change from our boarding house. The village pub offered a strong farmhouse cider, the like of which I had never tasted. An added bonus was a visit to a nearby village called Low Ham where a recently discovered Roman villa was being excavated by archaeologists; I was given a piece of Roman tile as a souvenir.

Life in London was exciting. With the war over, people were anxious for culture and entertainment. London had become the centre of a cultural revival. Theatres were putting on plays and concert halls were busy with recitals by local and visiting artists. One of the highlights among the musical events was a series of concerts, in 1946, by the famous Concertgebouw Orchestra of Amsterdam. I attended one and enjoyed it immensely. A recital at the Royal Albert Hall by the incomparable Yehudi Menuhin, in which he gave eight encores, was another unforgettable experience. In 1947 Richard Strauss came to London to conduct a concert of his own works. It was alleged that he had been a Nazi "fellow traveller", and I was wondering how the audience would react. When he turned and bowed to the audience at the conclusion of the concert — a small old man with a square head — the whole house erupted into a standing ovation. He was undoubtedly a giant among composers of the 20th century. Alfred Cortot, the great French pianist, visited London the same year and gave a recital of Chopin's works confirming beyond any doubt his reputation as the finest interpreter of Chopin.[9]

Yes, we were enjoying life in London, but by the middle of 1947 it became clear that our funds were running out. I was not earning enough to cover our living expenses and it seemed that we would have to move into cheaper lodgings. I sold my car, but it eased the situation only temporarily. The National Health Service Act, the grand idea of Aneurin Bevan, the minister of health, came into force in 1946 with the great slogan "from the

---

8. I was referring here to the future. Fifty years later, Sophie and I passed Stonehenge again. One could not get close to it. There were crowds of people around, shops, car parks, souvenir stalls, and Stonehenge itself was fenced off. Incidentally, I visited the farm where we stayed; it was now run by the son of our former hosts, whom I remembered well as a seven-year-old lad. The old pub still had the same strong cider; some things never change.
9. There were similar allegations about Cortot — that he collaborated with the Vichy government, but as with Richard Strauss, Alfred Cortot received, deservedly, a standing ovation.

cradle to the grave" (it was actually not put into effect until 1948), but jobs were still hard to get and salaries were pitifully low.

In June 1947 I obtained a job as casualty officer in St. George in the East Hospital, a small hospital in Wapping, a dockyard area. The doctors and nurses were very friendly and the working atmosphere was pleasant. Our patients were mostly Irish dockers and poor Jewish families from the nearby Whitechapel district. I was gaining an excellent all-round experience, but the salary was low, barely matching that of the bricklayers rebuilding the bombed section of the Hospital, though one had to admit that bricklayers were probably more useful than doctors in the bomb-damaged London. While our financial dilemma was still unresolved, I received a letter from a doctor in Hong Kong whom I had known before the war. "Ram" (short for Ramler), as he was known to his friends, came to Hong Kong in the 1930s, a refugee from Germany. He qualified in Italy and thus was able to practise in Hong Kong. It was ironic that before the war Britain had medical reciprocity with Italy and Japan — its two future enemies. Ram wrote that his general practice had grown to a size when he needed a partner. I knew Ram well and liked him, and his offer was very attractive. Moreover, I knew that Sophie liked Hong Kong and was keen to go back. I was, however, less certain. When we could not make up our minds, we agreed to take a holiday in France and visit my uncle Leon, and decide after we returned to London.

France

Uncle Leon was my mother's youngest brother. After escaping from Russia in 1918, during the Revolution (mentioned briefly in the "Siberian Childhood" essay) he made his way to France where he studied agronomy without finishing the course. He met and married Claire, a Frenchwoman, and they settled down in the small town of La Ferte-sous-Jouarre, where they opened a grocery shop. I had never met uncle Leon, but we exchanged a few letters during the preceding year. It seemed a good time to visit him, as well as to have a break from the monotonous English rations; uncle Leon's grocery was likely to be well stocked. We left London in August 1947, were met by Leon in Paris, then travelled by train to La Ferte — about an hour's journey north-east of Paris. Leon and Claire were both small, homely-looking people. Leon had twinkling eyes, a jutting jaw and a constant beret on his head (I wondered if he went to bed wearing it). Claire was plump, had blond curls and a lovely warm expression on her face. We spoke Russian with Leon and French with Claire. Fortunately, Sophie's French was far better than mine. La Ferte-sous-Jouarre had a population of about fifty thousand. With its old-style buildings and cobble-stone streets, it conveyed an air of a medieval town. Leon and Claire had a large house near the centre of the town. In the front portion was the shop, "Chez Leon", while the spacious rooms at the back served as their living quarters. The house was very old. It felt like going back a hundred years: we had a large room with a four-poster bed, ablution water was supplied in a basin and jug placed on a table. To reach the single toilet, we had to walk outside across the yard (I tried to imagine what it must be like to go to the toilet at night in the middle of winter). But these were minor inconveniences. We were enjoying the French food, the morning strong coffee with plenty of hot milk and a fresh baguette (I am addicted to baguettes to this day), and table wine at every meal. The slightly overripe fruit in the shop, which might not appeal to customers, would end up on our table, and there was a great variety of very tasty cheeses. We were having a wonderful time, exploring the town, fishing in the river Marne (La Ferte is actually between two rivers — Jouarre above and Marne below), and cycling in the countryside. One Sunday we travelled on the local *petit tren* (little train) to a small village ten kilometres away to visit Claire's parents. The little train, almost toy-like in size, actually served as the proper train for the local people. When it became derailed, which apparently happened quite often, the passengers got out and by common effort lifted it back on the rails.

Les Halles

As everyone knows a grocery must be regularly resupplied with fresh produce. To that end uncle Leon travelled twice a week to Paris's famous Les Halles, the wholesale fruit and vegetable night market, at that time still in the centre of Paris. When Leon offered to take me along, I eagerly agreed. Each time it went as follows: after an early dinner and a few hours' sleep, aunt Claire would wake us up at 1 a.m. Uncle Leon would drive his small pick-up van with empty crates, arriving in Paris around 2 a.m. Business at Les Halles would be in full swing. The first one or two hours would be spent in pricing the merchandise as the prices fluctuated according to the amount of produce arriving from the provinces. Once the prices stabilized, Leon would start buying fruit and vegetables and we both carried the crates to the van. By sunrise all purchases would be completed, the van loaded, and we would sit down to a hot mug of coffee with croissants, together with some of Leon's colleagues (or competitors) in the trade. Most were intrigued, or amused by uncle Leon's "English nephew" with his rudimentary French.

Return to Hong Kong

We returned to London after two marvellous weeks with Leon and Claire. At home, a cable was waiting from Ram urging an immediate response. The offer was very generous, and living in Hong Kong was, on the whole, an attractive option. I cabled back accepting the offer. I resigned from my job at St. George in the East with some regret as I truly enjoyed the work and the atmosphere in the Hospital. I sailed from Liverpool in September 1947 on one of the "Empress" (I cannot remember which) liners. Conditions on the ship were still basic, almost war-time, with eight persons to a cabin. The journey was far from uneventful: three infants died from diarrhoea and vomiting and dehydration. I was indirectly responsible for saving one, resulting in a life-long friendship with the father, and in being made the godfather of the little boy at his christening in Hong Kong. Shortly after my return to Hong Kong I received a letter from Sophie telling me that she was pregnant. Had we known this before I left England, I doubt if I would have left her to face the final examinations alone and pregnant. Sophie continued to live at 20 Holland Park. She took her final examinations in December 1947, passed, and shortly after flew back to Hong Kong. Our first child, Monica, was born in April 1948. She was probably conceived in France, carried in England, and born in Hong Kong; quite a record!

General Practice and the University

Ram was an excellent man to work with. A fine doctor, kind and considerate, adored by his patients, he was a generous partner and friend. The practice was busy and the income was good, yet I gradually found myself disillusioned with my work. It was difficult to pinpoint the cause of my dissatisfaction; perhaps it was simply not "my cup of tea". In the meantime Hong Kong University was gradually coming to life and the Medical Faculty was taking in students again. I had resumed my contacts with the University and some of the staff members became my patients. I was invited to conduct medical rounds with junior medical students at Queen Mary Hospital, the University's teaching hospital, which I continued for a number of years. Sophie was also recognized as the University's alumnus, and in 1949/50 she was able to undertake several internships, before herself going into private practice.

In 1955, the University decided to establish its own full-time health service for students and staff and dependants. I was invited to apply for the post of University Health Officer and without much hesitation I accepted. It was a challenging job in which I was given a free hand to organize a comprehensive and efficient health service; what I had in mind was a sort of a miniature version of the British NHS. After a short leave, spent in England where I visited and observed several student health services at work, I returned to Hong Kong to take up my appointment, on 1 January 1956, as university health officer, later retitled director, University Health Service; I stayed at this post until my retirement in June 1976.

10

MIRACLE AT ST. FRANCIS

This episode is from the period in my medical career when, after the Second World War, I was for several years engaged in general practice before joining the staff of Hong Kong University. Practising medical doctors have their successes and failures, the majority of which are not dramatic. Only on rare occasions does something happen which confounds all predictions and can truly be called a medical miracle. Such was my memorable experience which began one ordinary day in 1952 when I entered St. Francis Hospital on a routine visit to see my patients. Of course, I am exercising literary licence when I use the word "miracle", for by definition the word implies divine intervention. I claim no such connection, but the event was sufficiently far outside my normal experience to justify my use of the word. Since this is not intended to be a medical case report in the scientific sense, I shall try to use lay language and include as few medical details as possible.

St. Francis Hospital, where I normally placed my patients requiring hospital care, was a small hospital tucked away at the end of a short, narrow dead-end lane in a seedy part of Wan Chai, on Hong Kong Island. It was run by Italian sisters of the Canossian Order. They were all trained nurses, but what made the place especially appealing to me was their immense patience and dedication, spurred no doubt by their religious conviction. No hospital, in my view, could boast of better nursing care. The Hospital, by the way, is no longer there. It was closed in the 1970s, replaced by the larger and more modern Canossa Hospital located in the Mid-Levels.

To come back to that "ordinary" day: after I had finished my round, the matron of the Hospital approached me and said that a Chinese couple had brought their little boy who was very ill. They wanted to see a doctor, any doctor, and since I happened to be present would I please see them. The parents were waiting in the waiting room: a well-dressed couple, perhaps in their early forties; their child was lying on a hospital trolley. In fluent English they told me that their boy, Stephen (not his real name), aged seven, had been treated in another hospital for tuberculous meningitis and in spite of the treatment had steadily deteriorated. The doctors who treated Stephen pronounced the case hopeless, that nothing more could be done for him and advised the parents to take the boy "home to die". Instead, desperate and determined not to give up, they brought him to St. Francis Hospital. They begged me to treat him. I explained as gently as possible, that the hospital in which Stephen had been treated was well known and had a good reputation, that I had no reason to doubt the other doctors' opinion, and that perhaps they should follow their advice, but they begged me to examine the boy and treat him. With some reluctance I agreed to examine the child.

It was a pathetic sight. The boy was lying on his side with all four limbs bent close to his body. He was skin and bone, weighing about thirty pounds. He was in deep coma and did not respond to any external stimuli. There was no doubt in my mind that he was moribund and that death was imminent. I explained to the parents that there was nothing I could do and that they must accept the hopelessness of the situation. Again they begged me to treat him, assuring me that they understood the situation and placed no undue hope on Stephen's recovery. I was touched by their courage and their amazing determination not to give up as long as their child was alive. Against my better judgement I agreed to look after the boy. The sisters were delighted with my decision almost as if they expected a miracle.

I confirmed the diagnosis of tuberculous meningitis, by examining the cerebro-spinal fluid — the fluid which bathes the brain and the spinal cord. This is done by extracting some of the fluid with a syringe and needle inserted through a gap in the spine, usually in the lower back region — a procedure known as "lumbar puncture". The bacilli of tuberculosis could be seen in the fluid through a microscope, indicating the extreme severity of the case, as usually they can only be demonstrated by culturing the fluid, that is, allowing the bacilli to grow and multiply in a sample of the fluid placed in a special culture medium. This further reinforced my initial impression that the case was hopeless.

Until then tuberculous meningitis was invariably fatal. However, a recently discovered antibiotic called streptomycin was found to be dramatically successful in treating lung tuberculosis, though its effect in tuberculous meningitis was as yet uncertain. Although Stephen had been treated with streptomycin with no apparent response, I knew that there was no alternative but to resume streptomycin treatment. I decided to administer massive, sometimes in medical jargon called "heroic", doses daily and inject them into the muscles — the usual method — as well as directly into the cerebro-spinal fluid by lumbar puncture. Since lumbar puncture could only be done by a doctor, it meant daily visits to the Hospital. I informed the parents of my plan of treatment warning them that in the unlikely event of Stephen's recovery, streptomycin administered in large doses especially to children was likely to result in severe, if not complete, deafness. There was also, I added, a risk of brain damage after prolonged coma — a risk which I was unable to assess. They understood and were prepared to accept all the risks if they could only get Stephen back alive.

The sisters now busied themselves, giving their utmost attention to Stephen. He was fed through a vein, the chemical balance of his blood was monitored and kept as near normal as possible, oxygen was given through a face mask and his limbs were massaged at regular intervals. Twice during the first week I was called to the Hospital at night when Stephen's vital functions faltered and we thought we were going to lose him, but Stephen hung on. Those were times when modern life-support systems were unavailable and nursing was of crucial importance. At the end of the week Stephen was still in coma but, to my amazement, alive. At the same time lumbar puncture revealed a serious complication: the disease had produced a block between the fluid in the space around the brain and that around the spinal cord, and consequently streptomycin injected into the spinal canal was not reaching the brain. It was essential, I decided, to ensure that streptomycin reached the fluid surrounding the brain, which could be done by injecting the drug through an aperture at the base of the skull, a somewhat tricky procedure but necessary in the circumstances. So the daily intra-ventricular puncture, as it is called, was added to the lumbar puncture.

The treatment and the intensive nursing continued. There was little doubt in my mind that the sisters had made superhuman efforts to keep Stephen alive. When three weeks after the start of my "heroic" treatment, Stephen was still alive and beginning to respond weakly but definitely to external stimuli, I began to be hopeful that he might after all survive. Soon Stephen's limbs could be moved and straightened, and I noticed occasional spontaneous movements and grimaces of his face. I could hardly believe it but Stephen appeared to be responding to the treatment which was still on a "heroic" scale as I dared not reduce it. Six weeks after the beginning of treatment, lumbar puncture revealed that the blockage had cleared. It was a major success and a great relief for me as I was now able to discontinue the difficult and potentially dangerous intra-ventricular injections.

Stephen regaining consciousness, an event which might have been dramatic, had occurred so gradually, that I could not pinpoint the day or even the week when it happened. I believe it took place sometime between the third and fourth months. We were witnessing with amazement his slow recovery as his eyes began to take in his surroundings, as he began to move, to smile, to speak. The sisters were now able to feed him by mouth and the dosage of streptomycin was gradually reduced. At the end of the fourth month I stopped giving streptomycin by lumbar puncture but continued its administration by intramuscular injection. By this time he had put on a good deal of weight and was beginning to look normal. Paramount in our minds was the question of whether Stephen would show any adverse effects of his long illness and his treatment with streptomycin. Six months after the beginning of treatment, we were able at last to see the full extent of the "miracle" achieved. Stephen showed no mental impairment and — the biggest surprise of all — no appreciable hearing defect.

Stephen was discharged from hospital seven months after entering it in a terminal state. Tests revealed a child normal for his age. In fact he was a bright intelligent boy, though obviously he had missed out on schooling. Looking back at his remarkable recovery, I believe three factors were responsible: firstly the parents' absolute refusal to accept his inevitable death, secondly the dedication and skill of the nursing staff at a time when modern life-support systems were unavailable, and thirdly my almost reckless decision to embark on large doses of streptomycin administered by all possible routes. Perhaps one should also add an element of luck — bringing Stephen to St. Francis Hospital. No doubt the Canossian sisters would add their prayers to the list of contributing factors.

Not long after Stephen's recovery, the family left Hong Kong. Before leaving they presented me with a fine silver dish with Stephen's name engraved on it. I treasure it still. We kept in touch for a while, and I received a few letters from the family, one with Stephen's photograph enclosed, telling me about his progress, and then we lost touch for many years. Some thirty years later, I received a phone call from Stephen. He was in Hong Kong and wanted to see me. We arranged to meet for dinner. As I approached his table, he rose to meet me — a handsome young man in his late thirties; next to him was an attractive young Chinese woman. He introduced her as his fiancée. We sat down for dinner and talked. Stephen was a senior manager in a large well-known finance company and was doing very well. His parents were still alive, and he was on a short visit to Hong Kong. This unexpected meeting after so many years evoked in me an odd yet pleasing feeling. Looking at Stephen, full of life and promise, I thought that medicine, with all its ups and downs, was still, in the best sense of the word, a rewarding profession.

11

SINO-BRITISH CLUB OF HONG KONG AND ITS LEGACY

To understand the phenomenon of the Sino-British Club, one must examine the effects of the war and the subsequent occupation on Hong Kong and its society, since the SBC may be seen as the indirect product of these events.

At the time of the Japanese invasion of Hong Kong, in December 1941, Hong Kong's defending garrison consisted of some ten thousand regular British Forces and about two thousand Hong Kong Volunteers (Hong Kong Volunteer Defence Corps) who at the start of the hostilities were embodied in the regular forces and fought alongside them. The Volunteers were a polyglot body of many nationalities, in which expatriates and locals were thrown together with no social distinctions except ranks. Anomalies were frequent, such as employees outranking employers, locals outranking expatriates and, while in peacetime the social gap was restored when the Volunteers went home after their training and took off their uniforms, after the Battle of Hong Kong and the subsequent surrender, the survivors went straight into POW camps still in their uniforms. In camp even the rank distinctions became blurred, as all shared poor living conditions and insufficient food and suffered the same privations. There was even some advantage in being local since families outside the fence could send food parcels into camp. These were often generously shared with those who had no local contacts and received no parcels, which led to closer friendly ties. The two communities previously separated by a wide gap of social and job conditions, by colonial traditions and by different backgrounds, found common ground in the misfortunes of captivity. When men returned to camp from working parties, when the day's chores were done, they would sit and chat about food and the future — the two favourite topics. There was talk about "things being different after the war". I imagine that a similar situation occurred in the civilian internment camp at Stanley though to a lesser extent as the Japanese did not intern Chinese-British subjects and the internees were a more homogenous group than the prisoners-of-war. As a prisoner-of-war in Sham Shui Po Camp, I observed this interaction and wondered if those who survived the war and long imprisonment would learn from their experience.

After liberation things did seem to be different. Hong Kong, badly damaged by the war and the widespread looting, was experiencing many shortages, yet the overall mood was elated and hopeful. Feeling of general comradeship was evident and sharing of amenities was common. People with cars, of which there were very few, readily gave lifts to those without. Strangers found it easy to talk to each other and to share their feelings of joy at being free again from fear of war and brutal occupation. Social divisions were, for the time being, forgotten.

When Hong Kong began to recover from the ravages of war and occupation, among the many pressing needs felt was the need of cultural revival. It was in that new spirit of tolerance, understanding and co-operation that the Sino-British Club was born in 1946, its noble purpose to bring together the two main communities, the Chinese and the British, and "to promote cultural and social relations between all communities in Hong Kong".[1] The Club began to function in 1947 and was officially incorporated in June 1949. By this time a number of its activity-groups, such as Literary, History, Debating, Drama, Film, and the Music Group, were successfully launched, the latter to outgrow in time the SBC itself and give birth to the Sino-British Orchestra.

After liberation I spent two years in England working and studying, trying to fill the gaps in my medical training after nearly four years in the POW camp. When I returned, in the autumn of 1947, I found the SBC to be the centre of thriving cultural activities. The leading personalities at its helm were Kenneth Barnett as the chairman and Ma Man Fai as vice chairman, the former a brilliant linguist and a very capable civil servant, the latter a scion of a wealthy Chinese family with Wing On connections, who in his long Chinese gown and with a wispy beard cultivated an air of genteel literati of a bygone age.[2] Many other Hong Kong intellectuals from among academics, civil servants, business and professional people had become involved in the SBC activities and left their mark upon the Club, among them David Akers-Jones, Ruth Kirby, James Zee Min Lee, Brook Bernacchi, Professors Ma Kiam and

---

1. From the Memorandum and Articles of Association of the Sino-British Club of Hong Kong.
2. Wing On Company was well known for its chain of department stores in Hong Kong and several large cities in China.

R. K. Simpson, Colvin Haye, Geoffrey Bonsall, Jack Braga, Dr F. I. Tseung, K. P. Chan, Jesuit Fathers T. Ryan and F. Cronin. The British Council was clearly interested and offered help and advice. The Club's meetings were held variously in the premises of the British Council, and several clubs such as Hong Kong Club, Jewish Club, Club Lusitano and even Gloucester Hotel — a favourite place for afternoon teas and lunches. In 1950 the membership of the SBC was given as 150. The Club donated several school scholarships and awarded cups for literary competitions. Its involvement in the early Hong Kong Festival of the Arts, in the 1950s (as distinct from the later Hong Kong Arts Festival), is rarely remembered.

Sino-British Orchestra

The Music Group with which I became closely associated had been active from the start, with Professor Gordon King of the Hong Kong University, Eric Pudney of the Inland Revenue Department, Tony Braga, Arthur and Dolly Bentley, Betty Drown, Chan Kin Kung, Miss Bicheno, Yung Hei Kwong, all contributing richly to the musical life of Hong Kong. Their names have since become part of Hong Kong's musical history. Within days of my return from England, I was approached by Tony Braga, the tireless secretary of the Music Group, who informed me that the Group had started an orchestra and wanted me as leader. Tony was a member of a large and talented family. His father was a prominent Portuguese citizen and community leader; his mother a remarkable New Zealand musician. There was music in the family: sister Caroline a fine pianist and teacher, brother John a violinist. Tony's own musical ambitions were cut short by an unfortunate injury to his right arm; instead he devoted himself wholeheartedly to promoting music. His strongly held left-wing views marked him apart from his very conservative family, but his loyalty to it never wavered.

The Sino-British Orchestra, as it was named, had already held two or three rehearsals, at St. John's Cathedral Hall, when I took my place as the leader. I found a small strangely assorted group of some fifteen to twenty amateur players rehearsing Rimsky-Korsakoff's *Capriccio Espagnol*, a work I judged far too difficult for the Orchestra, under the baton of an obviously inebriated army bandmaster. It was not until this gentleman had staggered and nearly fallen off the podium, two rehearsals later, that I was invited to replace him and thus become the Orchestra's first permanent conductor. The Orchestra's public debut took place on 30 April 1948 at St. Stephen's Girls College (Lyttleton Road, Hong Kong Island). Although the Orchestra's first concert, it was in fact the fifth organized by the Music Group. The Orchestra contributed two items: Mozart's Overture to the opera *Marriage of Figaro* and Haydn's "Clock" Symphony, the others being solo items. The Orchestra by then consisted of thirty-one players, with only one oboe, one bassoon, and no double-basses but a tuba instead. Hope for a second bassoon was fruitlessly sustained until the very last moment when a trombone had to be recruited in desperate substitution! Several players, mainly of wind instruments, were borrowed from army bands.

The formation of the Sino-British Orchestra did not pass unnoticed by the press. "FHR" wrote in the *South China Morning Post* on 22 February 1948: "One of the most pleasing civic sights for the uncommercial traveler in this city is to be seen every Wednesday as six o'clock approaches, when hurrying holders of instrument cases converge. It is the Symphony Orchestra nearing rehearsal", while on the day before the Orchestra's first concert, the *SCMP* anticipated: "An event of some importance in Hong Kong's musical history will be the first public performance of the Sino-British Club Symphony Orchestra ... It is the intention ... to make their symphony orchestra a permanent fixture, with a view to raising the musical standard in the Colony to a fairly respectable height in the course of time". Four months later the Orchestra performed again and thereafter appeared regularly giving three to four concerts per season. At the end of 1950 Eric Pudney, the chairman, and Arthur Bentley, the secretary, both foremost in founding the Orchestra, returned to England. Two men came from the ranks of the Orchestra to replace them; Alastair Blair-Kerr became its chairman and for the next eleven crucial formative years helped to consolidate the Orchestra into a well-functioning team, helped by M. H. Fan as the secretary who devoted himself wholeheartedly to its affairs. In his first address as chairman, Blair-Kerr wrote: "A lot of responsible and influential people are watching our progress very keenly and critically. But we know we are just a 'promising child'. This orchestra of ours may very well be the nucleus (in years to come) of some future municipal orchestra of Hong Kong". We know today that this hope was amply fulfilled.

In 1953 I relinquished the baton in favour of Maestro Arrigo Foa, and became instead the Orchestra's deputy conductor and concertmaster. Foa was a distinguished musician and conductor who arrived from Shanghai to make his home in Hong Kong. The same year for the first time the Orchestra accompanied a world-renowned pianist in Beethoven's Third Piano Concerto. Louis Kentner took his place at the head of a long list of great artists with whom the Orchestra has had the good fortune to perform. K. C. Harvey wrote on this important occasion in the *Hong Kong Tiger Standard*: "For the first time in the musical history of Hong Kong, a world-renowned pianist has played in conjunction with a local orchestra ... A considerably improved SBO shared with Mr. Kentner one of the major honours of an illustrious evening". Although performing regularly, it must not be thought that the Orchestra's progress was one of steady, uninterrupted improvement. But despite periods of poor attendance at rehearsals, shortages of money, and occasional dismal performances, the Orchestra during the next few years grew steadily in strength, broadened its repertoire, and performed regularly with famous visiting artists, among them Pierre Fournier (cellist), Andor Foldes, Malcuzinsky, Julius Katchen (pianists), Ruggiero Ricci, Beryl Kimber, Maurice Wilks (violinists), Jean-Pierre Rampal (flautist). Most of these artists were brought to Hong Kong by Harry Odell, a colourful entrepreneurial personality who had set himself up as impresario in the 1950s. Nor were our own young artists forgotten, many making their debuts with the SBO, among them Chiu Yee-ha, Mimi Chow, David Oei, Enloc Wu, Nancy Loo, and Martin Stumpf.

As with most amateur orchestras there were incidents: some amusing when neither the music nor the music stands had arrived in time for the performance, players arriving without instruments, or when the tympanist fell asleep during the performance, and some not so amusing when the whole ceiling lighting installation crashed down to the floor where the orchestra was sitting only minutes before.

While the Sino-British Orchestra continued to develop, the activities of its parent, the SBC, were declining. By the late 1950s and early 1960s, the interest and membership were dropping as the early idealistic aspirations gradually gave way to the old ways of pursuing success and money. Some cultural groups, previously within the Club, including the Music Group, were becoming independent and new societies were becoming active. The SBC had largely fulfilled its mission of cultural revival: Hong Kong was no longer a "cultural desert", although Sino-British relations still left much to be desired. It was in this area and in the story of the City Hall that the Sino-British Club still had a vital role to play before it finally disappeared from the Hong Kong scene.

The Club's voluntary winding up was agreed upon in 1971 but was not officially confirmed, by a Special Resolution, until 1974.[3]

---

3. The Special Resolution was signed by Geoffrey Bonsall as joint-honorary secretary and chairman of the meeting on 14 October 1974 (information from G.B.).

Canton Visits

After the Communist victory in mainland China, in 1948, and the establishment of the People's Republic of China, relations between China and the "west", or more precisely the capitalist countries, had grown steadily worse. Hong Kong, still firmly a British colony, was deemed an enemy and relations between the two were at best strained and at worst hostile; communication between Hong Kong and its neighbour-city Canton was almost non-existent. It was therefore with considerable surprise that an invitation was received in 1956 by the Sino-British Club for the Orchestra to visit Canton to perform there. The invitation was from the Canton Arts Council and was described as an effort to establish a cultural link with Hong Kong. The SBC and its Music Group responded positively and enthusiastically to the invitation. Especially pleased was Tony Braga for whom this goodwill gesture reinforced his abiding hope for China–Hong Kong friendship. When the news of our proposed visit reached the media, its response was mostly negative and in some cases openly hostile. As we began to make plans for this visit, it became clear that the whole Orchestra would not be able to go. Members of the Orchestra who were employed by the Hong Kong government or by American and some British firms, and there were many, were told in no uncertain terms that they risked being dismissed if they went to Canton. I had recently joined the Hong Kong University staff and felt obliged to ask the vice-chancellor for permission to join the visiting group. Permission was given, albeit reluctantly and with a warning that China would undoubtedly use this visit, by well-intentioned but naive people, for her own political propaganda. In spite of our efforts, we were only able to recruit six instrumental performers who deserve to be mentioned by name because of this ground-breaking event: two brothers M. H. and C. H. Fan, violist and cellist; Dr C. K. Wong, flautist; Wong On Lan, bassoonist; Harry Ore, pianist, composer, and teacher; and myself as violinist. Joining us was also Barbara Fei, attractive and popular singer with a magnificent soprano voice, who was the niece of Mr Fei Yu-ming, the editor of a left-wing Chinese newspaper *Ta Kung-pao*.[4]

We were encouraged by the support and participation of the British Council in Hong Kong when its representative at the time, Janet Tomblin, a lady of stern aspect and forthright manner, declared firmly her intention to join

---

4. On my recent visit to Hong Kong, in June 2007, to conduct the Hong Kong Chinese Orchestra, I met Barbara who acted as presenter at the concert, and we recalled our trip to Canton fifty years ago. She was still attractive and still sang.

the group travelling to Canton. Leading the group was Tony Braga, happy and eager at the prospect of this exciting event, and there were others connected with the SBC whose names I do not recall, the final group numbering around twenty.

We set out from the Tsim Sha Tsui Railway Terminus on Easter Friday. The New China News Agency (NCNA) handled the travel arrangements and had managed to reduce border formalities to a minimum. Still, there being no "through train", we walked some hundred yards across the bridge at Lo Wu. A mere two-hour ride by train and we were in another world. Loud martial music, vaguely Russian in character, blared from thousands of loudspeakers; there was no rest or escape from it, it was in the train, in the hotel, and in the streets. Buildings and streets in Canton were pasted over with anti-foreign, anti-western and especially anti-American posters and cartoons. It seemed incongruous and unreal that in this hostile atmosphere directed at the world which our group represented, our hosts treated us with the utmost courtesy. On Friday evening after our arrival our group was welcomed at a banquet dinner at which speeches of goodwill and friendship were exchanged and toasts were drunk by both sides. The atmosphere was warm, friendly and relaxed. During the next two days we were shown places of interest around Canton interspersed with sumptuous lunches. Contrary to expectations of our critics in Hong Kong, our hosts behaved correctly at all times and made no political statements or innuendos.

Our small music ensemble gave two performances, on Saturday and Sunday evenings, in the magnificent Sun Yat-sen Memorial Hall to an audience of five thousand each night. It was truly an unforgettable experience. During Barbara Fei's performance, I sneaked out to the back of the hall to listen and observe the people. This was no captive audience; its delight and enthusiasm was obvious and genuine. I also noticed a number of Europeans in the front stalls and assumed they were from the diplomatic staff of East European communist countries. Their impassive faces revealed little emotion, but I doubted whether they enjoyed our amateurish efforts on the stage. At the end of each concert, the performers had to sit on the stage facing the audience and were presented with large bouquets of flowers accompanied by a great outburst of applause by the audience. After a farewell Monday lunch and assurances of lasting mutual friendship, we returned to Hong Kong. A few days later, the *South China Morning Post* reported, now in a friendly tone: "Members of the first cultural group from Hong Kong to visit Canton since the inauguration of the Communist government in China returned to the Colony with glowing accounts of their reception there". The newspaper also quoted Mr Noel Croucher, a prominent Hong Kong stockbroker and philanthropist who accompanied the group, as saying that " ... he had never seen a more enthusiastic or better mannered audience" (*SCMP*, 24 April 1956).

The following year, 1957, we were invited again and visited Canton as on the previous occasion on Easter weekend. While the music contingent was the same, the rest of the group was different, being led this time by Mr Percy Chen, a successful Hong Kong barrister. Son of Eugene Chen, a distinguished diplomat of the Imperial China period, Percy Chen was a strong supporter of communist China and always wore a Mao-style, tailor-made jacket. It was said, unkindly I think, that he must have found it convenient to be a communist while living in a capitalist Hong Kong in a luxurious mansion at Kowloon Tong, having a lucrative law practice, and his daughter being educated in Switzerland. In the event, he turned out to be a most effective leader of our group and had even taken a movie of the visit. The second visit was similar in every respect to the first, with two performances at the Sun Yat-sen Memorial Hall to an equally enthusiastic audience, with the same warm hospitality by our hosts, and bouquets of flowers presented to the performers on the stage. Later in the same year, the SBC in a reciprocal gesture invited a cultural group from Canton, and the Chinese responded by sending to Hong Kong a versatile group of performers who delighted the local audiences with dancing, singing and stage acting. Their performances at the Empire Theatre drew full houses on several nights. But thereafter these goodwill cultural visits ceased, as the political atmosphere continued to worsen, eventually manifesting itself in the 1967 riots.

Had our visits achieved anything? On the face of it, little. The opposing political forces proved far too powerful for the cultural aspirations. And yet...perhaps a small seed of better things to come has been sown though it would take long to germinate.[5] On a personal level, twenty years later, in 1978, shortly after the Cultural Revolution in China had ended, the NCNA arranged a sixteen-day tour of China for Tony Braga and me which was highly enjoyable and in which we were treated throughout like VIPs. When we wondered at this generous gesture, we were told that our participation in

---

5. Twenty years later, after the Cultural Revolution in China, the Sino-British spirit of co-operation was revived in Hong Kong in the form of regular dinner-meetings at the Mandarin Hotel under the name of Marco Polo Club. Inspired and organized by Percy Chen (still wearing the Mao-style jacket) they related chiefly to economic and commercial ties rather than cultural exchange.

the 1956 and 1957 Canton visits was still remembered and appreciated in China.[6]

Hong Kong Philharmonic Orchestra (HKPO)
Soon after our return from Canton in 1957, an important event took place in the history of the Orchestra, probably not directly related to that visit. The Sino-British Orchestra, already largely independent of the SBC, changed its name to Hong Kong Philharmonic Orchestra, thus severing its last ties with the Club, but with the latter's full blessing. The new name had no connection with the pre-war Hong Kong Philharmonic Society of which most of the members were unaware.[7] Separation from the Sino-British Club and the change of name dealt a severe blow to Tony Braga for whom "Sino-British" symbolized the ideal to which he had devoted many years of selfless work. He resigned from the Orchestra's committee and took no further interest in the Orchestra's future. We remained close friends until his death in the 1990s.

The Orchestra continued to thrive under its new title. The 1960s proved to be eventful years, both for the Orchestra and for me personally. In January 1965 I conducted a concert in which a distinguished young Australian violinist, Beryl Kimber, was the soloist in the Tchaikovsky concerto. It was by far the most difficult orchestral work the HKPO had so far been called upon to perform. Miss Kimber, playing on a Stradivarius violin, performed brilliantly, while the Orchestra acquitted itself creditably, so that the *South China Morning Post* was able to report: "The orchestra was breaking new ground by playing the Symphony in D Minor by Cesar Franck, and accompanying

---

6. We visited Beijing, Guangzhou, Shanghai, Shenyang and Harbin. The latter, in which I had spent the greater part of my schooldays, was at my request; we had subsequently found that we were the first Westerners allowed to visit Harbin since the Communist takeover.

7. The pre-war Hong Kong Philharmonic Society, which was formed around 1895, had only sporadic functions, an orchestra forming on occasions and conducted by whoever might be conveniently available, such as the current organist of St. John's Cathedral or one of the garrison's bandmasters; its first concert was conducted by George Lammert, the well-known local auctioneer. Its last concert took place a few days before the Japanese invasion of Hong Kong on 8 December 1941. The all-Beethoven programme consisted of Egmont Overture, Symphony No. 5 and the "Emperor" Piano Concerto with Harry Ore as soloist. The concert was conducted by Bandmaster Jordan, of the Royal Scots Regiment and led by me. In the violin section sat a young chemistry student, Rayson Huang — years later to be appointed vice-chancellor of Hong Kong University; Bandmaster Jordan was killed, tragically by our own sentry, in the first few days of the Battle of Hong Kong.

the visiting artist in the Violin Concerto in D Major by Tchaikovsky, both of these compositions being exacting and not hitherto in the repertoire of the orchestra. It is most satisfying to be able to say that the challenge was met with enthusiasm and a very fair degree of triumph".[8] In August 1969, a popular and charismatic conductor of the National Philharmonic Orchestra of the Philippines, Redentor Romero was the guest conductor of the HKPO. He reciprocated by inviting me to conduct his Orchestra, which I did in November of the same year.

On arrival in Manila, it was exciting to see large posters with my photograph, announcing the concert, displayed on many streets. The soloist for the concert was an internationally known harpist, Joseph Molnar, who was to perform Handel's Harp Concerto in B. At the first rehearsal, it soon became clear that, for the first time in my life, I was conducting a first-class professional orchestra. It was a thrilling experience. In spite of the near-disaster, when both the soloist and I became very ill after eating oysters at the cocktail reception given in our honour two days before the concert, we recovered in time to give a fine performance. The *Manila Times* wrote: "Mr Bard directed with sensitivity and skill ... attributes which were amply matched by the orchestra. Because he knew the work thoroughly (he conducted without scores the evening's major orchestral numbers), Mr Bard was able to give his full attention to the musicians and thus, elicit a more intimate type of music making".[9] Conducting without a score was a major effort on my part, as I do not have a photographic memory.

Arrigo Foa's appointment, in 1953, was welcomed and his initial training of the Orchestra was positive and helpful, but with the passage of time, he was found to be over-cautious and too conservative. To the players' increasing chagrin, he seemed disinclined to test the Orchestra with challenging works. The increasing dissatisfaction expressed itself in 1969 when in a popular vote at a general meeting of the Hong Kong Philharmonic Orchestra, Arrigo Foa lost his position with the Orchestra to Lim Kek Jiang, a Chinese/Indonesian conductor and violinist.

In 1973/74 the Hong Kong Philharmonic turned professional. At a press conference on 5 March 1973, speaking as the chairman, I announced: "The time has come to make a determined effort to up-grade it [the Orchestra] into a competent professional orchestra worthy of support. I believe there is a particularly strong desire on the part of the public for an orchestra as opposed

---

8. *South China Morning Post*, 29 January 1965.
9. *The Manila Times*, 24 November 1969.

to other forms of art. .... Initially it will consist of a nucleus of twenty to thirty professional musicians, but by September or October next year as many as fifty or sixty full-time professionals will be employed".[10] There still exists a misconception, especially within the ranks of the Orchestra, that this was the beginning of the Orchestra. Having played an active role in the whole of the Orchestra's evolutionary process, I can assert with absolute confidence that it has been one uninterrupted progress, from the Sino-British Orchestra's start in 1947 to the present professional Hong Kong Philharmonic, in which not a single scheduled concert was missed.

The City Hall

The crucial role of the SBC in the revival of the City Hall was, after the creation of the Sino-British Orchestra, perhaps its greatest contribution to Hong Kong's post-war cultural scene. As the momentum of artistic presentations in post-war Hong Kong gathered speed, the lack of a suitable venue was keenly felt. The Sino-British Orchestra and its successor, the Hong Kong Philharmonic, had variously used school halls, cinemas, and clubs until it finally settled on the recently refurbished and enlarged Main Hall of Hong Kong University (later renamed Loke Yew Hall). But its poor acoustics, limited capacity (around seven hundred), absence of a pit, inadequate backstage facilities, and other shortcomings made it far from perfect. Some may have wondered why Hong Kong, a thriving successful city with a large population, did not have a suitable cultural centre — a city hall. Indeed, Hong Kong did possess a city hall before the war; its story is one of government's callousness and public apathy.

Hong Kong's first City Hall, built in the classical style and partly financed by public subscription, was officially opened by Prince Alfred, Duke of Edinburgh, on 2 November 1869. Located prominently in the Central District, it was an imposing building containing a theatre, a museum, a library, and rooms for public functions. An ornate fountain, donated by the old and well-respected merchant house of Dent & Co., graced the front of the building.[11] The City Hall served the community well for over sixty years. Then, in 1934, in a move that showed callous disregard for public interest, the government demolished the building and sold the land on which it stood to the Hongkong & Shanghai Bank which until then had occupied a block

---

10. *South China Morning Post*, 6 March 1973.
11. Sadly, by the time the City Hall was completed, Dent & Co. no longer existed having failed in the severe commercial depression of 1867.

adjacent to the City Hall and was now able to use both blocks to erect a new and larger bank building. Surprisingly, there appeared to have been no public outcry. Perhaps the threatening world events — the rise of Nazi Germany in the west and of a militant Japan in the east — had obscured all else.

In the summer of 1953, I had occasion to discuss the subject of the City Hall with Tony Braga, suggesting to him that there appeared no signs of the Hong Kong government's intention to restore a city hall to the people of Hong Kong, and that some sort of action by the public may be needed. We arranged to meet for lunch at the Gloucester Hotel with Mr Robert Bruce of the British Council. After some discussion we agreed that concerted action was needed to persuade the government to build a new city hall and that the move would best be initiated and co-ordinated by the Sino-British Club. This lunch meeting, seemingly a minor event almost lost in memory, was to lead to significant results.[12] The Club took up our suggestion seriously and with marked enthusiasm. Invitations were sent to every club, society and association in Hong Kong (even trade unions were included) to send a representative to a meeting to discuss the subject of a city hall. In a remarkable response to what had become the "City Hall Campaign", over seventy representatives attended the meeting and elected a "City Hall Committee" of some fifteen members, chaired by Fr. Thomas Ryan, S.J., a well-known art connoisseur and critic, and including members representing various cultural interests.

At subsequent meetings, a long and difficult campaign was anticipated which would involve prolonged discussions with the government, problems of raising large funds possibly from private business firms, and a massive public relations exercise. Finally a letter was dispatched to the government containing a strongly argued case why the government should give back a city hall to the people of Hong Kong. It was with utter disbelief that we read the government's reply, a few weeks later, agreeing without any reservations to our request. The City Hall, they wrote, would be built on reclaimed land in the Central District, when the reclamation, then in progress, was completed. Moreover, the government made it clear that it intended to fund the entire project from its own resources. The SBC and the City Hall Committee were jubilant; the government had accepted its responsibility and deserved to be congratulated on its prompt response to rectify its past action with regards to the city hall.

---

12. Robert Bruce, when revisiting Hong Kong some years later, had no recollection of this lunch and Tony Braga had only a vague one.

But the Committee's job was not yet over. The government in its letter explained that it would seek advice from members of the Committee regarding various facilities in the proposed City Hall. All the Committee now had to do was wait. The reclamation was progressing satisfactorily but it took several years before the building, or more correctly, buildings, began to take shape, for there were two separate blocks, the low block containing a concert hall, a theatre and large exhibition halls, and a tall ten-storey block containing smaller halls and offices. Both blocks were contained inside a handsome enclosure and located on the waterfront opposite Queen's Pier and the Star Ferry piers. I have no idea what advice was sought from other members of the City Hall Committee, but Alastair Blair-Kerr (chairman of the Orchestra at the time) and I were asked to advise on the size of the concert hall and any other aspects relevant to musical presentations.[13] On one occasion, when the concert hall was almost complete, we were invited to inspect it. There were several people inside engaged in various tasks, presumably experts. We were surprised to see a soldier at one end of the Hall firing a rifle (blanks, of course), while at the other end I recognized Professor Deryck Chesterman, of Hong Kong University Physics Department making notes and looking worried. The acoustics tests were no doubt in progress. Deryck need not have worried: the acoustics of the Concert Hall, as we learned later from experience, either by design or by accident, turned out to be excellent.

The City Hall was opened on 2 March 1962. Any hope we might have entertained of the Hong Kong Philharmonic being asked to present an inaugural concert was dashed when instead the London Philharmonic with Sir Malcolm Sargent conducting was invited for this auspicious occasion. As a concession to Hong Kong, however, Miss Chiu Yee-ha, a talented local pianist performed a concerto with the Orchestra. At a reception after the concert, Sir Malcolm told the gathering that the Concert Hall's acoustics were excellent and that a poor orchestra should never be allowed to perform in it, and some of us wondered whether this was intended as another slight at our orchestra. In any case, the first performance of the Hong Kong Philharmonic in the new Concert Hall took place on 12 April 1962 when Sir Thomas Armstrong

---

13. In the event, our recommendations were not followed. For instance, we strongly urged a concert hall to seat at least 2000 and preferably 2500; it was built to seat just under 1500 and was found to be too small. We recommended an orchestra pit; one was built much later at the expense of some of the front stalls further reducing the seating capacity. We recommended large back stage space; the one built was found to be woefully inadequate.

directed the Orchestra jointly with the newly formed Combined Christian Choir in Handel's *Messiah*.

The new City Hall Concert Hall ushered in a new era of concert presentation in Hong Kong. For the Hong Kong Philharmonic it provided a permanent modern venue. In 1965, the Urban Council initiated a series of low-priced concerts with the Orchestra in the forefront of this outstandingly successful enterprise. At ticket prices of $1, 2 and 3, these concerts brought music within reach of a large, eager, and mainly young audience, at the same time taking away from the Orchestra the financial burden of managing its own concerts.[14] The Hong Kong Philharmonic Orchestra never looked back.

By 1970 the SBC had virtually gone from the Hong Kong scene, but its legacy lives on in the many cultural undertakings, not the least of which is the Hong Kong Philharmonic Orchestra.

---

14. The idea belonged to Mr Darwin Chen, a very capable and enterprising government officer.

12

ERIC COATES

"I heard a London cabbie whistling the Knightsbridge
March."

Eric Coates to the author

Eric Coates (1886–1957), the English composer, was undoubtedly the king of
English light music. Some people erroneously confuse light music with bad
music. Light and serious music are two different genres, though the dividing
line between the two is not always clear-cut. Either can be good or bad. Eric
Coates's light music was certainly good, very good.

I met Eric Coates through his son Austin. Although brought up in a
vibrant musical environment (his mother was a fine pianist), Austin's talents
were channelled into history and writing. As a young man he felt strongly
the lure of the Orient, and what better way to learn about the East than to
join the British Colonial Service? That is what young Austin did, arriving in
Hong Kong in 1949 as a cadet officer of the Service, and proceeding to serve
in various capacities including that of a magistrate in the New Territories.
However, Austin's independent and non-conformist temperament seemed
unsuitable for the somewhat rigid colonial administration, and he resigned
from the Service in 1962 to devote himself entirely to writing, which he did
with considerable success. He described his experience as a magistrate in the
New Territories in a witty and amusing book, *Myself a Mandarin*, which is a
literary gem.

In the 1950s Hong Kong was often described as a "cultural desert". This
was certainly true when applied to music. There were many pressing needs for
public amenities which had to be addressed. Cultural matters were for people
and private organizations to initiate, so the government reasoned. There was,
therefore, no question of a government-funded symphony orchestra. In this

bleak cultural environment, a start was made by members of the Chinese
and European community, who founded the Sino-British Orchestra in 1947.
Shortly afterwards I became its conductor. The Orchestra's progress was slow
and difficult. In the 1950s it was still struggling to assert itself.[1]

Austin was well aware of the Orchestra's problems. He was interested and
encouraging, though not personally involved. We met and became friends. I
told him more than once how I admired his father's music, but, alas, could not
perform any of it as the Orchestra had not yet reached a sufficient standard
of skill. One day, in 1952, over a lunch at his flat, I told Austin that I was
shortly due to go to England on leave. "Would you like to meet my father?"
he asked. "I would, very much," I replied. "And so you shall," he said. He
explained that he had bought for his father a box of cigars and would like
me to deliver it personally to his father in London.

The day after I arrived in London, I rang Eric Coates's house. A male
voice answered. Startled, for a moment I thought it was Austin's. I expressed
my surprise, and Mr Coates, who answered the phone, said, "Ah, yes, that's
what Austin's girlfriends used to say when they rang the house." I explained
who I was and that I was carrying a box of cigars and a personal greeting
from his son. Eric Coates then invited me for lunch the following week at a
club in London's Mayfair; I think it was called either International Music or
International Musicians Club.

At the Club, I was warmly greeted by Eric Coates and his wife, as I handed
over the box of cigars. Eric Coates was a short, slightly built man in his sixties.
The resemblance between father and son was striking: unmistakably, Austin
was a younger version of Eric. Mrs Coates was a beautiful woman of great
charm and considerably younger, I thought, than her husband. It was obviously
a high-class club, stylishly furnished inside, and a favourite meeting place, as
I was soon to discover, of celebrities, especially of the musical world.

At the table, nervous at first, I was soon put at ease by the charm and
easy manner of my hosts. They asked about Austin, and I told them about his
interest in the orchestra I was conducting. Apologetically, I explained that it
was only an amateur one, but that I hoped it would serve as the nucleus of a
future professional symphony orchestra. The food and wine were excellent,
and the conversation flowed easily. Then Eric began to talk about his early
difficult times as a viola player in the old Queen's Hall Orchestra, of his efforts
at composing, of his struggle for recognition. The latter came dramatically
in the 1930s with his London Suite, the music which captured so faithfully

---

1. Described in my essay "Sino-British Club of Hong Kong and Its Legacy".

and tunefully the essence of London, and endeared him to thousands of listeners throughout England. Fascinated, I listened as he warmed up to the subject with Mrs Coates inserting occasional details. He described how while recording the Suite with the BBC Orchestra, the musicians stopped playing and began packing their instruments at one o'clock, when the last movement — the Knightsbridge March — had not been recorded. He then begged the musicians to stay for another five minutes to record it. Grudgingly, they agreed. The London Suite was an instant success, and Eric Coates famous. It was at this point, he told me about London cabbies whistling his March, using the words I quoted at the head of this essay. Many might still remember that the Knightsbridge March was used by the BBC Radio as a signature tune for its popular programme "In Town Tonight", which ran for an incredible twenty-seven years.[2]

At one point, during our lunch, a tall, ramrod-straight man with a military-style moustache passed by our table and waved to my hosts; I recognized him as Adrian Boult, at the time the principal conductor of the London Philharmonic Orchestra (LPO). Eric Coates beckoned him saying "Adrian, come and meet a young conductor from Hong Kong." We shook hands, and Adrian Boult said something, but I cannot remember what it was. I do remember, however, being awestruck.

Near the end of our lunch, Eric Coates asked me whether there was anything I especially wanted and whether he could help. There was, indeed. I told him that I wanted very much to attend a rehearsal by one of the symphony orchestras in London. He thought for a moment then glanced around the dining room and said: "Ah, there is Basil Cameron. Let us walk over and talk to him." We walked across the room to the table where Basil Cameron, another distinguished British conductor, was sitting. I was introduced and my request was conveyed. Apparently, attendance at rehearsals by non-players had recently been strictly curtailed. But when informed that I came from the far-away Hong Kong, Basil Cameron agreed to arrange my attendance at his rehearsal. He took my name and told me to come to the stage door of the Royal Albert Hall on a specified date. The man in charge there would admit me.

For a conductor like myself, who was still learning the mysteries of conducting, and with no guidance available in Hong Kong, attending a rehearsal is much more revealing and informative than a concert. I was therefore looking forward to it with eager anticipation. Two days after the lunch

---

2. 1933–1960.

at the Club, I presented myself at the stage door of the Royal Albert Hall and was duly admitted by an important-looking, uniformed commissionaire. Basil Cameron was conducting the London Symphony Orchestra (LSO). The details of the rehearsal are no longer clear in my memory, but I remember savouring the experience, as I listened to the exchanges between the conductor and players, and watched the conductor and his movements. During a break I was allowed to go backstage where I talked to several players. I was also able to thank Basil Cameron again for allowing me to sit at the rehearsal.

Meeting Eric Coates and Mrs Coates, and attending a rehearsal conducted by Basil Cameron, were certainly the highlights of my visit to London that year. Eric Coates died in 1957, while his beloved Knightsbridge March was still played every Saturday night on the BBC's "In Town Tonight".

Austin Coates wrote many books, mostly historical and mostly excellent. One, *The City of Broken Promises*, a novel about a Chinese girl in Macao, was made into a successful musical. He loved the Far East, and although he travelled extensively, Hong Kong and Macao remained his favoured homes. We remained friends till his death in 1997.

9.1 Shanghai, 1945. Seated: my mother, Leo and Luba's children Alik and Becky, my father, my brother Leo. Standing: myself, my wife Sophie, Leo's wife Luba.

9.2 Stonehenge, on Salisbury Plain, England, 1946: my wife Sophie, a friend, and myself. The massive ancient monument is truly an awesome spectacle.

9.3 Uncle Leon and aunt Claire in front of their shop "Chez Leon", La Ferte-sous-Jouarre, France, 1947.

9.4 In front of Claire's parents' house at St. Antoine, a small village near La Ferte, 1947. Claire's parents are sitting with Claire's small niece in front. Standing are Leon, Sophie and Claire.

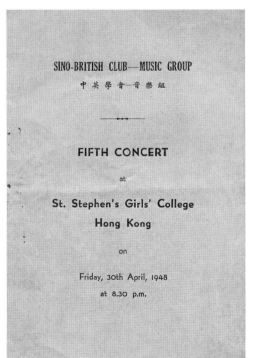

11.1 Front page of a programme of the Sino-British Club Music Group's Fifth Concert, featuring the Sino-British Orchestra's first public performance, in which the Orchestra contributed two items.

SINO-BRITISH CLUB—MUSIC GROUP

中 英 學 會—音 樂 組

FIFTH CONCERT

at

St. Stephen's Girls' College

Hong Kong

on

Friday, 30th April, 1948

at 8.30 p.m.

11.2 Hong Kong's first City Hall, c. 1925. The picture shows the City Hall's southern façade facing Queen's Road Central. The ornate Dent Fountain is seen in front of the Hall. (Photograph courtesy of the Hong Kong Museum of History).

11.3 Sino-British Club Music Group's Fifth Concert, 30 April 1948, showing the Sino-British Orchestra on the stage of St. Stephen's Girls' College, Lyttleton Road, Hong Kong Island. Myself, the conductor, is standing in the centre; M. H. Fan, the leader, is on the left front desk. This was the Orchestra's first public performance, in which it contributed two items.

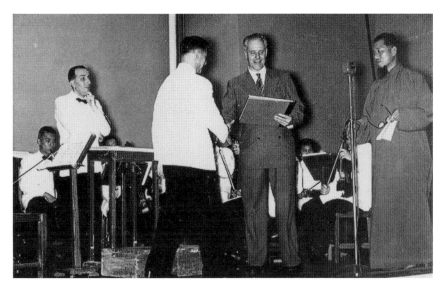

11.4 As leader of the Sino-British Orchestra, I am receiving an album of gramophone records for my services as conductor from 1947 to 1953, from Professor Gordon King, chairman of the Sino-British Club Music Group. Mr Ma Man Fai (on the right), vice-chairman of the Sino-British Club, is watching the presentation. Arrigo Foa, who succeeded me as conductor, is standing on the left. The photograph was taken in 1953 (the exact date is uncertain) during an interval of one of the Orchestra's concerts.

11.5 Canton visit in April 1957. Performing on the stage of the Sun Yat Sen Memorial Hall are Sino-British Orchestra's four musicians: C. K. Wong, Solomon Bard, M. H. Fan and C. H. Fan.

11.6 Canton Visit in April 1957. Performing a sonata for violin and piano, on the stage of the Sun Yat Sen Memorial Hall, are Harry Ore and I.

11.7 Hong Kong Philharmonic Orchestra performing in one of the school halls in Kowloon in 1961. The performing pianist, in front on a specially added platform, is Malcuzinsky, one of the world's greatest exponents of Chopin's music. Arrigo Foa is conducting (behind the piano) and I am leading.

11.8 Hong Kong's second (the present) City Hall, 1962. The low block containing the Concert Hall is on the left; the tall, ten-storey block is on the right. In front is Queen's Pier. (Photograph courtesy of the Hong Kong Philharmonic Society).

11.9 I am conducting the National Philharmonic Orchestra of the Philippines, Manila, 18 November 1969.

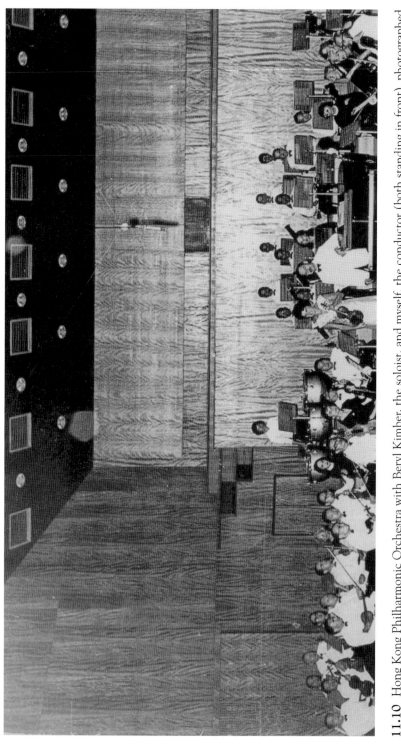

11.10 Hong Kong Philharmonic Orchestra with Beryl Kimber, the soloist, and myself, the conductor (both standing in front), photographed after the concert, 27 January 1965.

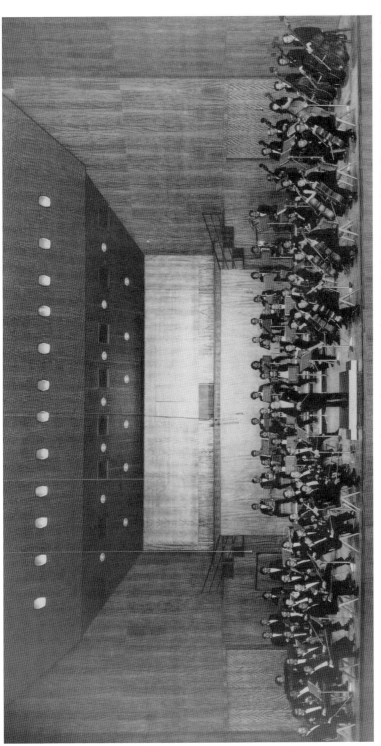

11.11 Hong Kong Philharmonic Orchestra in its first professional year, 1974, photographed in the City Hall's Concert Hall with the newly appointed conductor Lim Kek Jiang. The concertmaster is his brother, Lim Kek Ting.

13.1 Hong Kong, 1953. The governor, Sir Alexander Grantham, presenting the Efficiency Decorations (ED), for officers, and the Efficiency Medals (EM), for other ranks, to the Hong Kong Volunteers. I am on the extreme right. These awards are earned after twelve years of efficient and commendable service, the war service counting as double.

13.2 Hong Kong, 1963. The RMO (myself, second from left) with three members of the Regimental Aid Post (RAP) in front of the Land Rover–ambulance.

13.3 Hong Kong, 1963. The RAP members pose after practising evacuation of the wounded by helicopter.

13.4 Hong Kong, 1966. The governor, Sir David Trench (in the centre), with members of the RAP during his inspection visit of the Hong Kong Volunteers during a field exercise in the New Territories.

13.5 1972. The RMO (myself), assisted by Sergeant Cheuk, treating village children during a Village Penetration Patrol (VPP) in the New Territories.

13.6 1982. Myself as the honorary colonel of the Royal Hong Kong Regiment (The Volunteers).

13

HONG KONG VOLUNTEERS AFTER THE WAR: FROM THE NOTES OF A REGIMENTAL MEDICAL OFFICER*

> Sergeant-major, in a loud commanding voice,
> to a young recruit: "Get cracking".
> Young recruit, some time later:
> "Sorry, Sir, can't find Mr Cracking".
>
> (Overheard during Volunteers' training)

Regiment

For those who are not familiar with the British army system, it is sometimes difficult to grasp the full meaning of the term "regiment". It is not a battle formation, defined by strength or number, like a platoon, a company or a battalion. A regiment's numbers vary widely. In Britain and its Commonwealth, regiments are generally formed within a particular locality or county, with which they have strong affiliation, for instance The Royal Scots, or The Royal Hampshire Regiment. Some regiments have a very long history, all have strong traditions and esprit de corps. Members usually maintain lasting attachment to their regiment, which continues after they leave the army, through regimental associations formed as extensions of the regiments to allow present and past members to keep in touch with each other. In some respects, a regiment and its association may be viewed as a club with members who share common interests and experience. The latter may be a very strong bond, especially when forged on a battlefield. Viewed in this light, the Hong Kong Volunteer Force was certainly a regiment, its roots and traditions embedded firmly in Hong Kong and its people.[1]

---

* I am indebted to the Leisure and Cultural Services Department of Hong Kong SAR for permission to use my article "Medical Section: Recollections of a Regimental Medical Officer" in its publication *Serving Hong Kong: The Hong Kong Volunteers* as the basis for this essay.

1. It must be added that Britain and the Commonwealth are not unique in the custom of regiments with long-standing histories and traditions. It exists in many other countries.

The Hong Kong Volunteers were essentially a part-time volunteer force, formed in 1854 when the Crimean War led to a reduction of British military presence in Hong Kong. An appeal by the governor to join a Volunteer Corps was answered by ninety-nine citizens who volunteered to defend Hong Kong.[2] Since then, with short interruptions, and until its disbandment in 1995, the Volunteer Force had been a permanent military force in Hong Kong, and on several occasions was called out to help maintain law and order. In December 1941, the Hong Kong Volunteer Defence Corps (HKVDC), as it was then called, met its severest test in the Battle of Hong Kong when it fought alongside Hong Kong's regular garrison against the invading Japanese forces. The Volunteers acquitted themselves well, earning nineteen decorations and eighteen "mentioned-in-dispatches" for gallantry and good service. But the price was high: out of the mobilized strength of 2,200 all ranks, 289 were listed as killed or missing and many others became prisoners-of-war.

Post-War Volunteers

My service with the Hong Kong Volunteer Defence Corps during the Second World War and subsequent imprisonment by the Japanese are described in the essays "Battle for Hong Kong" and "Behind the Barbed Wire". I was back in Hong Kong, after a spell in England, when, in 1949, the Volunteer Force was re-established as the Hong Kong Defence Force, and I immediately rejoined it. With conscription enacted in 1951, the HKDF had to absorb and train conscripts. In spite of this its strength was only around a thousand men, compared to more than two thousand at the time of the Japanese invasion in December 1941.

The composition of the revived Force was also different. Instead of a polyglot, but mainly European, pre-war body of men, the rank-and-file was now predominantly Chinese; Europeans still formed the majority of the officers. The men were assigned to six Companies, identified as A, B, C, D, Home Guard (for older members), and Headquarters (HQ) Companies, the last consisting of small supporting units, such as Motor Transport (MT), Signals, Intelligence, and Medical—designated Regimental Aid Post (RAP).[3] Later a Women's Section and the Band were added to the HQ Company.

---

2. The toast to "The Ninety Nine" was proposed at all formal Hong Kong Volunteer functions, and continues to be drunk at similar functions of the Hong Kong Volunteer Associations.
3. In the army, several platoons, each of around thirty men, form a company (or a squadron). Several companies (or squadrons) form a battalion, and several battalions form a brigade.

The Volunteers' Regimental Headquarters (RHQ) was located in Happy Valley, on Hong Kong Island, close to the Race Course. It consisted of a two-storey building with offices, a spacious parade ground, several training rooms, and a miniature firing range for small-calibre weapons. The full-time training staff — all seconded from the British regular army for an average period of two years — were responsible for the overall military bearing and efficiency of the Volunteers. Headed by the commanding officer (CO) with the rank of lieutenant-colonel, they comprised several officers and senior non-commissioned officers (NCOs).[4] The second-in-command, however, was always a Volunteer. The regimental schedule of training, applied to all units, consisted of fortnightly four-hour periods at the regimental headquarters, monthly weekend field exercises, and an annual camp of two to three weeks, usually in the New Territories.

In 1961 conscription was discontinued and the Force resumed its fully volunteer status. Shortly afterwards it was renamed the Hong Kong Regiment (The Volunteers), later to be honoured by the title "Royal", or the RHKR(V). The Regiment's time-honoured motto — NULLI SECUNDUS IN ORIENTE (Second to None in the Orient) — embodied the Regiment's aspirations and its goal.

Training the RAP
The Medical Section, designated Regimental Aid Post (RAP), numbered around twenty, including a regimental medical officer (RMO), five NCOs and twelve to thirteen other ranks with myself as the senior medical officer (SMO), called from time to time to assist when extra help was needed as, for instance, in the pre-enlistment medical examination of recruits. When in the early 1960s the then RMO, Captain Eddie Gosano, resigned, I was asked to revert to RMO and take over the RAP. There was no longer an SMO. Eddie was popular with his men in the RAP and in the Force generally, and his departure was regretted. For me it was a welcome "demotion" since I was happy to be put directly in command of my medics. All were young Chinese men who, except for the senior NCOs, had little or no previous experience in medical matters.

---

4. Officers, from second lieutenant to general, hold the reigning sovereign's commission or authority. Hong Kong Volunteer officers hold the governor's commission. Non-commissioned officers, from lance-corporal to sergeant-major, do not hold a commission.

The war had taught me that the medical training of our medics in peacetime fell short of the needs in real emergencies. The RAP could be called upon at any time to treat real casualties, which are not infrequent in regimental field exercises.[5] I resolved that the training of our small RAP unit should be made as realistic as possible. To begin with, some of the men had probably never seen serious injuries or real fractures, and might even react badly at the sight of blood. I was able to arrange regular visits by small parties, of two to three men, to the Casualty Room at Queen Mary Hospital, where they could see real injuries and possibly witness minor surgical procedures. A team from the Royal Army Medical Corps (RAMC) agreed to come to our training sessions to demonstrate wound simulation techniques, by which injuries are simulated on a "casualty" using a special make-up kit. Subsequently we acquired the make-up kit and four of my medics learned to make-up very convincing "injuries". The men took very seriously the new realism in medical training, almost too eagerly as the following incident illustrates. During one regimental field exercise, Lieutenant-Colonel Ivor Daniel (known generally as Colonel Danny) sportingly volunteered to act as a "casualty". The RAP was relayed a message that "Danny" was seriously wounded, was unconscious and required immediate treatment and evacuation. His location was given (in code), as grid reference, in the Castle Peak area. In spite of it being a dark moonless night, the medical party sent to locate Danny found him with the minimum of delay. After a quick examination, a safety pin was produced and Danny realized to his horror that the medics were about to pierce his tongue (as required in an unconscious casualty to prevent the tongue falling back and obstructing the airway). Danny promptly "regained" consciousness and fought off the over-zealous medics. Were they really going to pierce his tongue? I wondered afterwards, but Danny was adamant that they were.

I laid emphasis on how to use first aid in serious life-threatening conditions, such as blood loss, asphyxia, severe fractures and so forth. Every man in the RAP had to be thoroughly familiar with CPR (cardio-pulmonary resuscitation) which was repeatedly practised either on volunteers or using a dummy. Two of RAP's senior NCOs were sent to the British Military Hospital to learn how to use an intravenous drip — a procedure used on casualties in the field before reaching hospital. Trying to keep pace with new developments, I managed

---

5. Even a fatal injury can occur. During one field exercise in the New Territories, in the 1970s, a young Volunteer was crushed to death, when the armoured car he was in overturned. The RAP medics were quick to respond, but unfortunately were unable to save the man.

occasionally to borrow a helicopter from the Royal Auxiliary Air Force for a very brief stop at the RHQ to allow my medics to practise evacuation of the wounded by helicopter. While the major part of my medics' training was devoted to medical skills, they also had to be instructed in military skills. They were trained in map reading, radio communication and weapon handling. Medical personnel are non-combatants, but allowed to carry personal weapons for self-defence and protection of the wounded in their care. Apart from regular lectures and training at the Regimental HQ, and participating in regimental exercises, the RAP was encouraged to have its own field training. The men and I enjoyed these field trips immensely, getting to know the unfamiliar remote areas of the New Territories and the Islands, and practising map reading.

From Companies to Squadrons

In the early 1960s the regiment's role was changed from infantry to reconnaissance, and the companies became squadrons. The change was also marked by the granting of a guidon, a standard normally carried by a reconnaissance regiment.[6] It was justifiably argued that the Volunteers, being mostly locals and familiar with the local terrain, were especially suitable for setting up and manning well-concealed forward Observation Posts (OPs) from which they could pass information on movements of the enemy to the Battalion Headquarters.[7] They would not engage the enemy and only fought when discovered or ambushed. Henceforth, the training was oriented to meet this new role, though the regiment would still be available to assist the police and the army in internal security and times of civil unrest.

Discussions were held at the RHQ on how best to employ, or deploy, the RAP. One suggestion was for the RMO and his men to train a few men in each squadron to act as medical orderlies. When put into practice, this soon proved a total failure as the assigned men had no interest in medical work and resented having to perform different duties from those of their comrades.

---

6. A guidon is a flag or a pennant, originally carried by the cavalry. With the role of the cavalry passing on to armoured corps and reconnaissance and tank units, so also did the guidon. The equivalent in the infantry is the Regimental Colours. Both Colours and guidon are regarded as symbols of the spirit of the regiment. In the past they were carried into battle, but are no longer in modern warfare. In the case of the RHKR(V), the guidon replaced the previously carried two Colours (Queen's and Regimental), the latter then being laid up.

7. The RHKR(V)'s numbers being roughly a battalion strength, the Battalion Headquarters was its field command centre, coordinating and directing movements of its various units.

The next move was to attach two to three RAP men to each squadron either permanently or on rotation basis. I opposed this plan. The RAP had, in the past few years, developed its own esprit de corps and worked best as a team; splitting it up would destroy that spirit. In the event, when put to the test this too proved a failure: my medics were treated as outsiders, and I had to put a stop to it when I found that they were used for all sorts of unpopular tasks such as cleaning up and sentry duties. In the end, the RAP remained intact as a unit within the HQ Squadron, always deployed close to the Battalion HQ, ready to take off in its Land Rover–ambulance to treat a casualty, real or simulated.

Riots and Natural Diasters

James Hayes, in his article "A Short History of Military Volunteers in Hong Kong", describes how during the 1966 riots a call-out came "on an evening when at least two squadrons were holding chows".[8] I remember well that evening, for one of these squadrons was the HQ Squadron. Along with the others, I had too much to drink and had managed to get home with difficulty. My summons came at about 2 a.m., from the CO, Col. Laurence-Smith, who spoke on the telephone. He sounded calm, almost matter-of-fact, when he informed me that the "O" Group (Orders Group) meeting would be held at the Regimental Headquarters at 6 a.m. and that I was required to be present in uniform and ready to be deployed. My wife, Sophie, and daughter, Monica, helped me to dress and drove me to the Headquarters (for I was in no condition to do either); I noticed that I was not the only bleary-eyed officer at the meeting that morning. The RAP stayed on duty for two days, attached to its squadron, but there were no casualties. The Volunteers were again mobilized in 1967 when the riots lasted longer and were more serious. The RAP was on call-up duty for a whole week. There was a curfew at night, and I recall having an eerie feeling when driving along empty streets, all of us wearing steel helmets, as objects were sometimes thrown at us from balconies and windows.

June 1972 brought disastrous floods and collapse of buildings with many casualties. One of the worst areas affected by flooding was Happy Valley, where torrential rain had turned the RHQ on Sports Road and the adjoining Race Course into a large lake, in some places four to five feet deep. The RAP happened to be spending its training weekend at RHQ when we were

---

8. *Serving Hong Kong: The Hong Kong Volunteers*, produced by the Hong Kong Museum of Coastal Defence, 2004, p. 24.

awakened at night by water surging into the ground floor. We began to work at once, moving papers and archives to the upper floor, managing to save most of the records. The next morning we found ourselves "marooned" in the HQ Building with the parade ground under four feet of water; light rain was still falling. Two scenes from that morning come vividly to mind: one of the adjutant, Major Hugh Lohan, floating into the HQ on an inflated rubber mattress paddling with both hands, the other of Corporal Choy Bee, of the Motor Transport Troop (and the mainstay of the regimental water polo team), wading through the HQ up to his armpits in water, but holding an umbrella over his head.

That evening we were urgently summoned to help at a landslide on Stubbs Road where a number of people were buried under a collapsed building. When we arrived, the police and the fire brigade were already on the scene. We worked frantically, using army trench tools, extricating several bodies and applying resuscitation, but sadly with little success. Then success! An elderly Chinese woman, who appeared dead, suddenly responded to our efforts. She was sent to hospital in a stable condition. It is difficult to describe adequately the joy and the satisfaction we felt at the first sign of life in her seemingly lifeless body. We learned later that another disastrous building collapse occurred on Po Shan Road with many deaths.

Village Penetration Patrols (VPPs)

Started in the early 1970s, during the disturbances, the Volunteer VPPs consisted of small parties which visited remote villages in the New Territories, generally inaccessible by roads. The VPPs served as useful exercises in familiarizing the squadrons with remote areas of the New Territories, while at the same time learning about the needs of the villagers, helping them on the spot when possible, and generally forging good working relations with them. The Volunteers were not the first to adopt VPPs. The regular army units and the Hong Kong Police had been visiting remote villages regularly for some years, but I believe the Volunteers, with their knowledge of Cantonese, were more successful in this role, at least more so than the regular army.

I was able to persuade the CO that the RAP could also be usefully employed on a VPP to provide occasional medical care in remote villages situated far from regular medical clinics. In practice the RMO and three to four medics, with camping equipment and a small mobile dispensary, would be dropped by helicopter close to a selected village where we would spend a weekend treating villagers for a variety of generally minor medical conditions. We found that already most of the young, working-age men had left these villages, which then contained mainly women, old people and children.

Our mobile clinic proved very popular with patients, who came for treatment from a large area around. Many children had skin infections and by the time we left, many of them would be walking about painted in bright violet and red colours (from applications of gentian violet and mercurochrome). Along with our medical supplies, there was always included a mahjong set to occupy my team in the evening after the clinic's work was done; I recall being lulled to sleep in the tent by the noise of mahjong pieces clicking on the table. Our village visits stopped after a few years as, with increasing urbanization of the New Territories, the remote villages had gradually emptied.

The New Territories Races

These contests became very popular in the 1960s and 70s when teams from Volunteer squadrons and from the regular army raced in army vehicles around the New Territories, the prize going to the fastest team to complete the course. In a later version of the contest, the competing teams were tested for various military skills at check points along the course, including one manned by the RAP with the RMO and the medics testing the contestants in elementary First Aid and CPR. Some surprising answers were elicited, but the one I particularly remember was given by one team: when asked to describe treatment for a snake bite: "Take the snake to the hospital", came the reply.

It was during one of these contests that I came across a strange case of "obeying orders without question". Driving in Shek Kong, in the evening, I noticed a lone soldier, clearly a Volunteer, standing by the roadside. Thinking nothing of it, we drove on. Twelve hours later we were driving on the same road, on our way back to the RHQ at the end of the contest. To my astonishment the same man was still standing on the same spot. When asked, he replied that he was dropped there by his squadron and told to wait until picked up later; that he had, indeed, stood there for twelve hours waiting! I ordered him into my Land Rover and brought him back to RHQ. As I suspected, his squadron simply forgot to pick him up. There is no substitute for common sense!

Stonecutters Firing Range

It has been said, I believe correctly, that the Volunteers spent more time practising shooting on Stonecutters Island Range and other firing ranges than did Hong Kong's regular garrison. A day on the Range was always eagerly anticipated and was sometimes made into an open day with the families invited. On such occasions the regiment used to hold shooting competitions. The HQ squadron had a sniper section with volunteers like Henry Sousa, Peter

Rull (Snr) and Reggie Remedios, among others, renowned as sharpshooters. Home Guard Squadron, too, had good marksmen among its members. On one particular occasion, the squadrons were competing in the "falling plates" events, in which eight-member teams must "shoot down" eight metal plates. The Officer Commanding (OC) the HQ Squadron formed two teams, placing all his best shooters, mainly the snipers, in "A" team with himself in command, and putting me in charge of the "B" team selected from the rest of the squadron. No doubt the OC expected to make a clean sweep of the prizes. In a surprising turn, the Home Guard team was eliminated, and the "A" and "B" teams found themselves in the finals. Then the incredible happened: with one salvo my B team brought all our plates down, while the A team was still struggling with theirs. Against all expectations, we won the Holmes Cup. Each member of the winning team received a small shield, which I still treasure as a reminder of a memorable experience.

Some Unusual Events

The Russian Sputnik.[9] In October 1957 the Russians sent *Sputnik*, the first man-made satellite, into orbit around the Earth. That month the regiment had its usual annual training camp at Sai Kung, New Territories. In Camp, Major "Sonny" Capell and I, after dinner and a few drinks, stepped out of the Mess. Somewhere outside the Camp, night firing was in progress; tracers flashed across the dark background. I happened to glance at the sky and saw a faintly lit object moving slowly but steadily across the sky. "This is not an aircraft, and certainly not a meteor or a tracer bullet," I thought. I drew Sonny's attention to it, but he was baffled. It could only be the Russian *Sputnik*, I decided. By now the object in the sky was no longer visible. We went back into the Mess and described our experience, but were immediately told that we had either had too many drinks or had mistaken tracers for a satellite. However, I rang the Royal Observatory and was told, surprisingly, that they had not so far observed the *Sputnik*, but would look out for it the next night. Later the Royal Observatory confirmed that the object was indeed the *Sputnik*, while the *South China Morning Post* reported that two Volunteer officers (our names were given) were the first in Hong Kong to spot the Russian satellite.

The Governor's Adze.[10] In the 1960s and 70s, when the regiment's annual training camp was usually held at Sai Kung, in the army's so-called "Battle

---

9. "Sputnik" (Russian) means "fellow-traveller".
10. An adze is a cutting implement shaped like a chisel, generally hafted onto a wooden handle. They were made of stone in the Stone Age, and bronze in the Bronze Age.

School", our field firing practice took place at a specially assigned area, the Ha Tsuen Range. Red flags were put up at high points around the perimeter of the Range to keep local people and hikers out of the area. As a general rule, whenever live ammunition was used, for instance in field firing or on a firing range, the RAP with the RMO were always standing by in full readiness. The weapons fired at Ha Tsuen were machine-guns and two-inch mortars, with an old metal tank used as a target. The medics were always stationed close behind the firing men, ready to, but hoping they would not, be called upon to treat injuries. Ha Tsuen Range also happens to be a known archaeological site of relatively minor importance. By this time, I had already developed a strong interest in archaeology, and sometimes while on duty at Ha Tsuen firing, would pass the time by keeping my eyes open for possible ancient artefacts. On one occasion, the governor (Sir David Trench) was visiting the regiment on Ha Tsuen Range. Lunch was arranged in the open on a knoll near the firing positions. When the CO asked me if I had found anything, I produced a stone adze picked up that morning. The adze was passed on to the governor and somehow landed in his soup! Embarrassment was followed by general laughter. I wondered what had happened to that adze, for I never saw it again.

   The RMO and the Field Binoculars. During its training periods, the regiment used to be visited by various VIPs. On such occasions the regiment would usually be spruced and made to look busy with various training activities for the visitor to observe. On one such visit, by the Commander British Forces (CBF) in Hong Kong, the CO, possibly short of officers, asked me to give a lecture on the use of field binoculars to a group of trainee-recruits. Actually, it was a subject I knew well. I was fully engrossed in my task, enjoying teaching a subject different, for a change, from a medical one, when I became aware that the CBF had stopped by our group and had been listening for some time to my lecture. He must have liked my presentation and commented on it to the CO. The offshoot of this was that henceforth, I was instructed to repeat my performance with the binoculars at all VIPs' visits, while demonstration of the RAP's medical skills was delegated to my senior NCOs.

Postscript

I retired from the regiment in 1976 on reaching the requisite age of sixty, but continued to keep close links with the RAP, and with the regiment as a whole, by attending mess nights and regimental association functions, and helping occasionally with medical tasks when extra help was needed. In 1982, I was appointed honorary colonel for two years (1982–84) and recalled back as honorary colonel for one year in 1990. It was an honour beyond my expectations, but one which I cherished and of which I was proud. It was especially gratifying to be "on active service" again.[11]

The Royal Hong Kong Regiment (The Volunteers) was disbanded on 3 September 1995 after 141 years of distinguished service to the people of Hong Kong. As I sat among many old comrades that evening of 3 September, watching with heavy heart the regiment's last parade, I reflected on my long association with the Volunteers. I was fortunate to have been a Hong Kong Volunteer from the date of my enlistment on 3 September 1939, through the Battle of Hong Kong and the dark months of imprisonment which followed, through the post-war revival of the regiment, till its final, in the words of the last Hong Kong governor, Chris Patten, "march into history" exactly fifty-six years later. They were meaningful, sometimes difficult, but always rewarding years. What made the Hong Kong Volunteers so important in my life? I ask myself. I am not by nature a military man. I abhor violence and intolerance. Yet I joined a military force and rejoined it after the war. The answer to the first is easy: in September 1939 it was simply the sense of duty. Moreover, I joined not to kill but to heal. The motivation for rejoining in 1949 is more difficult to understand. Perhaps it was the spirit of camaraderie, the sense of common purpose, in the Hong Kong Volunteers that I found so appealing. I always felt at home among them. But was there something else? I wondered. I suspect that many men, and perhaps some women, still contain within themselves a young boy (or girl) who admires uniforms and likes to play soldiers.

The spirit of the Hong Kong Volunteers I believe lives on in the regimental association and its branches, while each of us who had served in the regiment can look back with pride for having been a Hong Kong Volunteer.

---

11. Appointment of honorary colonels is yet another regimental tradition. A regiment appoints an honorary colonel, generally for a fixed period of time, as a sign of honour and respect. The appointee usually has had a long and distinguished service with the regiment, and becomes a sort of father-figure, always ready with useful advice or help. Sometimes, the appointee may have little direct connection with the regiment, but is an important person who adds prestige to the regiment. The RHKR(V) had had both types of honorary colonels (I belonged firmly to the first type).

14

MARIA CALLAS AT EPIDAUROS

In the summer of 1960, while travelling in Greece, I was very fortunate to be present at the performance of Bellini's opera *Norma* at Epidauros, with Maria Callas singing the star role.

The old port of Epidauros lies in Peloponessos, on the southern shore of the Saronic Gulf. Four miles inland from the old port, and off the main road, lies the famous Theatre of Epidauros, the largest and best preserved of the ancient, open-air Greek amphitheatres. Untouched by modern restoration, its steeply rising tiers of hewn rock spread upwards and outwards like a fan, and can accommodate up to sixteen thousand spectators. The acoustics are so remarkable that the softest voice spoken in the centre of the circular stage can be heard clearly from the topmost tier. All around is beautiful, fir tree–covered land, and Nature itself seems to be the stage of this magnificent theatre. Nearby are the ruins of the temple of Aesclepios, the god of healing, and it is tempting to think that perhaps the ancient Greeks regarded theatre as a valuable aid in the process of healing.

During the preceding years, an annual festival of ancient classical plays was held in Epidauros in summer time. The dramas of Aeschylus and Sophocles, the comedies of Aristophanes, had all been given superb performances in these beautiful surroundings. This was the first time, however, that an opera was presented in the Theatre of Epidauros. The production was part of the Athens Festival of Arts which lasted from 29 July to 15.September. The Festival included some twenty musical and stage presentations, but *Norma* with Maria Callas was undoubtedly the highlight of the Festival. There were to be only three performances, all at Epidauros, and special coaches were provided for the journey from Athens, which takes nearly four hours.

Maria Callas was immensely popular in Greece. The Greek people regarded her as one of them and were very proud of her. Probably the surest way of being lynched in Greece was to suggest that Maria Callas was American. In fact, though of Greek origin, she was born in New York and had some of her training in America. But her early studies and training, and the formative years of her art, were in Greece, and she was justifiably considered in Greece to be their prima donna. She first emerged as a singer of importance in 1947 and subsequently won world fame in a number of roles. Her greatest, which established her as a great performer, were in Bellini's *Norma* and Cherubini's *Medea*. She had a rich voice of great range and remarkable purity. Her technique was excellent, but what made her a truly great artiste was her amazing dramatic talent.

It was not surprising then, that all the numbered seats for *Norma* were sold out in Athens well in advance. I had been travelling around the Peloponessos, visiting sites of historical interest. While at Nauplion, which is only twenty miles from Epidauros, I found that the second performance of the opera was to be held that evening. To my surprise and delight, tickets for un-numbered seats could still be bought at Nauplion. I spent the rest of the day looking at the ruins of the temple of Aesclepios, determined to be one of the first to get into the theatre and get a good seat. By six o'clock in the evening I was seated high up on one of the uppermost tiers, watching the sun sinking behind the purple hills and the shadows slowly creeping over the land.

Gradually the theatre filled with people, their voices filling the air. One hardly noticed when it became dark. Suddenly the stage was flood-lit and a white-haired little man strode to the rostrum and bowed to the applauding audience. Tullio Serafin, the conductor, at eight-two was still full of vigour. A few moments later the majestic introductory chords of the overture set the solemn mood of the opera.

The scene of the opera is laid in Gaul, in approximately 50 BCE during the Roman occupation. The story centres around Norma, the Druid high priestess, who is betrayed by her lover, Pollione, the Roman proconsul.

In the first act, the druids assemble to await the arrival of Norma. It is difficult to convey the full impact of this majestic scene. The stage is lit by flaming torches held by the soldiers; their spears are raised in salute. Norma enters with her attendant priestesses, her hair streaming over her shoulders, a wreath of vervain around her brow, and carrying a golden sickle. As Maria Callas appeared on the stage, looking tall and magnificent, the whole theatre exploded into wild applause which lasted for a long time.

In the second act, a very dramatic scene is enacted. After a prelude, the chief melody of which is later sung by Norma, the curtain rises on Norma's dwelling showing her two children, by Pollione, sleeping. Norma, wounded by love and hate, enters, dagger in hand, and tries to bring herself to kill them. As she raises her hand to strike, there is a wonderful moment in the music — a simple figure for strings — and a most vivid and dramatic piece of acting, as she realizes she cannot do it. The dagger drops from her hand and she kneels to embrace the children.

In the final act, Pollione, who has been captured by the druids, is brought in to be offered as a human sacrifice, but Norma announces that as a priestess who has broken her vows she must die too. This is the beginning of a marvellous finale in which all the voices and the chorus join. Pollione's love for Norma has returned and together they ascend the funeral pyre.

The whole audience stood up and cheered, and, if I remember correctly, Maria Callas was called back no less than ten times. Everyone connected with the production was called to take a bow, and at the end a short stocky man came on the stage whom Callas embraced and kissed. I guessed he was the shipping magnate Aristotle Onassis, no doubt a very proud man at that moment.

The entire cast, the orchestra, and the chorus were excellent. Maria Callas was superb and showed once more that she possessed that unique combination of a great voice and a great dramatic talent. As I drove slowly, in a long line of cars, back to Nauplion, I thought that this evening alone had made my visit to Greece worthwhile. The unusual stage settings, the supreme artistry of Maria Callas, and the magnificent surroundings of the Theatre made it an unforgettable artistic experience.

PART 3

15

INCAS OF PERU

"...the glory of the Children of the Sun had departed forever".

From *History of the Conquest of Peru* by
William Prescott (1796–1859)

Background

In these dramatic words William Prescott lamented the demise of one of the most extraordinary empires the world has ever seen — the Inca Empire of South America.

Like most people I was vaguely aware of the fascinating subject of the Inca Empire, but South America was not in my field of archaeological interest, which centred predominantly around Hong Kong and South China. It was the family and not the Incas that brought me to Buenos Aires, Argentina, in the summer of 1960. My parents had migrated to Argentina, from Harbin, in 1935, whilst I pursued a different course — graduating in medicine from Hong Kong University, returning to Hong Kong after a spell in England, and eventually joining Hong Kong University in 1956, as the director of its Student Health Service. My elder brother Leo had established an optical shop in Shanghai which he ran throughout the war, but when the Communists prevailed in China in 1948, he saw no future in Shanghai for foreign businesses. Married with a family, and still stateless, he migrated to Israel, the only country to accept them without a visa. After my mother died in 1954, he moved yet again to join father in Argentina.

Long distances made reunions difficult. I was married and had three children. Fortunately, mother was able to visit us in Hong Kong in 1950 and father in 1955. My opportunity to visit the family in Argentina came in 1960 when I had leave from the University to attend a conference on Student Health in Canada and to visit several student health facilities in the USA. An extra month of leave, applied for and granted, allowed me to travel from the USA to Buenos Aires to visit father and Leo and his family. Leo and father had opened an optical import company under the name of "Mateo Bard e Hijo" (Matthew Bard & Son). I was looking forward eagerly to my first visit to South America and to meeting them after a gap of several years. My wife Sophie agreed to look after the children; I promised to do the same on my return, when she would visit her parents in Australia. They had migrated there from Shanghai in the early 1950s.

Buenos Aires

I arrived in Buenos Aires early in June 1960 and immediately became totally immersed in family affairs. Not having seen father for five years, and Leo for even longer, it was not surprising that I was fussed over. After a couple of days, when the initial excitement of the reunion had subsided, I had time to see something of the city, nearly always in Leo's company; he had taken time off to be with me. Buenos Aires is a beautiful city, well planned, with many handsome ornate plazas. All South American cities have plazas named after, and adorned with statues of, either San Martin (accent on the last syllable) or Simon Bolivar (accent on the middle syllable), the two liberators of South America from Spanish (and Portuguese) rule. It is still hotly debated how many countries were liberated by each, or even who liberated what. Central Buenos Aires is laid out in a regular square grid, and crossed diagonally from corner to corner by a wide, tree-lined avenue called, predictably, Diagonal. A trendy pedestrian mall called Florida (accent on the middle syllable), usually packed with strolling people, contains many artists' studios, where, if one is lucky, one can pick up early works by artists of future distinction. I found the general atmosphere friendly and congenial. People enjoyed being outdoors late in the evening, restaurants were full, and having the evening meal at 11 p.m. seemed normal.

While in Buenos Aires, I met a man by chance who rekindled my interest in the Incas. He talked enthusiastically about the Incas and the succession of early civilizations which had flourished in South America before them. He urged me to visit Peru — the centre of the Inca Empire, and to Peru I went. The family was sorry to let me go, but, frankly, by that time we had exhausted our topics of conversation, and I was ready for my next adventure. I promised to come back (and I did, three years later).

Peru and Lima

Peru stretches along the western coast of South America and comprises three parts: the long and narrow desert, the mountains with their deep valleys and long grass, and the eastern slopes of the mountains which are jungle. The coastal region is a rainless desert with a uniformly brown arid landscape. It used to be said "when you no longer see any trees, you are in Peru". This is certainly not true of Lima, the capital of Peru. Although located in the western desert region, the city is beautiful, with many trees, parks, wide avenues and, of course, the inevitable plazas with statues of San Martin or Bolivar. My first visit was to the Museum of Anthropology and Archaeology. Founded by Julio Cesar Tello, Peruvian archaeologist of international renown, it is an excellent museum of South American cultures and probably the best of its kind in South America. I spent nearly a whole day at the Museum looking at the wealth of material depicting the peoples and the ancient cultures of Peru, of which my friend spoke to me in Buenos Aires.

Ancient Cultures of Peru

Man did not originate in the American continent. No fossils of primitive human species have ever been found there; nothing but *Homo sapiens*. It is generally agreed that human migration into the New World took place from Asia across the frozen Bering Strait, probably about thirty thousand years ago. By that time man was already a skilled hunter and maker of fine stone tools. It took considerable time to spread to the southern continent, where man's presence probably did not occur before 9000–8000 BCE. Early settled neolithic cultures began to emerge around 3000 BCE. These, I thought, were relevant to my main interest, which was the rise and fall of the Inca Empire. To summarize briefly: one of the earliest formative cultures of prominence was Chavis in the Northern Highlands, around 1000 BCE, when pottery and weaving crafts were already well developed. A number of distinct cultures followed between 400 BCE and 400 CE — a dynamic period known as the "Experimental". Then came the period of high development, from 400 to about 1000 CE, when cities and fortifications emerged and to which the famous Mochica and the early Nazca cultures belong. The Mochica is well known for its remarkable portraiture pottery. These cultures were named later. It is unknown what these people called themselves, for there are no written records in South American archaeology of that period. Finally, from about 1000 to 1400 CE, Nazca and Tihuanaca ushered conquest, political and social unification, and the emergence of the Inca Empire.

Before leaving the Museum I bought in the museum shop William Prescott's *History of the Conquest of Peru*. First published in 1847, it is a classic and an absolute "must" for anyone interested in the history of the Incas. As I read it in the following days, its exciting narrative in beautiful, slightly antiquated English left me completely enthralled by the incredible story of the Inca Empire.

I had time to visit only one of the remains of a pre-Inca civilization. Twenty miles from Lima, near the coast, lie the ruins known as Pachacamac, believed to have been a great religious centre, probably of Chimu culture, immediately preceding the Incas. It is a huge pyramid constructed of sun-baked bricks. When the Incas conquered the area, such was the veneration of this shrine that they permitted the continuation of the worship, but built on the top their own temple to the Sun.

The Pageant

Early the following morning I flew to Cuzco, the heart and ancient capital of the Inca Empire. It was 24 June; at the time I did not know how fortunate I was to arrive in Cuzco on that date. It was a two-hour flight in a small passenger aircraft operated by Faucett Airlines. We flew at an altitude of between 20,000 and 25,000 feet holding oxygen tubes in our mouths and marvelling at the incredible beauty of the Peruvian Andes. Then suddenly the plane swooped down into a magnificent valley with Cuzco before us bathing in the morning sun. After landing, we were warned that we were now at an altitude of 11,000 feet and therefore must "take it easy" and not exert ourselves for a couple of days until we got used to it. Several of the passengers, I noticed, had bleeding from the nose, and complained of shortness of breath. Strangely, apart from feeling slightly lightheaded, which passed after an hour or so, I felt no ill effects and decided that "taking it easy" was not on my agenda. Disdaining a couple of hotels, close to the main square, I set off at once to find a room in a private house and was lucky to find one in less than an hour. It was a boarding house, a *pension*, run by two young and rather attractive sisters. Inside there was a commotion, as everyone was preparing to leave. I was then told that it was 24 June, the day of the Inti-Raymi, an annual pageant enacting the coronation of the Inca king. The ceremony was about to begin soon, and off we all went, the two sisters and the lodgers, to a large open ground in front of a ruined fortress, on the hill above Cuzco. The Incas did not surround their cities with walls, but built a fortress, a "pucara", outside each city into which people retired in the event of an attack. The pucara above Cuzco was called Sacsahuaman. We found a spot near the pucara's long northern wall, which my fellow-lodgers told me was 1500 feet long, with some stones 20 feet high and weighing as much as 20 tons. I was astonished at the enormous polygonal stones so perfectly fitted together. The unfinished stones were pushed up the hill, it was believed, and then cut accurately to a finish. Sufficient of the walls remained to leave one amazed at the massive structures which can fairly be described as cyclopean.

The pageant began at two o'clock in the afternoon. The pucara walls and the rising ground above were covered with a multitude of spectators. The whole of Cuzco must have turned up to watch this ancient rite. The ceremony opened with colourful processions and dancing, the actors using the original Inca masks and costumes. The dancers were followed by a procession of "soldiers", also in the original coloured tunics, who performed what was presumably a "war dance". This went on for some time accompanied by loudspeaker-transmitted music. Finally the "Inca King", holding a long ornate staff, was led to an artificial platform of stones which he ascended. The soldiers knelt as the new King was proclaimed. The King was then carried in a litter several times around the parade ground accompanied by musicians playing on a mixture of old instruments, such as seashell trumpets, special drums and tambourines, as well as modern fiddles and trumpets. In spite of some modern concessions, such as microphones and loudspeakers, and hundreds of clicking cameras, the display was both impressive and enjoyable. It was also very clear that the people of Cuzco enjoyed the festival very much.

Back at the *pension*, we all sat down to a sumptuous meal amidst much joyful talk and laughter. The sun was setting in glorious red colours; it was getting chilly. At this altitude, as I was to experience in the coming days, it was hot sunshine by day and biting crisp cold by night. A fire was lit in the lounge and we all relaxed in comfortable armchairs in the warm and cosy atmosphere. I was now able to take stock of my company. The two pretty and vivacious sisters, Mariela and Isabella, managed the place for their parents who were political exiles, hiding in neighbouring Bolivia. Once a month, the sisters hiked across the mountains into Bolivia to see their parents and bring them supplies and other necessities, a strenuous and dangerous adventure for such young girls, I was told. There were three lodgers: a young blond German globetrotter Klaus, without, he explained, a definite itinerary; a young Peruvian girl, Inez, a trainee tourist guide, on a short holiday from Lima; a short stocky man in his middle thirties, whose name I cannot recall and whose nationality remained a mystery, but who seemed to be of a very jolly and friendly disposition. At forty-four, I was the oldest by a good margin, but soon felt totally at ease with everyone. The conversation was in English in which everyone appeared comfortable. Soon wine appeared which further helped the relaxed and happy atmosphere. One of the sisters switched on music and we danced until three o'clock in the morning. I had completely forgotten that I was 11,000 feet up and enjoined to "take it easy". I could not recall a more enchanting evening in many years.

Cuzco

I was awakened at 6 a.m. by the sound of a bugle. Surprised, I looked out of the window and saw that across the street were the army barracks. From now on, I thought, there would be an early wake up call by bugle every morning! I went back to bed and managed to sleep for another few hours. When I came out for breakfast, I was alone except for the sisters who served very good coffee with freshly baked bread. My fellow-lodgers had all gone on their various excursions. I had hardly seen anything of Cuzco the previous day and so set off to see the city. Cuzco, the sacred city of the Incas, is an attractive and interesting city located in a peaceful highland valley. The Incas had erected in it many fine imposing buildings, some of which were destroyed by the Spaniards, their finely-cut stones used to build churches and private houses. But the main damage to the city was inflicted by the earthquake in 1650, and more recently by one in 1950. In spite of this, some of the original walls and many doorways survived and were incorporated into new buildings, bearing witness to the remarkable building skills of the Incas. Referring to the little guide-book I borrowed at the *pension*, I found the remains of the palaces, one of Manco Capac, the legendary founder of the Incas, the other of Inca Roca, both well preserved. The latter contains a remarkable piece of masonry — the Stone of 12 Angles — set perfectly without any mortar. There was a group of tourists around the stone taking photographs; I did too. As I walked the streets of Cuzco, I could see other examples of the architectural skills of the Incas. Interesting features were their use of polygonal stones interlocked with amazing precision, and the total absence of an arch in the construction.

It has been generally presumed that the arch was unknown to the Incas. Neither did they possess the wheel, and the massive blocks they used for building were probably transported on wood and stone rollers pulled by ropes. Personally, I believe it is unsafe to assume that because the Incas did not use the arch or the wheel, they did not know about them. Among the post-Inca buildings, the magnificent Cathedral, with two widely spaced towers, stands at the top of the main square, the Plaza de Armas, while to the right of it is the almost equally impressive church Compania de Jesus. I had time for a short visit to the Regional Museum (Museo de Historia Regional) which, though small, was very informative. The Plaza was filled with local people. Cuzco's population was said to be about a hundred thousand, but it seemed as if half of the population was out in the streets. There was still a festive air about, perhaps a spillover from the great pageant of the previous day.

I returned to the *pension* late in the afternoon pleased with my day out. The sisters were lighting a fire in the lounge and soon the rest of the lodgers were returning for dinner. Afterwards we all settled comfortably in the lounge, with wine and music, for another delightful evening.

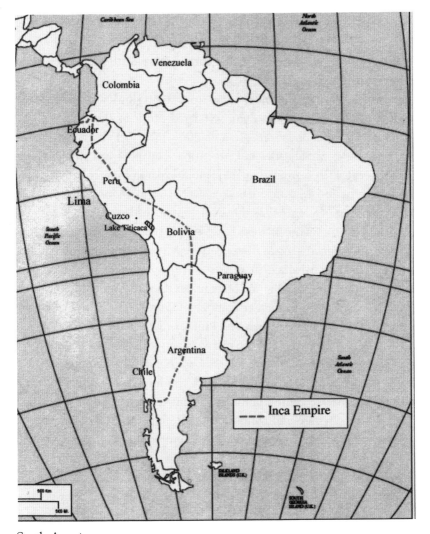

South America.
The dotted line, superimposed on the map of modern South America, outlines the extent of the Inca Empire at its zenith, c. 1500 CE.

The Rise and Fall of the Inca Empire

Curiously, little is known about the origins of the Incas, and this is true to some extent of all South American prehistory, for not one of their cultures had writing; no writing of any form, and therefore no records. Even the name "Inca" is problematical, for it was applied only to the rulers. To avoid confusion, I shall use "Inca" in singular form for the king, and "Incas" plural for the people.

Records began with the Spanish conquest in 1532, first by the conquerors (conquistadores) and later by the new, mixed Indian and Spanish generation. Among the latter the best known is Garcilase de la Vega, who wrote his "Royal Commentaries of Peru". Serious archaeological studies began at the end of the 19th century, but even then, the early history of the Incas remained a mixture of fact and legend.

It is believed that the Incas came from the region of Lake Titicaca, in the high plateau of southern Peru, wandered north to the valley of Cuzco and there laid the foundations of an empire which included most of today's Peru, parts of Bolivia, Equador and Argentina. The move had probably started as early as the 13th century, but their rapid expansion, mainly by conquest, began with the first historical emperor Pachacuti in 1438. When Columbus discovered America, in 1492, the Inca Empire had extended 2,300 miles along the South American west coast. Their rulers bore the title of Inca. For some 150 years the Incas ruled, with remarkable organization and unity, a totalitarian state in which there was no private ownership of land, where nearly everything belonged to the State under the direction of the Inca family. When the Spanish arrived under Francisco Pizarro, in 1532, the country was involved in a civil war between two brothers, which the Spanish exploited and which partially explained the extraordinary collapse of the empire. Still the conquest of such an immense area by a handful of adventurers, said to number less than two hundred, is one of the most extraordinary events of history. The extreme centralization of the empire may have also contributed to the disaster. By ruse and cunning the last emperor, Atahualpa, was lured into the Spanish camp. All authority was centred in the emperor and when he was captured, resistance did not materialize. Atahualpa was executed by the Spaniards in 1533 and the conquest was complete.

Although there have been attempts to originate Incas from elsewhere (from the lost tribes of Israel to the Egyptians), there is little doubt among scholars that the Incas were the product of the Andean civilization. The Incas arrived late and built successfully on a succession of cultures before them.

They could be looked upon as organizers rather than creators of Peruvian civilization.

Field Adventure

Klaus, knowing my interest in archaeology, suggested for the two of us to have a field day in the countryside outside Cuzco searching for artefacts. I liked the idea, so early in the morning we set off armed with nothing more than a couple of penknives. Klaus had already been in Cuzco for several weeks and knew the surrounding countryside well. I explained to Klaus that we should look for eroded or terraced surfaces where artefacts might be exposed and thus avoid any actual digging, which was illegal. We walked and climbed among beautiful scenery for hours without finding anything. Then, suddenly, luck smiled upon us. We spotted a vertically cut slope with several terraced plots, prepared for cultivation — this is a common cultivation method used in hilly terrains. The freshly cut surfaces showed a number of potsherds sticking out. They appeared to be typical Inca pottery with painted geometric designs. I was satisfied that we broke no law: we did not dig but had only taken out loose sherds, which would have been washed down the hill with the first rain and lost. We also saw some bones which Klaus wanted to prize loose, but I persuaded him to leave them. I did not know, and did not wish to know, whether they were human or animal bones.

Pleased with the results of our excursion, we headed home. Klaus talked about his plans, or rather lack of plans. He would stop at a place when he wanted, or take off again when he felt like it. He wanted to feel "free as the wind", as he put it. For the present he liked Cuzco and the *pension*, and was going to stay on for a while. I, too, liked my present situation, and for a moment, I must confess, I had wished I could be like him.

The Life and Organization of the Incas

What were the Incas like? They were described by the Spaniards as American Indians of chocolate to brown colour, of medium height, inclined to be thickset, with large chests (probably an adaptation to high altitude), large heads, high cheekbones and proud prominent noses. It struck me that when I walked on the streets of Cuzco, I could see them everywhere. One had the feeling that the Incas had not gone, but rather that they lived in the people of today's Cuzco, though they called themselves Peruvians.

The Incas wore tunics and capes, some very simple like the present-day "poncho" — a piece of cloth folded across the middle, with holes for head and arms. The tunics of the better-class people were beautifully woven of colourful yarn. It was said that the Inca himself, whose tunic was made of the finest vicuna wool, never wore the same one twice. The weaving skills occupied both men and women, the weaving industry being strictly controlled by the state officials. Llama wool was used for rough articles, blankets, sacks. The white wool of alpaca was used for clothes, and vicuna wool — soft and silky, the finest in the world — was reserved for the highest luxury weaving. The wool was dyed but the dyeing processes used are unknown.

Inca pottery was well made, fine-grained and hard. The wheel was never used, and the pots were made by shaping the body around a sausage-shaped core. The pottery was made in a variety of shapes and distinctive painted patterns, mainly geometric. The flower designs are said to have appeared after the Spanish conquest. Of the two pottery sherds in Figure 15.7, which Klaus and I found on our field trip, the one on the left has a geometric design, while the other one, with what looks like a plant design, is probably of a later type.

Animals, the llama and the related alpaca and vicuna, played a vital part in Inca economy. There were no draught animals, like horses or donkeys, in South America, and the wheel was unknown. This may seem inconceivable in the 15th century CE, but it has been asserted in reputable publications. Perhaps having migrated into the New World before the invention of the wheel, and not having draught animals, the people did not need the wheel? And is the absence of an arch and potter's wheel a consequence of, or related to, the absence of the wheel? These are interesting questions, to which there are no satisfactory answers. The llama is a peculiar animal, with a camel's head and a sheep's body (or close to it). Apparently it is related to the camel but has no hump. There are no records of the llama's first appearance in South America and it is not known in a wild state. Thousands of them were bred on high plateaus and used to carry loads, and still are. The animal does it patiently and compliantly, but, I am told, will not carry more than 100 lbs; if overloaded even slightly, it will lie and not move until the extra load has been removed! To the Incas, llama was much more than a beast of burden: its wool was used for heavy blankets, its meat for food (if dead from natural causes, for it was forbidden to kill them), its dung for fuel. The alpaca and vicuna were used chiefly to supply wool.

Quechua, the language of the people before the Incas, was adopted and used by the Incas. It is still the language of the people in the highlands of Peru. Like the other South American cultures before them, the Incas possessed no writing. Quechua tradition and "literature" were verbal, though the Spanish introduced writing after the conquest. "Quipus", which means "knot", is a method of counting, a device by which knotted strings were used to aid memory. Quipus was perhaps the closest Incas got to writing, but it was not writing. Verbal message had to accompany quipus or it had no meaning. Quipus made communication easier, since in any message, numbers would be the most difficult to remember. Spanish sources refer to the ability of knot-string readers to interpret them.

Iron was unknown to the Incas, as well as to other indigenous Americans. Other metals were worked, especially gold. The land was known as the land of gold, which undoubtedly attracted the Spaniards. Bronze was used for weapons and tools, but stone continued to be used as a tool. One of the outstanding achievements of the Incas was construction of roads, in which they could truly be compared to the Romans. As far as can be ascertained, no roads existed in Peru before the Incas. Like the Romans, the Incas needed roads for efficient centralization of power. However, not having wheeled vehicles, they did not need good paving, width or strong bridges. There were two main roads: the Royal Road which stretched through the Andes for 3,250 miles! And the coastal road which ran for some 2,500 miles. There were also many laterals. These roads were used for sending "chasqui", or couriers, who could run, in relays, 1250 miles in five days, or an average of 246 miles per day, and that at an altitude of 6,000 to 17,000 feet — seemingly an incredible feat! Yet the chronicles seem to agree on the figures. Actually, it has been found that stations existed at one to one and a half mile intervals, so that each runner had only to run between two stations. Even so, they ran, at an average, a six-and-a-half minute mile.

The Inca people were primarily farmers, growing mainly corn and potatoes. Meat was scarce, since it was forbidden to kill llamas. Guinea pigs, which apparently were plentiful, served as the main source of meat. Women helped in the fields and also did the cooking. Polygamy was only possible for the upper classes. In the mountainous areas, terraces were cut into slopes and used for cultivation, an obvious method used in other countries, where little flat land is available. The Incas had no money and probably used a barter system. Taxes were paid in agricultural work and on special days the whole village would band together to work the fields of the Inca. For ordinary people the incessant toil was inseparably tied to ritual and local deities, the latter manifested in animistic forms of nature. However, religious hierarchy was present and formal ritual was enforced. The sun god was foremost among the deities of the earth, the sea and the heavenly bodies. Animal sacrifices were practised, but not human, except possibly at times of extreme calamity.

The social organization of Inca society was based on a primary social unit called ayllu, which was like an early commune, in which families living together shared land, animals and crops. For ordinary members of the ayllu, who were tied to the earth, it was hard work throughout. Ayllus were united into larger units and so on until a large domain was formed answerable to the King. Upon this land division was also built the political system, which rose like a decimal pyramid in which every ten units were controlled by an official, continuing until the apex of the pyramid occupied by the king or Inca. It was calculated that for every 10,000 people there were 1,331 officials. This efficient system was the keystone to the Incas' rise to power; it was also probably the main cause of the kingdom's downfall, for when Inca was captured, by ruse and cunning, the administrative pyramid collapsed.

Machu Picchu

North of Cuzco, about three hours by rail-car, across sixty miles of breathtaking scenery, lie the ruins of an Inca city called Machu Picchu (meaning "Old Peak" in Quechua language). Anyone visiting Cuzco, and interested in the story of the Incas, would almost certainly visit this remarkable site. When, after a few days in Cuzco, I mentioned my intention to visit Machu Picchu, Inez offered to come with me. We travelled on the single narrow-gauge rail-car which was only half-full. It made frequent stops to allow us to enjoy the scenery, observe people, and take photographs; the journey was most enjoyable. Our first sight of the ruins of Machu Picchu was an unforgettable experience. Lying on a narrow precipitous ridge between two sharp mountain peaks, in one of the most inaccessible parts of the Andes, it seemed unbelievable that such a city could have been built and occupied. The city was never discovered by the Spanish conquerors. But here it was — a fortified city lying just as it had been left by its last inhabitants. It is believed to have been the last stronghold of the Incas, though it is not known why they left, or where they had gone. Outside the city walls one could see the terraced fields which were cultivated and had supported the Machu Picchu population. Inez and I wandered among its nearly two hundred granite buildings, consisting of small palaces, shrines, barracks, and ordinary dwellings, among its maze of ancient walls, marvelling yet again at the remarkable skill of Inca architects and stonemasons. There were not many tourists like us looking over the ruins, but a professional photographer suddenly materialized, and Inez and I had our photograph taken sitting, irreverently, on what was reputed to be a sacrificial stone.

The story of Machu Picchu's discovery is an intriguing one. In the outside world, Hiram Bingham, an American historian, is generally credited with the city's discovery, which is sometimes described as accidental. In Cuzco one hears a different story. Bingham came to Peru in 1911 with the initial purpose to collect material for his book about Simon Bolivar, the great South American hero and liberator. Like many others who had come in contact with Inca history, Bingham became fascinated with the subject. He read books and listened to folklore about the Incas. He became convinced that after they were conquered, some of the Incas took refuge in a city which was never discovered by the Spanish and eventually lost to posterity. Tales of "the lost city of Incas" had circulated in Peru for many years, but were never regarded seriously. Bingham, however, took them seriously and became obsessed with the idea of finding this "lost city". He went back to the USA, raised money, and returned to Peru to search for it. When one considers the vast expanse of the country with its innumerable, often inaccessible valleys buried in dense jungle, it was no wonder that after two years of searching, Bingham was ready to give up. But just then he had a stroke of luck, when he met a roguish Peruvian gentleman by the name of Arteaga. Bingham was aware that Arteaga had been quietly selling some Inca artefacts. Surprisingly, and this was Bingham's real achievement, he was able to persuade Arteaga to reveal the latter's source of artefacts, and was led to Machu Picchu.

The ruins were almost totally hidden by dense vegetation, and it took Bingham several years to uncover them. Hiram Bingham deserves full credit for winning Arteaga's confidence, for it could hardly have been in the latter's interest to reveal his well-concealed source of Inca artefacts.

Farewell

A day or two after our visit to Machu Picchu, Inez and the nice, stocky man went back to Lima, after a small farewell party the evening before. Instead, an elderly Peruvian lady joined the household. She kept very much to herself, never joined us in the lounge, and apart for an occasional "buenos dias" (good day) never spoke to us. The evening chats by the fireplace continued, but the sisters suddenly looked worried; perhaps the time for their monthly trip to their parents in Bolivia was approaching. It was time for me to leave. On the day, I kissed the sisters goodbye, promising to return — the promise I knew I was unlikely to keep. I thought they were close to crying, and Klaus too looked sad. Then I walked away from the house. I had spent twelve happy days in it. I knew I would miss the fireplace chats, the music and the dancing, the sound of the morning bugle. I learned a great deal about the Incas, and enjoyed thoroughly exploring Cuzco and Machu Picchu. But unlike Klaus, I was not free "like the wind".

Conclusion

The Incas, some of the most paradoxical empire-builders in the world, people who lacked writing, wheel and iron, had succeeded in conquering a vast domain. They lost it in an even more incredible way, though not without a parallel: a generation before, another Spaniard by the name of Hernando Cortez conquered the Aztec Kingdom of Mexico in almost exactly the same manner. Probably inspired by the exploits of Cortez, Francisco Pizarro, with a handful of men (said to be exactly 170 in number), desperate and brave, achieved as much and destroyed a great realm. How could it be, one might ask, when the sheer weight of the people could have crushed the invaders? Historians have been speculating for years about the reasons: Spaniards on horses were thought to have caused terror among the Incas, for they had never seen horses, let alone mounted men, and might have taken them for some sort of half-men, half-horses centaurs, the civil war raging in the country, the ancient prophesies, which told of white gods coming to take over the Inca kingdom — all these, singly or collectively, were blamed. But above all, the cunning Spanish manoeuvre, by which the Inca, who was the apex of an immense organization, was lured into a trap and captured. Historians will probably continue to speculate on this amazing event.

Finally, it is probably wrong to imagine that the Spanish had totally destroyed the empire. Although much looting and vandalism took place, especially in search of gold, although many important leaders were killed — Pizarro himself among them — or executed, the empire itself was so well regimented, that when the Inca was replaced by a Spaniard, the government machinery continued to function, and the common man continued to live and farm as before.

16

BEAUTY PAGEANT IN SOUTH DAKOTA

"Beauty is altogether in the eye of the beholder."
Margaret Hungerford (1855–1897), *Molly Brown*

"Beauty is only skin deep."
Attributed to Thomas Overbury (1581–1613)

The first phrase has become a cliché, but in the case of a beauty contest it can surely be regarded as apt. The second, also a common cliché, is not as apt since beauty contests, as I have found, seem to seek beauty beyond skin depth. Acting as one of the judges at a beauty pageant was undoubtedly among my more unusual experiences, especially since at no time in the past had I shown any particular interest in beauty pageants or beauty contests of any sort. The events I am about to relate took place in the summer of 1963 in South Dakota, USA, and how I came to be in this somewhat less noticeable part of the United States deserves a page or two.

Hong Kong University Health Service
In 1956, in Hong Kong, I left general medical practice to take up the post of university health officer at the University of Hong Kong. My job was to organize a comprehensive full-time medical service for students, staff and the staff's dependants. In this, the University was falling in step with most of the world's tertiary educational institutions, which, in the post–Second World War era, had established student health services. A departure, by Hong Kong University, from the usual model was the addition of staff and dependants to the panel — a sensible measure in view of the absence in Hong Kong of any national medical insurance. The University Health Service provided straightforward general practice facilities for staff and families, but for students it entailed much more. The Service was concerned with the students' physical, mental and emotional wellbeing, and consequently provided help

and advice in health education, sports medicine, preventive medicine, and simple counselling.

It was in simple counselling that I felt the lack of professional help. The post-war university environment was much more stressful and competitive than the pre-war one. Instead of the affluent student body of prewar days, the university now catered for poorer students, many studying on scholarships or bursaries. The demand for university places far exceeded their supply. The academic demands and the pressure on students to succeed were enormous. I soon became convinced that the Service needed trained professional counsellors for students who were increasingly weighed down with financial, family and other problems such as poor study skills. Counselling services were already accepted in many universities abroad, especially in America and Australia, where returning servicemen and women entering universities, some traumatized by their war experience, required counselling. When I proposed a counselling service for university students, I received no support at all from the University's academics or administrators. They clung steadfastly to the old notion, strongly entrenched in British red-brick universities, that the students' best counsellors were tutors or hall wardens. I was amazed at how British academics accepted psychology as a subject, but were suspicious of its practical application, as in clinical counselling. However, I persisted. Finally, in 1963, after the Asia Foundation, an American educational institution working in Asia, offered to send me and pay for my attachment to a counselling service in the USA, the University agreed to give me three months' paid leave to take up the Asia Foundation's offer and to report my findings to the University on my return.

University of Minnesota Counselling Service
I apologize to my readers for being slow in getting to the main subject of this essay, the Beauty Pageant, but I still have a good deal of interesting material to impart. The Asia Foundation had arranged for me to be attached to the Counselling Bureau ("bureau" — an ugly term, I thought later; a "centre" would have been more appropriate) of the University of Minnesota, Minneapolis, widely regarded in the field as the "Mecca of Counselling". I was to be guided and advised by its head, Professor Ralph Berdie, and there I proceeded in May 1963.

The Bureau was housed in a large old-fashioned, three-storey red-brick building and served by a large staff of professional and clerical personnel. The ground floor was allotted to clinical counselling, where students were seen by qualified and trainee clinical counsellors, either by referral or by open entry.

The middle floor was occupied by the research section, in which numerous aptitude, ability and psychological tests were designed, tested and re-tested in an almost non-stop vigorous fashion. The Bureau, I learned, was famous for its invention of the widely used MMPI test, a rather cumbersome title which stands for Minnesota Multiple Personality Inventory. It was a three-hour questionnaire test which claimed to reveal the tested person's total personality, aptitudes and predispositions. The top floor contained a most interesting section — Research and Development of Study Skills, in which new methods and devices were evolved and tested, designed to improve students' ability to read and comprehend faster, and learn how to study more effectively. A curious fact — while in other sections the staff appeared to be equally divided between men and women, in the Study Skills, the psychologist in charge, who for some reason reminded me of the Hollywood actor Donald Sutherland, was the only man, surrounded by some twenty or thirty female staff. In a witty allusion to this, he had a ceramic figurine of a rooster on his desk.

During the three months of my attachment to the Counselling Bureau, I was initiated, with ruthless efficiency, into all aspects of the Counselling Bureau's very impressive organization. I observed and studied the philosophy and methodology of counselling programmes, until I was familiar with, or at least aware of, some of the complexities of University Counselling.

The University and the City

The University of Minnesota is a huge institute, with an enrollment, at that time, of some forty thousand students. It is located in a picturesque, well-wooded campus on the bank of the Mississippi River. Surrounding the campus are many lodging houses for students; I rented a room in one of them. I met many people and was overwhelmed by kindness and invitations. Had I wished I could have been out for dinner every night. I joined a small group of fencers at the University who were trained by an excellent professional coach twice a week after classes. As a result, my fencing, which had become my passion after the war, improved enormously.

Minneapolis, Minnesota, is a large but very friendly city. Together with Saint Paul it forms the Twin Cities along the banks of the Mississippi River. The climate, in late spring, was pleasantly warm and trees and shrubs were in bloom. The "City of Lakes", as it is called, has strongly entrenched Scandinavian and German traditions, and may be viewed as somewhat stolid and puritanical, but its warm hospitality refutes this. There was plenty of cultural activity: the Guthrie Theatre, recently imported from England, opened its season with Shakespeare's *Hamlet*, which I was fortunate to attend. I also very much enjoyed several concerts given by the Minneapolis Symphony Orchestra, a first-class professional body.

Beauty Pageant

My attachment to the University's Counselling Bureau did not pass unnoticed. Although Hong Kong was generally well known and was well established on the tourist circuit, a person from such a far-away place was still bound to excite some interest, if not curiosity. A number of people questioned me about my life and work in Hong Kong. The University must have had many foreign students, but the Bureau's staff appeared to be entirely American. Perhaps because I stood out as a stranger in the all-American team of the Bureau, I was picked out for a role in a beauty pageant. One day in June, about a month after my arrival, a young man and a woman came to see me. They said that I was just the sort of person they were looking for — faring from a far-away place with no connection to local events or people — a totally neutral person. They asked if I would agree to join a panel of judges of a beauty pageant to elect Miss South Dakota. The event would shortly take place in Mitchell, South Dakota and would take three to four days; they would drive me there, lodge me in a comfortable hotel and then return me to the Bureau. They promised a most exciting and interesting experience, and I had no doubt they were right. Without a moment's hesitation I agreed. Two days later we drove 260 miles west, first through the handsome fields and small lakes of Minnesota, and then through monotonous, seemingly endless, corn fields of South Dakota.

During the long drive, of about five hours, my two companions briefed me partially on the beauty pageant process, but warned that full briefing for the five judges would take place the following morning. I was told that the five selected judges comprised three men and two women, that there were seven finalists-contestants, and that the full pageant would take three days. I also learned a little about the history of beauty contests: although some were apparently held sporadically in the 1890s in America, the modern beauty pageants date from 1920s, also originating in the USA. They later spread internationally, to become, in the 1950s, Miss Universe Beauty Pageants. We arrived at Mitchell late in the afternoon. After a short rest at the hotel, I was fetched and taken to a splendid dinner at which I met members of the organizing committee and the other four judges, two men and two women. Strangely enough, I remember very little about them, except that they were Americans from other states; one of them, a woman, was, I recall, from California.

I kept neither notes nor a diary of the following three days and will be relying on my memory to relate the events of the Pageant as they unfolded. After more than four decades, there are blurred spaces, of course, but on the whole I remember it well enough to describe the entire process day by day.

Day 1: Corn Palace

On the morning after my arrival in Mitchell, I and my fellow judges were fetched from the hotel and taken to the famous Mitchell Corn Palace for a meeting with the organizers of the Pageant. The Corn Palace, where the Pageant events were to take place, is the pride and show-piece of Mitchell and South Dakota. A large building surmounted by several strange-looking domes, and reminding me slightly of the Brighton Pavilion, its exterior is completely covered with millions of cobs of corn forming various patterns. I must confess, I found the Corn Palace somewhat grotesque, but then, I was not a native of South Dakota. For the people of South Dakota, for whom corn was the source of livelihood and wealth, it was no doubt a splendorous edifice.

At the meeting we received a detailed briefing. The organizers emphasized that this was not merely a beauty contest, but also a test of personality and talent; that the winner would proceed to compete in the Miss America Pageant, and would subsequently be likely to achieve a successful career. Each of the judges was given a file with details of the contestants, their photographs and short biographical sketches, as well as notes on criteria and scoring. During these three days, the judges would have ample opportunity to mix with and observe the contestants at various functions. The judges should note their manners, poise, and other social graces.

The first of these functions took place the same afternoon in the form of a cocktail party, and we were able to meet the contestants for the first time. The girls wore badges with their names, while they were as yet unaware of our identities. As expected, they were attractive, but personally I did not find any of them exceptionally beautiful or stunning. Perhaps too much corn in the diet is not conducive to good looks.

In the evening, the first "beauty parade" was held on the stage of the main hall of the Corn Palace. The hall, which I estimated could hold about seven to eight hundred people, was about three quarters full. The Master of Ceremonies (MC) introduced the seven contestants who walked slowly, wearing swimsuits, before the judges sitting at a special table in front of the stage. By the standards of present-day beach attire, those swimsuits were very conservative. Then, each contestant was recalled individually onto the stage and asked to make a short speech about herself, and her aim and ambition in life. Not surprisingly some appeared self-conscious. After an hour's break, when the contestants changed into informal frocks, we all had dinner at the Palace. The judges were placed next to the competitors, so we were able to talk to them and further observe their behaviour at the dinner table. It was a very full and busy day; I was glad to be back at the hotel and went to bed.

Day 2

The morning was free. I spent the first part of it making notes in my file about the contestants, and then went for a stroll. Mitchell is a small town, with a total population, at that time, of about ten thousand. I was not impressed by it. The houses were mostly nondescript, pedestrian in style, and the surroundings unattractive. I came back bored, but perhaps I did not explore the town well enough. In the afternoon the five of us, judges, were taken to a tea party where again we were expected to mix with the competing girls and further observe them. By this time, my attention was drawn to three of the seven competitors, and especially one of them — a blond girl with a very pleasant and modest bearing. I was, however, determined to keep an open mind as long as possible.

In the evening, at the Palace, the Pageant continued with another parade, the girls this time wearing informal, afternoon frocks, some of which we were told had been fashioned and made by themselves. The audience was bigger than on the previous night, but the hall was still not packed. The second part of the evening was devoted to talent tests, when each contestant had to perform some artistic act. I recall that the blond girl, whom I favoured, performed rather well on a guitar. Another girl played an accordion, indifferently I thought. One danced some sort of tap dance, and one or two sang. None was outstandingly good, but they bravely did their best, and earned generous applause from the audience.

Day 3: The Gala Event

In the morning the judges had a breakfast meeting at the hotel. We discussed our findings to date and compared notes. On the whole, there was general agreement as we found our gradings of the contestants were for the most part similar. I noticed that the blond girl was among the top three. We arrived at the Palace at five o'clock in the afternoon for a preliminary meeting with the organizers and the MC. At the meeting we were reminded of the percentage marks allotted to the different aspects of the competition and asked to adhere to them, as far as possible, in our judging. I do not remember the exact figures, except that talent was given a higher percentage (it might have been 40%)

than the swimsuit and physical appearance. At the Palace, preparations for the final night were in full swing. Lavish decorations and glimmering coloured lights had been installed. It was going to be a big gala event.

By 6.30 p.m. the Hall was packed with people. Many in the front row were wearing dinner jackets and black ties — presumably the city's dignitaries. The show opened with the MC introducing the judges. As he called out our names and briefly described each one's background, we stood up one by one and acknowledged the applause. I am not entirely a stranger to limelight: on many occasions, when conducting the Hong Kong Philharmonic Orchestra, I stood on the podium receiving the audience's applause, but the elation I felt on this occasion was altogether of a different nature — more like a thrill.

Then came the parade of the contestants in swimsuits, followed by a short break, after which they came on the stage slowly one by one wearing evening gowns, smiling and looking splendid. Each one was introduced by the MC and received a rousing applause from the audience. After the introduction came the questions-and-answers event, which purports to test the competitors' mental agility by responding with quick repartees to questions. On this occasion the event had a surprising and ingenious twist. Each competitor was given an answer, and asked to improvise a question to it. I recall one which was: "No, I will most certainly not". Most competitors assumed that it was an answer to a proposition of some sort and devised appropriate questions, which I thought displayed little ingenuity.

Finally came the climax of the event — choosing the winner. We, the judges, huddled together for a consultation. By this time we had a consensus and it only took us a few minutes to agree on the final list and the winner. Only three top places were to be announced. I was pleased to see that my favourite, the shy blond girl, was our unanimous winner. The MC informed the public that the three top winners would now be called, and he did so in the usual way, beginning with the third, then the second, leaving the winner to the last. As Miss South Dakota was announced, the audience erupted into a long and enthusiastic ovation. Smiling, she stepped forward to have a garland of flowers and a crown placed upon her. To my shame, I cannot remember her name. The judges were then conducted onto the stage where we shook hands with and congratulated the three top performers. After thanking the audience and the participants, the MC announced that the Pageant was over. The people dispersed. The organizing committee and the judges had dinner together and all agreed that the Pageant was a great success. It was late when I finally reached my hotel. It was a night to remember.

As we drove back to Minneapolis the next morning, I had ample time to reflect upon my recent experience. A beauty pageant was, of course, one of mankind's many light, frivolous activities, like sports or games, some of which, however, are often taken very seriously indeed. Waste of time? Hardly. In a world beset with many profound problems, pursuits which relax and amuse serve a useful purpose. The beauty pageant in which I had just participated was interesting, entertaining, a pleasant diversion from the concentrated work at the Counselling Bureau: it was, in a word, FUN. I later learned that our Miss South Dakota did not win the Miss America title, and was thus ineligible for the Miss Universe contest.

Postscript

My report and recommendations regarding a Counselling Service were well received by Hong Kong University, but setting one up was far from plain sailing. I had gained some converts, but there was still considerable opposition to the idea. I then suggested that a counsellor should be invited to talk to the University staff. The Asia Foundation again came forward with funds and some time later a counsellor from an American university arrived in Hong Kong and appeared before a selected group of the University staff. The meeting was a total disaster. The Asia Foundation's choice was ill-advised and the hapless man said everything possible to antagonize his audience. I thought our case was sunk. But now there were several of us and we pressed on, suggesting that this time the University should listen to a counsellor from a British university who might be more in tune with the conditions in the largely British-oriented Hong Kong University. This was agreed to, but none could be found in the United Kingdom, so a counsellor from Australia was invited to repair the damage. This he did with stunning success and in due course the first University Student Counsellor was appointed. He too was an Australian. The University went even further, by appointing a dean of students — a position common in American universities, but virtually unknown at the time in British universities. All this took time — four years in fact, since my trip to the USA — before a Counselling Service was set up, separate from the Health Service. Having kept in touch with the University for many years after my retirement, I witnessed both services flourish.

17

EASTER ISLAND/RAPA NUI

"Easter Island is the loneliest inhabited place in the world."

From *Aku-aku* by Thor Heyerdahl[1]

I cannot recall when the wish to visit Easter Island first stirred in me. It may have been many years ago when I was still a young man and when exploring remote, little-known places held a special fascination. Later, my strong interest in archaeology further impelled me to fulfil this wish, for Easter Island had a reputation of being a bizarre place with mysterious large stone figures which held a unique place in the study of early civilizations. But getting there was a problem until I heard, in 1969, that a Chilean airline had recently started regular flights between Tahiti Island and Santiago in Chili with a stop at Easter Island. My parents had settled in Argentina in 1935. My mother had passed away, but father was still living in Buenos Aires. It seemed a good plan to combine my visit to him with a short stop on Easter Island, and this I resolved to do.

In March 1970 I flew from Sydney, Australia, to Tahiti (town of Papeete) in French Polynesia, and after spending a night there, boarded a LAN Chile flight to Santiago via Easter Island. Knowing that Easter Island was a small island, I was surprised to see that the plane was a large Boeing 707; there were only twenty passengers out of the normal capacity of some 180, and I was the only passenger to disembark at Easter Island. We landed on the Island on a glorious sunny morning of 21 March, and I had the immediate feeling that this was going to be an adventure beyond my best expectations.

---

1. "Aku-aku": Polynesian islanders' unseen guiding spirit (Thor Heyerdahl). I must admit that during my eight-day stay at Rapa Nui I have not heard "Aku-aku" mentioned.

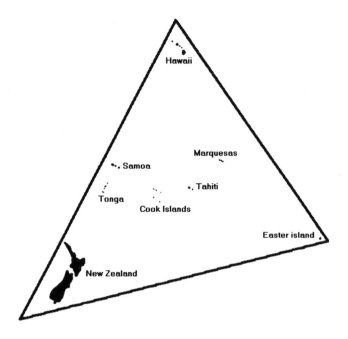

Map 17.1 Pacific Ocean, the Polynesian Triangle. Most islands with Polynesian populations lie within this triangle.

Rapa Nui

Easter Island is a small hilly and relatively treeless island located in the South Pacific about 2,300 miles off the coast of South America. If you draw a triangle on the map of the Pacific Ocean, with Hawaii at the apex, New Zealand at the western angle and Easter Island at the eastern angle, roughly within this triangle lie the Pacific islands of Polynesian populations and cultures (Map 17.1). Easter Island thus represents the easternmost outpost of Polynesia. It is a typical oceanic island of volcanic origin — a volcano which rose at some very distant past from the depth of the ocean by a series of distinct eruptions. Roughly triangular in shape (it is supposed to resemble a paddle, though not to me!), the Island measures about fourteen by seven miles covering about forty-five square miles. There are two large and three smaller craters; none is active. The Island is covered by lava rocks of various sizes. The climate is temperate, mild, and very pleasant. A tiny solitary dot in the vast spread of the ocean, the nearest islands to it lie hundreds of miles away.

Discovered to the Western world in 1722, on Easter day, by Captain Roggeveen, a Dutchman, it became known as Easter Island, or sometimes, in Spanish, as Isla de Pascua. But to the people who live on the Island, or those closely associated with it, it is Rapa Nui, or Big Rapa, meaning big paddle. As I now regard myself among the latter, I shall from now on refer to it only as Rapa Nui. The name naturally begs a question: is there a small Rapa? Indeed there is — Rapa Iti, located more than two thousand miles to the west. Captain James Cook anchored at Rapa Nui in March 1774, during his second voyage. He wrote in his journal that the natives called their island Rapa Nui to distinguish it from Rapa Iti, many miles to the west, whence according to tradition their forefathers had come. But here we meet another mystery: why did the islanders name their original home "small rapa" before they knew they would later discover "big rapa"? I do not know the answer, but perhaps the adjectives "iti" and "nui" were bestowed on the two islands later.

To many people who have heard of Rapa Nui, the name conveys an idea of mystery, of a large number of gigantic stone statues the origin of which is unknown. Stone statues are known on other Polynesian islands, but nowhere do they occur in such profusion — hundreds of them — as on Rapa Nui. Therein lies its main, perhaps its only, mystery. Rapa Nui is marvellous, beautiful, and in some ways unique, but painstaking scientific research in recent years has dispelled much of its "mystery", even if the popular press from time to time continues to refer to the Island's arcane secrets.

Arrival

I looked around as I got off the plane. There were no buildings near the single airstrip on which we landed, not even a hut to mark an airport terminal. A small crowd of onlookers observed me with friendly curiosity. Then a young man approached me and introduced himself as Mark, an American, a representative of Lindblad, a tourist company well known for its specialized tours: Rapa Nui was obviously regarded as one. I was both surprised and delighted when Mark suggested, instead of a primitive but expensive "hotel" — actually an assembly of small huts — to take me to the home of Nico and Rosita. This he did, and soon I was comfortably installed in a clean bright room. Mark went back to the airstrip where he would take the other passengers around the Island in his station wagon, the only motor car on the Island. This was apparently the routine: the plane usually stopped for four hours to allow passengers a quick tour of Rapa Nui before taking off again.

I liked my hosts Nico and Rosita instantly. Nico, whose father was a Scotsman, was a young, good-looking, vigorous man, who during the day worked at the Island's little harbour and the rest of the time looked after a small "pub" in the annex of their house. His wife Rosita, also of mixed blood, was a tall good-looking woman; they had two children, also called Nico and Rosita. The house was spacious, cool, with a splendid internal patio and a garden adorned by bright hibiscus bushes. My hosts spoke but a few words of English, while my Spanish was only slightly better than their English. In spite of the language barrier we were getting on splendidly. Rosita produced a small, well-worn, and obviously much-used, English-Spanish dictionary and told me that it was used by Kenneth Emory some years before when he stayed at their home.[2] This delighted me — the idea that I was in some way following in the footsteps of one of the most famous scholars of the Pacific region.

After unpacking and settling down, I took a walk through Hanga Roa, Rapa Nui's single village, then northwards along the shore and saw my first stone platforms, the "ahus" — Ahu Orongo, Ahu Tahai and Ahu Koteriki — with the famous giant stone statues, the "moai", upon them (Map 17.2). The moai looked majestic and noble, though my excitement was somewhat tempered since I knew that they were not in their original state but were reinstalled on the ahus recently by an American archaeologist with the help of a local team. I found later that, elsewhere on the Island, more moai were restored by him at great expense of time and money. It was well known to those interested in the subject that when the earliest scientific expeditions visited Rapa Nui, in the early 20th century, they found all the moai on ahus toppled over. From an aesthetic point of view, I am in favour of only partially restoring historical structures; in this case — a few moai at most.

Back at home, after a delicious dinner of local fish and crab, Mark arrived with his wife whom he called Me Me, a stunningly beautiful Italian girl. We drove in his station wagon right through the middle of the Island in the dark. Here and there, groups of horses staggered off the road at our approach like dark shadows. There were so many of them! Mark told me that there were twice as many horses as people on the Island. We arrived at the beach at Anakena, on the northern shore of Rapa Nui. One solitary moai stood on the beach. It was put up in 1956 by the villagers, supervised by Thor Heyerdahl, the intrepid Norwegian scholar/explorer, who was attempting to show how these large figures were erected. We sat on the beach under a full moon and talked about the Island, its secrets, its past turbulent history and its future. Except for the sounds of our voices and the waves, there was absolute silence. I was entranced by the new sensation, as if the air itself was filled

---

2. Kenneth Pike Emory (1897–1992): eminent American pioneer and anthropologist of the Pacific area.

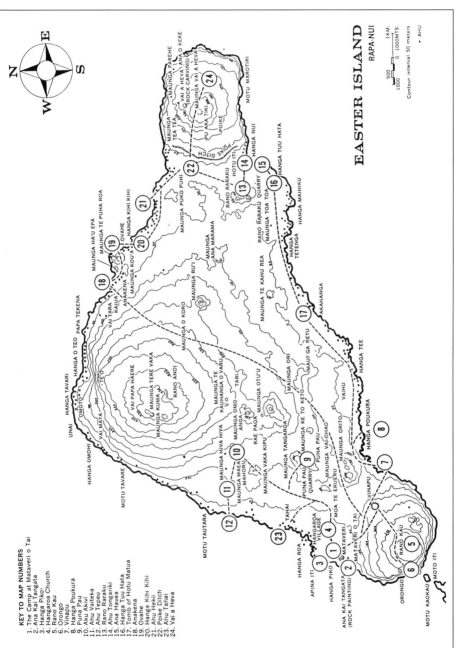

KEY TO MAP NUMBERS
1. The Camp at Mataveri o Tai
2. Ana Kai Tangata
3. Hanga Piko
4. Hangaroa Church
5. Rano Kau
6. Orongo
7. Vinapu
8. Hanga Poukura
9. Puna Pau
10. Aku Akivi
11. Ahu Vaiteka
12. Ahu Tepeu
13. Rano Raraku
14. Ahu Tongariki
15. Ana Havea
16. Hanga Tuu Hata
17. Tomb of Hotu Matua
18. Anakena
19. Ovahe
20. Hanga Kihi Kihi
21. Ahu Hekii
22. Poike Ditch
23. Ahu Tahai
24. Vai a Heva

Map 17.2 Easter Island (courtesy of Lindblad Expeditions).

with the mystery of this amazing Island. Mark believed that Rapa Nui could be developed as a major tourist attraction, but at the same time he did not want to see it spoilt. He did not know how to reconcile the two; nor did I. Although I was one of them, I believed tourists were a modern plague and every place they favoured in big numbers was ruined beyond recall. I fear this will be Rapa Nui's eventual fate. But for the present, the Island was a largely undiscovered Pacific "shangri-la". Back to Mark and Me Me's house for a hot cup of coffee and more talk. They are delightful people. I could not recall a more pleasant evening in a long time.

Sunday, 22 March

I have started a diary. It is a beautiful sunny morning. As I sit and write now, the sound of singing is reaching me from the little church nearby, and I suddenly feel happy and peaceful. Rosita's brother, Samuel, has come to take me to the southern portion of the Island, to the crater Rano Kau. Nico junior joins us.

We travelled on a tractor which has only one seat, for the driver, Samuel. Young Nico and I perched ourselves on the two mudguards. The tractor is slow and has a vicious clutch. Unprepared, I fell off twice before getting the knack of staying on. On Rapa Nui tractors are multiplying fast. The islanders clearly prefer them to other vehicles as they serve both as tractors and as cars, and are suitable for the unpaved roads. At Rano Kau the view of the ocean from the edge of the volcano is spectacular. The inside of the crater — nearly half a kilometre wide — looks peaceful, almost sleeping; marshy water covered with reeds occupies the floor of the volcano. Around the tops of the cliffs, on the slopes of the volcano are situated the remarkable strong subterranean dwellings of the Orongo-cult people. The openings are just big enough to admit a single person. On the rocks there are superb carvings depicting the bird-men motifs. This was an important ceremonial centre of the bizarre Orongo cult, reputedly of a long history, though there were no radiocarbon dates to determine its antiquity. Rano Kau overlooks the three tiny rocky "bird islands", Motu Nui, Motu Iti and Motu Kaokao. Rites and dances were a prelude to the climax of the bird-cult ceremony centred upon the eggs of the "manu taru", or the sooty tern whose breeding grounds were on the three little rocky islands. For weeks celebrants chanted and danced waiting for the sacred bids to settle in their nests. Then at a signal the contestants swam to the islands, many possibly jumping from the cliffs, competing for the season's first egg. It is said that the last ceremonies of the cult were practised as late as 1866.

After the Orongo site we drove to the nearby Ahu Vinapu — the finest ahu on the Island. Although some of the stones were displaced, the general construction is stunning in its majestic concept. The great two-tier wall is perfectly fitted with massive stones. I was strongly reminded of the Inca walls in Cuzco, Peru, which I saw several years before. It was easy to see how Thor Heyerdahl might have been influenced by the resemblance of the two when he suggested the South American influence in Rapa Nui.

It was past midday when we arrived at Rapa Nui's small museum, located in the Island's only school, where Herman Hotu was waiting for us; he had specially opened the museum for me. Herman, who always wears a tropical cork helmet, worked with William Mulloy, the American archaeologist, on several excavations and on the restoration of moai on the ahus. Herman's English is limited, but we got by. The museum is small and crammed with various artefacts, including a couple of small moai. Afterwards, to the great delight of Herman, I presented him, for the museum's collection, with a good specimen of "Bondi Point" from Australia.[3]

Back at home we had a light lunch. It took all my Spanish vocabulary and Samuel's limited English to impress on Rosita that I did not wish to have my meals separately like a VIP, but would prefer to eat with the family. The food is simple and tasty, with some excellent seafood, and there is too much of it. The meat comes from the sheep which Scottish farmers introduced into the Island years ago. Sheep also provide the milk from which cheese is made; the latter is an acquired taste, but one which is easily acquired, as I discovered. The only drawback is water: although soft and pleasant for washing, it has a bad taste. However, it is usually disguised with a little pineapple juice, making it a good refreshing drink.

In the evening Rosita, Nico and I went to church where the congregation sang beautifully, like a trained choir. After church we attended a wedding and a party afterwards. There was plenty of dancing and wine drinking and altogether it turned out to be most enjoyable. If anything, the islanders are inclined to drink too much. I am told that this has become a problem. Nico's little "pub", in the annexe of the house, is doing good business and probably contributing to the problem. One cannot exactly blame the people: there are no cinemas, no television or radio. They are generally happy in disposition, but after the day's work is done there is little to do except sing and drink.

---

3. "Bondi Point": Australian aboriginal stone implement; small, triangular in section with a trimmed back. Precise use not known; possibly used as spear barbs.

European Contacts

Rapa Nui's history of European contact is not a happy one. It is a story of violence, murder and enslavement. From the time it was discovered, in 1722, ruthless adventurers brought disease, violence and death to the Island. Finally, slavers carried away thousands of men to work on the islands off Peru. In 1877 it is said that only 111 inhabitants were left on the Island. They were living in caves, frightened and beaten, all their past greatness crushed together with their stone statues. Peace finally settled over Rapa Nui when Chile annexed it in 1888. By a miracle a small handful of islanders had survived to revive and replenish the population. To be fair, not all calamities were brought from the outside. Some early visitors came peacefully, among them Captain Cook (1774), and La Perouse (1786).[4] They found the island already torn by internal strife and many moai toppled over, though some were still standing on the ahus. However, by the time the first scientific expeditions arrived, early in the 20th century, not a single moai was standing upright on an ahu.

The Island belongs to Chile which governs it with a firm but paternalistic hand. There are only about two thousand inhabitants all living in the single village of Hanga Roa in the south-western portion of the Island. The Island is administered by about two hundred Chilean officials headed by a governor. They seem to keep themselves apart and appear to have a colonial attitude towards the "natives". Occasionally one can see Chilean uniformed policemen, usually in pairs, riding stiffly erect on big handsome horses, obviously disdaining the local ponies. My impression is that Chile's rule is regarded as benevolent and is not resented by the islanders. The islanders are primarily Polynesians, but many show an admixture of various European races. They are charming, hospitable and happy in their ways. There is always plenty of music, singing and fiestas. News of my presence on the Island spread quickly and I was readily accepted and invited to every festive occasion. The people are proud of their beautiful small whitewashed church. Father Sebastian Englert, the scholar, priest, and spiritual king of the Island for thirty-five years, lies buried in his beloved churchyard. He lives on, however, in the heart of every islander. I had just missed him for he died the previous December.

---

4. Jean-Francois de La Perouse (1741–1788): French explorer who visited Rapa Nui in 1786. He was lost at sea with his two ships in a storm, probably near the Solomon Islands.

Monday 23 March

Herman Hotu came at 8.00 a.m. to the house. He wanted to take me to see a few more ahus with moai along the west coast, not far from Hanga Roa. I asked him whether we were going to walk, but he replied "certainly not, I do not want to ruin my shoes", or something to that effect. The sharp, craggy pieces of solidified lava on the ground play havoc with shoes. Two horses were brought for us. I had not ridden for some twenty years, but the horses were small and seemed docile. Instead of a saddle, a sheep skin with stirrups was slung over and there was a bridle. All islanders are skilled riders, starting to ride from early childhood, almost before they learn to walk. I found getting up on the horse was not as easy as it used to be twenty years ago, and certainly not as easy as it looks in the western films, but I refused help and finally made it. Herman and I rode slowly through the village. People smiled and waved to us; after only two days, I felt at home here. Out of Hanga Roa, we changed into a light trot and proceeded along the coast. It was another perfect day, the sea was a beautiful deep blue, and I felt I could break into song! As we rode past Ahu Tahai, which I had already visited on foot on my first day, Herman explained that he had helped William Mulloy to put the moai on the ahu (which I already knew). He added that even the red hat, or top-knot, on the moai's head was not the original, but was made at the same time (which I did not know). We got off the horses and Herman took a photograph of me standing next to the moai: I served as a human scale for its size. The stone blocks of the ahu, and the sloping foreground with pebbles, have been stabilized with cement. My aesthetic inclination rebels against excessive modern restorations, but restoring a few as an example was probably a good idea. Back on horseback (this time I am more adept at getting up) we trotted on and briefly stopped at two more ahus — Ahu Tepeu and Ahu Vaiteka — then rode inland towards the important Ahu Akivi. It is a fine ahu with seven moai standing on it: all were restored, but none were wearing a red top-knot. Herman told me how it took several months' work, but I am still unhappy about this wholesale restoration. I must admit, however, it is an impressive sight — the seven giants looking all alike standing with their backs to the sea, as if observing their domain. As we slowly rode back side by side, Herman talked about life on Rapa Nui, of stories and traditions, and of the islanders' hopes for the future.

Anthropologists nowadays tend to regard folklore seriously as it often contains a kernel of truth. Rapa Nui is rich in folklore. Local tradition relates the story of the first arrivals on the Island led by the chief Hotu Matua from far away in the west. (I have heard no mention locally, however, of Rapa Iti). They sailed eastwards in search of new land and after many months finally reached Rapa Nui. They landed on the north shore of the island, now called Anakena (where I spent my first evening on the Island with Mark and Me Me). So emaciated (and bearded) were the travellers after their long journey that Hotu Matua ordered the artists to carve a figure commemorating their ordeal and appearance. The carved wooden figurine of an emaciated bearded man called Moai Kavakava is traditional on Rapa Nui and is made in many sizes; I bought a foot tall one for myself.

It was still early afternoon when we arrived back at Hanga Roa. There was excitement in the air. People on the quay were staring at something in the distance: it is a ship, they said. Trying hard as I could, I saw nothing. There are scheduled ships which bring provisions and goods once or twice a month, but visits by unscheduled vessels are rare and always cause excitement. After a while, the ship came into view and dropped anchor. It turned out to be an American scientific ship *Oceanographer*. Within hours Mark, Me Me and I were invited aboard by a very pleasant petty officer and we spent two very interesting hours being shown all the latest scientific instruments for exploring and studying the ocean floor. After the ship, I had tea with Mark and Me Me at their home. I told Mark that I should like to collect some artefacts, perhaps some stone flakes or adzes, but he laughed and said that there was not a chance: "the archaeologists had gone through the Island with a fine tooth-comb and picked up everything; there are no artefacts to be found, except some crude picks, called 'toki' around the main quarry of Rano Raraku". However, I could buy some imitations from the villagers, he added, which they make for tourists. I resolved to prove him wrong.

In the evening, Nico, Rosita and I walked to the little harbour. It was full of people chatting and laughing and we joined in. The *Oceanographer* had sailed away, but the villagers were still talking about her visit. It was a pleasant evening with a gentle breeze easing the heat of the day. We ended the evening at a celebration (I am not sure of what event) at the home of one of the neighbours; more singing and dancing!

Tuesday, 24 March
Today Samuel, young Nico and I are going to Rano Raraku. I have been impatient to visit and examine it, for it is undoubtedly the most impressive feature of Rapa Nui. I noticed with some consternation that the tractor would again be our mode of transportation. I much preferred a horse, but made no protest: to Samuel and young Nico, riding a horse was commonplace, but the

tractor was still a novelty and therefore more exciting. About nine-and-a-half miles east of Hanga Roa, and close to the southern coastline, the Rano Raraku mountain rises a thousand feet above a flat plain. It is a volcanic cone with steep sides. My first sight of it almost took my breath away; it was unforgettable. As we approached the mountain, the scene was incredible: scattered all around the foothills were numerous moai, some standing partly buried, some leaning, others lying on the ground; there must have been at least a hundred of them. As we began our climb, we encountered everywhere unfinished moai in various stages of completion still cradled in their rocky beds. Several were practically finished, connected to the rock only by a thin stony pedicle, as if ready to be launched. It is a steep, difficult climb but Samuel and Nico reached the top easily and quickly; they have obviously done it many times before. I took my time but finally joined them at the top without a mishap, where another amazing sight met my eyes. On top is a large crater with a small and rather beautiful lake, and on the inner slopes of the crater more moai scattered about. The total picture defies reasonable explanation. It does suggest a sudden cessation of activity as if the moai had been abandoned before they could be moved, due perhaps to an imminent calamity. Could it have been due to an intensification of the warfare which is known to have taken place on the Island and to which I shall refer later?

I was loath to tear myself away from this amazing place, but after about an hour on top of the mountain, Samuel persuaded me to descend. I took a close look at the structure of the mountain: the basic rock appeared to be grey volcanic tuff interspersed with intrusions of harder dark basalt. The tuff is not very hard and would make carving the figures not too difficult a task.[5] It is known, in fact, that the initial estimate of the weight of the moai was exaggerated. It is certain that virtually all the moai of the Island were quarried from its rock. I noted that they have been numbered with white paint, (by Fr. Sebastian), in some cases, I thought, somewhat too conspicuously. Samuel told me that there are 160 uncompleted moai; the largest sixty feet long. On the ground there was much debris and hundreds of crudely chipped picks of basalt, called "toki" — undoubtedly the tools with which the initial crude work was carried out. I picked a small one for my collection. The fine finishing work must have been done by polished adzes but, trying hard, I could not find one: as Mark said, they must have all been assiduously collected some time before, leaving the crude tools behind as of no interest.

---

5. Tuff: Essentially a volcanic ash with mineral fragments, consolidated into a rock. It is found in volcanic eruptions.

We drove to Ahu Tongariki on the coast, only a short distance from Rano Raraku. It had originally fifteen moai on it but all were shattered and overthrown, and the ahu itself was partially destroyed during the final, violent period of the Island's history. To add to this, in 1966, Samuel relates, a huge tidal wave struck the coast at this point and with terrific force had lifted and scattered the moai still further, some of them at present lying more than a hundred feet from the ahu.

We visited two more ahus nearby — Ahu Hekii and Ahu Tepito te-kura. At the latter Samuel showed me a feature which he said was little known outside the Island: it is a large, fully eighteen inches in diameter, perfectly spheroidal stone called "tepito te-kura" (from which the ahu derives its name) which means "the navel of the light". Samuel said that because of this stone, the locals sometimes described Rapa Nui as the "navel of the world". I noticed the number "120" painted in white on the stone; it was obviously known to Fr. Sebastian. I took a photograph of Samuel standing on the stone.

We climbed back on the tractor and headed home. Mindful of the horrible clutch, I hung on hard with my hands to whatever I could grab on the tractor. As we approached Hanga Roa, we discerned a commotion: people at the quay were again staring and pointing. Surely not another ship, just a day after the last one! Again I could not see anything. When the vessel finally docked, it was a moderately sized yacht with an American family of four — a husband and wife and two teenage children, a boy and a girl, on board. That evening they were invited to our place for dinner, and what a remarkable story they had to tell — of enterprise and adventure! They had set out to travel around the world which they expected would take them between two and three years. "How do you manage with the children's schooling?" I asked. They had an ingenious plan: educational papers and even tests were sent in advance to places where they were scheduled to stop.

Ahus and Moai

The Orongo bird-cult no doubt presents some unsolved problems and may be of special interest to anthropologists studying Rapa Nui, but to the less-initiated, the stone platforms — ahus — and the giant stone figures — moai — are more impressive, more closely associated with the Island, and have certainly caught the popular imagination.

A typical ahu consists of a narrow, one- or two-tier raised rectangular platform with or without low wing extensions. On the side facing inland, a paved ramp slopes down, while the side facing the sea is vertical, built of well-fitted dressed masonry. There are altogether about 260 ahus that can be counted, scattered around the periphery of the Island in various stages of collapse and destruction. Very likely not all were built during the same period in the Island's history.

Even more impressive than the ahus, are the moai — the numerous massive stone figures — for which the Island is famous. Moai do occur elsewhere in Polynesia: they are known in Raivavae, Pitcairn and Marquesas Islands, but nowhere have they reached the dimensions or the profusion of those at Rapa Nui. It would be no exaggeration to say that the moai of Rapa Nui are the most remarkable phenomenon of its kind in Polynesia and, indeed, in the whole world. The number of moai on ahus varied from one to as many as fifteen. Ranging from twenty to forty feet in height, all are half-bodied, highly stylized in type — sharp features with long ears — and many are further enhanced by a top-knot of red scoria which was added to the top of the head as a separate component. These top-knots were quarried separately in the Puna Pau crater. Fr. Sebastian who studied and numbered the moai all over the Island counted around six hundred. It is likely that the actual number is higher, as some almost certainly lie completely buried in the accumulated debris and soil. No stylistic difference was found among the moai, except that those at the quarry of Rano Raraku had eyes unmarked. Probably the eyes were ceremonially carved after the moai were in position on the ahus.

Wednesday, 25 March

Herman arrived early to show me subterranean caves on the Island. I have so far found very few artefacts on the surface, and these were mostly obsidian flakes. I believe I should find more inside the caves. Rosita is fussing over me, insisting that I come back for a proper lunch instead of taking sandwiches with me, but I manage to overrule her.

We rode out, what a relief — I much prefer a horse to a tractor. Herman took me to an area around the middle of the Island, where there are several large caves. I assured him that I should be perfectly safe and persuaded him to leave me. He promised to come back for me in the early afternoon. I explored several caves. Inside the caves it is dark and I had to use a torch. I was particularly anxious to find a few "mataa". They are implements roughly triangular in shape with a shaft, made of obsidian. At first glance they resemble crudely made spear-heads and are so referred to by the islanders, but their asymmetry and crudeness make it unlikely that they had the power to penetrate. Most likely they were used as weapons: hafted to the end of a flexible stick, they would be capable of inflicting serious injury. Villagers make them of various sizes for tourists, but I was looking for genuine ones.

I was correct in my assumption, for there were many artefacts on the floor of the cave: masses of flakes, some of which had been worked and trimmed to form scrapers. I also found several fine mataa. I was very pleased with my success, even though I did not find a single polished adze. It was stuffy and uncomfortable inside but I persevered until my bag was full of stone artefacts. Finally I emerged into daylight and had my sandwiches while waiting for Herman. When he arrived, I showed him my haul: a dozen very fine mataa and a mass of obsidian flakes. He was impressed. Obsidian is plentiful and comes mainly from Maunga Orito — a hill two miles east of Hanga Roa. It is my favourite stone: in its purest form it is like lustrous black glass.

We rode on to Poike which is the eastern headland of the Island. Poike stands out in marked contrast to the rest of the Island because of its smooth grassy slopes devoid of black outcrops of rock and loose lava stones. It is separated from the main body of the Island by a depression known as the Poike Ditch. Archaeological work revealed that originally it was probably a natural depression, but was later deepened artificially. While we took a rest, Herman related to me a local legend of the two rival factions of Hanau Eepe (the bulky or fat people), who occupied the Poike area and Hanau Momoko (the slender or thin people) who occupied the rest of the Island. A quarrel between the two, over the clearing of stones from the Island, flared into open conflict. In a battle at Poike Ditch, in which treachery played a part, Hanau Eepe were annihilated. It is a simple, artless story, such as might have been told to children by an old sage, but one which may conceal within it the real and far more serious cause of conflict between clans. When I asked Herman what he thought of the story, he dodged the question, but told me that archaeological excavations several years before had confirmed that a battle did take place at Poike Ditch. Later I read, in a book borrowed from Mark, that, indeed, excavations at Poike Ditch unearthed a significant amount of burned or charred material and charcoal, but no skeletal remains. The radiocarbon tests of the charcoal indicated circa 1670 as the approximate date of the "battle". Poike Ditch is close to Rano Raraku, and it seems to me at least possible that the apparent abrupt cessation of work there could be the direct result of the Poike battle.

As Herman and I rode back, I attempted to nudge my horse to canter, but to no avail; gentle trot is all we got. As we parted, I thanked Herman profusely for a wonderful rewarding day. The Nico and Rosita family were at home and we had dinner together. Samuel is leaving for Santiago the next morning and we all drank to him, wishing him a safe journey.

Thursday, 26 March

Very early, at 6.00 a.m. we all accompanied Samuel to the airport; there was a beautiful sunrise over the ocean. After breakfast, Nico junior and I rode to Puna Pau; it is a short ride from Hanga Roa. Nico rides bareback, no saddle or stirrups, and he is very good at it. Puna Pau is a small crater. It consists entirely of red scoria and is the factory where the red topknots were made.[6] The picture here reminds one, in a smaller way, of Rano Raraku: many topknots, some half-buried, lying about as if the work was suddenly abandoned. After Puna Pau we rode on to the coast, but it started to rain and we decided to return home. After lunch, the weather was still overcast and I decided to remain at home, reading up about the archaeological work at Rapa Nui from the books lent to me by Mark. In the evening I had dinner with Mark and Me Me. In their cosy lounge, over glasses of wine, we talked about the Island and its future.

So far there is only a trickle of tourists visiting Rapa Nui, most of whom do not stop on the Island. This is largely due to the Chilean government's "go slow" policy, and the uncertain attitude of Mark's tourist agency.[7] There are no shops, newspapers, radio or many of the other features of civilization to which we are accustomed. There is no motorized traffic and no paved roads. Nevertheless, there have been signs of impending changes in the past year or two, since the start of regular air flights which stop on the Island. There is increasing prosperity and a new look on the Island. Electricity has been installed, a small bank opened, a couple of cafes have sprung up, and a proper hotel is being planned.

Scientific Work on Rapa Nui

Scientific expeditions to study Rapa Nui's unique cultural features began in the early 20th century. Among the most important early expeditions was one by a resolute Englishwoman, Catherine Routledge, who arrived at the Island in her own yacht, and produced a thorough, detailed and penetrating study of the Island's ahus and moai. Among the more recent expeditions, Thor Heyerdahl's in 1956 merits special mention: Heyerdahl assembled a brilliant team of archaeologists, mainly from the USA, which carried out

---

6. Scoria: A lava froth formed in volcanic eruptions and hardened into rock. Light in weight, it resembles pumice, though slightly heavier than the latter.

7. I kept in touch with Mark for a couple of years, and knew that he was recalled from Rapa Nui by Lindblad about a year after we had met there. I do not know whether Lindblad sent anyone to replace him.

careful painstaking field work on the Island over a period of years. Curiously, Heyerdahl's purpose in choosing Rapa Nui was to prove a theory that the Island and other Polynesian islands were settled from South America by pre-Columbian migrants. While his interest was soon transferred to other parts of the world, some members of his original team continued intermittently to work at Rapa Nui, together with Chilean archaeologists. The results of their work did not bear out Heyerdahl's theory, but in fact pointed to a purely Polynesian origin of Rapa Nui's culture.

Archaeological work at Rapa Nui has established tentatively three periods in the history of the Island: the Initial Settlement, or Early Period, circa 400–1100 CE, the Development, or Middle Period, circa 1100–1680 CE, and the Disintegration, or Late Period, circa 1680–1868 CE, the last marked by overpopulation, intensified warfare, and finally the destructive contacts with the outside world.

The Early Period is characterized by large, precisely fitted ahus built with astronomical orientation: their finest masonry faced the sea and the rising sun either at the time of the equinox or the summer solstice. The evidence strongly suggests that at this stage the ahus served as important ceremonial structures, perhaps as altars, and that there were no moai upon them. One of the finest examples of ahus of this period is Ahu Vinapu. The Orongo ceremonial site of the bird-cult also belongs to the early period.

The Middle Period saw an extraordinary proliferation of the massive figures — the moai — for which the Island is so famous. New ahus were built, no longer so soundly or precisely designed, nor having an astronomical orientation, while the early ahus were repaired and rebuilt and both now served as platforms for the moai which were placed facing inland. The number of moai upon the ahus varied and so did their size; the largest was about forty feet high, though one unfinished at Rano Raraku was estimated to be sixty feet long. The initial estimate of their weight — a hundred to four hundred tons — was later revised to around sixty to seventy tons for the heaviest ones. It was also found that the stone implements were most plentiful during the Middle Period.

The Late Period was one of strife and decline during which most of the moai were toppled over. The period overlaps with the European contacts which no doubt aggravated and hastened the downfall of the Island's culture and population. The period was truly a black one for the islanders. Disease and cannibalism were rife and the population had dwindled to a handful living in caves in fear like savages. What caused this terrible state? Both the folklore and the archaeological evidence suggest internal warfare culminating in the battle of Poike Ditch. There is little doubt that the war eventually resulted in the abandonment of whatever religious practices were formerly associated with the moai. The stones of the neglected broken moai and of the partially destroyed ahus were reused for other purposes. By the time Captain Cook visited the island in 1774, he reported that the islanders seemed indifferent to the big moai which appeared to play no part in their religion.

One could only speculate on what the conflict was about, though further research may shed more light on it. As in other similar cultures, it may have developed over kinship or succession, or rivalry of some sort. If we turn to folklore, we get an interesting but probably highly simplified story, such as that related to me by Herman, which I mentioned above. Occasionally, outside Rapa Nui, one reads about the rivalry between the people of "the long and the short ears". I have asked on the Island about these, but the local folklore does not mention them. However, they do repeat Herman's tale of the two rival factions, the Hanau Momoko (the slender people) and Hanau Eepe (the fat people).

Friday, 27 March

A large group of tourists from Scandinavia arrived this morning and Mark asked me to help him to show them around the sites while the plane was on the ground. I enjoyed my role as a tour guide. We took the tourists in batches to Rano Raraku. I tried to explain to them about this great quarry of moai, but no one listened; they were too busy running around like excited children and taking photographs. Finally, we left and on the way back stopped at Ahu Tahai. To my utmost delight I found, at last, a polished adze; the butt of the adze is broken but the sharp edge is intact. I have proven Mark wrong!

In the evening Mark, Me Me and I were invited for dinner at the American army weather base. The Americans live in prefabricated huts with all modern conveniences and, of course, a permanent and abundant supply of ice-cream. Every morning they send a weather balloon high into the air. Colonel Horne, in charge of the base, met us and we spent a very pleasant evening with him and several officers. Colonel Horne told us that the airstrip on the Island was built by the Americans. I had been wondering whether the weather study was the real purpose of the American base on Rapa Nui, but eventually had to concede that perhaps it was. I am not sure to what extent the small American contingent mixes with the local population, but Mark has told me that one member, the base's doctor, has made himself very popular by attending to the islanders' medical needs, and even delivering babies on a number of occasions.

Saturday, 28 March

Today is my last full day at Rapa Nui. Herman arrived and we rode out in search of the only moai made of red scoria rock. He was not sure where exactly, but thought it was somewhere on the plain east of Ahu Tahai. It did not take us long to find it. Compared to other moai it is not big, about ten feet high, but a good portion of it is probably hidden buried in the ground. It stands entirely by itself and is strikingly red in colour. I wonder whether it was an experimental type, like the small ones in the museum? I took a photo of Herman standing next to the moai. Then we rode on to Rano Raraku which I wanted to see once more before leaving the Island. As I wandered among the moai in the foothills, I reflected that I should probably never see anything comparable to this scene. Before returning home, we visited Rano Kau, the site of the Orongo bird-cult, once more.

Reflections

The extraordinary story of Rapa Nui is not fully understood, but some conclusions may be drawn. To begin with, the concept of Polynesian migrations from South America must be discounted. The weight of archaeological evidence points to migration in the opposite direction — from Asia eastwards. The successive radiocarbon dates show later dates as we move eastwards, with Rapa Nui, at the easternmost end of Polynesia, giving 400 CE as its earliest date. The study of artefacts of Rapa Nui supports entirely their Polynesian origin. Archaeological work and some of the verbal folklore present a general picture of the rise and decline of an isolated community.

In its early history, a small but cohesive community established a stable order, erected fine stone shrines in the form of well-fitted platforms, the ahus, and practised a mysterious Orongo bird-cult. The middle period of its history saw the Island at the height of its development with an extraordinary proliferation of large stone figures, the moai. During this period, it is estimated that the population probably never exceeded thirty thousand, and might have been much less. With the limited economic resources and neolithic technology, it is truly amazing what a small human group, such as the Rapa Nui islanders, was able to achieve: carving hundreds of moai, transporting them to, and erecting them upon, the ahus.

The moai were transported from the quarry at Rano Raraku by placing them on tree logs and rolling them to their assigned ahus along the coast. How they were lifted and placed upright on the ahus without modern appliances was demonstrated by the villagers to Thor Heyerdahl in 1956. It was an ingenious method in which small stones and pebbles were pushed, painstakingly one by one, under the moai so that the latter gradually rose on a growing heap of stones, until it was in line with the top of the ahu. It was then levered into an upright position.

Archaeological and historical research has established that the moai were carved by the Polynesian inhabitants — the forefathers of the present people. We know, or at least have a good idea, how they were transported and put up on their ahus: the methods were ingenious but perfectly feasible. But the questions — why were they built? why so many and so big? why did their production suddenly cease? and, finally, whom did they represent? — still remain to some extent in the realms of speculation. Some of the answers may be hidden in the Island's folklore and traditions.

The archaeologists working in Rapa Nui, however, did not leave the answers entirely to idle speculation. Study of comparative cultures and, where possible, excavation field work provides some possible explanations: among various theories on the symbolism of the moai, the most likely is that they represent ancestors and that some might have been considered divine. There is some evidence, though not fully conclusive, that the early moai, like the two I saw at the Island's museum, were smaller than the later ones. The most probable explanation for the profusion and size of the moai is the rivalry between clans or factions, which finally exploded into a full-scale war. The excavations at Poike Ditch support this view.

There is little doubt that the inhabitants of Rapa Nui had sowed the seeds of their own destruction. Beginning probably during the Middle Period, they had wasted their natural and human resources on a wasteful and excessive production of large stone figures which resulted in deforestation, erosion and denudation of the land. Over the years, spurred by increasing rivalry, the warring tribes desecrated their rivals' moai, toppling them off their ahus. The internal war extended through the period of initial contact with Europeans, leading to the final and tragic downfall of the Island's culture and population.

Goodbye

Early on Sunday, 29 March, the whole family took me, on the tractor, to the airstrip. It was a sad journey; no one spoke. "How," I wondered, "can one get so attached to people who only a week ago were total strangers?" Mark and Me Me were waiting at the airstrip to bid me farewell, but Herman was nowhere to be seen. We embraced and kissed all around. Rosita cried. I promised I would return one day. Then, suddenly, it was all over. I was in the air and saw through the window, my beautiful Rapa Nui receding fast and then disappear from view. I felt sad and lonely.

Santiago, Chile

On arrival at Santiago, the passengers had to go through customs check. I was carrying masses of rock fragments, including a number of mataa and other obsidian flakes. Concerned that their combined weight would tip me over the allowed baggage weight, I crammed them into the pockets of my overcoat which was slung over my arm. To my horror, after examining my suitcase and passing it, the customs officer motioned to me to hand him my overcoat. I felt sweat gathering on my forehead and for a moment or two had visions of jail in Santiago. I handed over my overcoat. The customs officer weighed it up and down in his hand with a puzzled expression on his face, then turned it upside down over the counter. Out came a cascade of rock fragments. My heart sank; I shall now be charged with illegally taking artefacts out of the country, I thought. Then, incredibly, the customs officer began to laugh. He called another officer and pointing to the hoard on the counter, they both laughed — at what I assume they regarded as a mass of useless rubble, and at a madman who carried it in his overcoat. I gathered the stones back into the pockets and left relieved, with the sound of laughter still in my ears.

Postscript, November 2005

Rapa Nui has changed much since my visit. There are now cars, tour buses, and motorcycles on the Island, running over its as yet mainly unpaved roads. There are souvenir shops, telephone and television, a new airport terminal, and several well-equipped hotels. Recently I have learned that Rosita is alive and well, that she owns and operates a hotel with Nico Junior's help, but that Nico senior died three years ago. I have not kept my promise to return to Rapa Nui. I have waited too long and now, after three decades, it seems unlikely I ever shall. I fear the disappointment of finding that the quiet unspoilt Rapa Nui has become just another popular noisy tourist place. And yet a tiny flicker of hope, of seeing Rapa Nui once more, still lingers in my mind...

Terms:
ahu: ceremonial stone platform
hanga: bay
maunga: hill
moai: statue, figure
moai Kawakawa: a figurine of a thin wasted man with a beard — traditional carving
rano: crater
toki: basalt adze, crude handpick

18

OLD CHINESE FORT REDISCOVERED

> Archaeology is a scientific study of material remains from the human past.

Introduction

This is a story of heritage conservation: a story of challenge and achievement, in which an old ruin was rescued from neglect and decay, restored and protected for posterity as a valued historical site. I must confess that heritage conservation did not occur to me as a possible avocation, until well into my thirties. When the time came to consider an occupation, soon after leaving school, music was high on my list of priorities, but in the end, I was persuaded by my family to embark upon the long and difficult path of medical studies. I recall being always interested in history. In my early teens, I discovered the world of Alexandre Dumas (père) and revelled in his tales of musketeers, deadly plots, and gallant fights; I memorized the names of the French kings in correct order.

In the early 1950s, while engaged in general medical practice in Hong Kong, I became interested in archaeology. The interest arose through friendship with two geologists, both lecturers at Hong Kong University, whom I followed on many weekends around the Hong Kong hills and valleys as they surveyed Hong Kong's rock formations and knocked off bits of rocks with special hammers for more detailed examination. From them I learned how to tell hills of granite from those of "volcanics", and distinguish igneous from sedimentary rocks. The field trips were interesting, informative, and physically exhausting.

Archaeology in Hong Kong

One day, during a field trip, I picked up from the ground a well-shaped polished stone adze.[1] We were astonished to find that artefacts of Stone Age and old pottery shards, exposed presumably by erosion or washed down by rain, were common. These intriguing finds seemed to indicate substantial human activity in the area in ancient times. My attention began to shift from rocks to human-made artefacts. Hong Kong promised to be even more interesting than I had imagined. At the time I could find no evidence of local interest in Hong Kong's ancient past, but several articles and published papers pointed to abundant archaeological research conducted in Hong Kong before the Second World War. Beginning in the middle 1920s, when the study of Chinese prehistory as a whole was still in its infancy, in Hong Kong several talented amateur archaeologists, working in their spare time, had achieved remarkable results. Joseph Shellshear, professor of anatomy at Hong Kong University; Dr Charles Heanley, medical practitioner; Walter Schofield, civil servant; and Jesuit Fathers Daniel Finn and Rafael Maglioni, mostly working independently, had excavated prehistoric sites and distinguished a sequence of cultures. Schofield, in an amazing feat of endurance and observation, had mapped more than one hundred sites with archaeological finds in the Hong Kong region. Only Maglioni continued archaeological research after the war, in Hoifung about a hundred miles north of Hong Kong, until his death in 1953.

At the end of 1955 I left general medical practice to join Hong Kong University as director of its newly established Health Service. By this time I had completely embraced archaeology as a chosen avocation. The following year the University Archaeological Team was founded by a small group of enthusiasts, mostly members of Hong Kong University staff, and archaeological work in Hong Kong, interrupted by the war in the Pacific, was resumed. As one of the founders of the Team, I recall well this diverse group of academics led initially by Professor F. S. Drake of the Department of Chinese and later by Professor S. G. Davis of Geology and Geography. Archaeology was still a weekend pursuit; the Team, rarely more than twenty-strong, re-visited previously recorded sites and searched for new ones. A landmark in the Team's work was the discovery and excavation in 1958 of a new site at Man Kok Tsui, a late Neolithic and Bronze site on the east coast of Lantao Island.[2]

---

1. Adze: A stone tool with, in cross-section, an asymmetrical cutting edge like a chisel, as opposed to axe which has a symmetrical cutting edge.
2. Man Kok Tsui site was discovered by me, in 1958, at the end of a long walk from Mui Wo (Silver Mine Bay). Incredibly, the site's valley and low hills were strewn

No teaching in general archaeology or prehistory was available locally. A long service leave in 1966/67 in Australia, spent almost entirely working in the Anthropology Department of the Australian Museum in Sydney under the then curator David Moore, an experienced archaeologist and inspiring teacher,[3] strengthened enormously my grasp of the subject and gave me the first professional experience in archaeological field work. Popular books describing "lost civilizations" discovered by renowned archaeologists tend to give archaeology an aura of romance. But great discoveries are far from every-day events. I have learned that for most of the time, excavation is a painstaking, laborious task which needs to be carefully and scientifically recorded and documented. Digging up an ancient refuse pit is hardly glamorous, but may yield a wealth of information about the daily life of an ancient people. However, in all excavations an anticipation of an important discovery is always present and that is what makes the work so fascinating.

In 1967 the University Archaeological Team was wound up and the Hong Kong Archaeological Society was formed, open to members of the public who were interested in archaeological work. As with the Team, I found myself again a co-founder of the new Society. The following year I was invited by the Extra-Mural Department of Hong Kong University to give a course of lectures entitled "Introduction to Archaeology". It continued yearly for twelve years and proved to be an excellent recruiting ground for new Society members.[4] The Society's excavations at Sham Wan on Lamma Island, in 1971/72, revealed clearly for the first time the full profile and relative sequence of Hong Kong's prehistoric levels. By the late 1970s, a sufficient number of radio-carbon dates was available to identify in Hong Kong the Middle Neolithic (c. 6500–4500 BP), the Late Neolithic (c. 4500–3000 BP), and the Bronze (c. 3000–2000 BP) periods. At 2000 BP, finds of Han Dynasty pottery usher the Chinese historic presence.[5]

---

with stone and pottery artefacts, many exposed on the surface; one could hardly walk without stepping on pottery shards.

3. After David Moore's retirement, we continued to meet, and sometimes conduct excavations together whenever I visited Australia. Forty years later, and myself settled in Australia, we continued to meet weekly for coffee and a chat.

4. The course consisted of ten to twelve lectures and three field trips. I continued lecturing after these twelve years but with an emphasis on local history rather than archaeology.

5. Radio-carbon testing is a highly complex scientific method of determining the age of an object, applicable only to organic matter — in archaeological context usually charcoal — with a ten to fifteen percent margin of error, and an age limit of about fifty thousand years. BP, meaning "before present" is preferred to BCE, when describing archaeological dates.

Hong Kong's Heritage and the Antiquities and Monuments Office

Although a number of Hong Kong scholars and historians had written about Hong Kong's significant historical heritage, of both the Chinese and British periods, the Hong Kong government so far had taken no steps to protect it. The Archaeological Society had long been a firm advocate of legal protection of archaeological sites and of Hong Kong's historical heritage generally and had pressed the government to act accordingly. When the latter, in 1972, was at last persuaded of the need to adopt these measures, members of the Society sat on the Provisional Antiquities Advisory Board, formed by the government to advise on the drafting of the appropriate legislation. The resulting Antiquities and Monuments Ordinance was promulgated in 1972 and came officially into force on 1 January 1976. At the same time the Antiquities and Monuments Office (AMO) was set up to implement and supervise the provisions of the Ordinance. After several unsuccessful attempts at recruiting a suitable person to head the Office, I was invited to apply for the post which was given the name, too long and ponderous I thought, of Executive Secretary (Antiquities and Monuments) or ES (AM). It so happened that I had just retired from my University post. I believe it was truly a case of being "in the right place, at the right time". I could not have wished for a better opportunity to pursue my favoured hobby as a full-time occupation.

I was appointed ES (AM) and placed in charge of the AMO in October 1976. I had become a civil servant of the Hong Kong government. The AMO was initially placed with the Home Affairs Department but almost immediately transferred to the Urban Services Department, a strange placement I thought, in which it shared its position with such sections as Street Cleansing, Markets, Hawkers Control, and Public Toilets! I was provided with a minuscule staff, consisting of a clerk and a typist, later augmented by a photographer and an assistant curator. There was no job description of my post as my employers seemed uncertain as to what my duties were. Someone even suggested that all I had to do was to take minutes of the Antiquities Advisory Board's infrequent meetings. But it soon became abundantly clear to me that I was facing an enormous task of searching, identifying and recording, throughout the territory, a wide range of items specified by the Ordinance to be of archaeological, historical, and palaeontological interest.[6] What was less clear

6. I was against including protection of palaeontological, i.e. fossil, sites in the Antiquities and Monuments Ordinance believing that only man-made antiquities should be included in it, while the fossils would be best included in the Country Parks Regulations. However, the Hong Kong government would not be moved, and fossil sites remained in the Ordinance.

was how to do this. There was no time to be lost. In the post-war prosperity and re-development fever, Hong Kong's heritage was disappearing fast. Even as I was taking up my new post, wreckers were busy demolishing one of the finest of the old buildings on Hong Kong Island — the General Post Office.

My archaeological experience did not prepare me for Hong Kong's rich historical heritage. Fortunately, some records and lists of historical sites and buildings, compiled by British and Chinese scholars and historians, were available and proved very useful as a starting point. It was my plan now to embark on extensive field surveys to check whether previously recorded items were still extant and to search for and record new ones. This was not to be an arm-chair job, nor did I want one. Using the above sources and my own field notes, I was able to compile a formidable "inventory" of heritage items to be recorded, which included: historic buildings (of Chinese and Western style), archaeological sites, ritual buildings (Chinese ancestral halls and temples), ancient tombs and graves, Chinese traditional villages, historical stones (boundary, foundation and others), ancient rock engravings and inscriptions, forts, bridges, and old kilns. Nor were the odd items such as street furniture (lamp-posts, letter pillar-boxes), and old cannon forgotten. Using my previous experience with Hong Kong University and relying a good deal on common sense, a recording system was devised which has stood the test of time and has remained the basis of the AMO's subsequent recording methods.

After eight months on the job, having more questions than answers, I requested an attachment to the Department of Environment (DE) in England (later called English Heritage) and was granted three weeks. A great deal of basic information had to be crammed into this short period. My hosts and teachers at the DE were patient, sympathetic and very efficient. Not a minute was lost as they took me through various sections and stages which they regarded as important in the present state of development of my Office. Another four-week attachment to the DE at the end of 1978 proved enormously useful in the further organization of the AMO and, most importantly, in helping me to understand the philosophy of conservation and restoration of heritage. The AMO's task would no longer be limited to recording Hong Kong's heritage but would include, with the assistance of relevant government departments, repair, restoration, and maintenance where necessary, of those items listed for protection under the Ordinance. I felt the time was ripe for the AMO to undertake one such major repair and restoration. My choice fell on an old ruined Chinese fort on Tung Lung Island, at the eastern approaches to Hong Kong harbour. Its existence has been known for some considerable time; its location marked as a "ruin" on the government ordinance map.

Chinese Coastal Defences

Little is known of the early Chinese coastal defences, but it is generally accepted that the Chinese authorities became seriously concerned about the safety of their southern regions during the Ming Dynasty (1368–1644 CE) and began to fortify their maritime defences along the coast. There were two reasons for this: the increasing menace of piracy, the plague of the South China seas from early times; and the new threat posed by the appearance in local waters of Europeans supported by heavily armed ships, ostensibly to establish trade but at the same time, the Chinese suspected, to gain footholds on the mainland. Ruins of four old Chinese forts exist in the territory, three on Lantao Island and one on Tung Lung Island, but none, however, can be dated beyond the early years of the Ch'ing Dynasty (1644–1912 CE).

Tung Lung Fort

Tung Lung Island is rugged and sparsely populated, and has some of the most picturesque scenery to be found in Hong Kong. The Fort is located on high ground, on the northern promontory of the Island, from which it overlooks the narrow Fat Tong Mun passage, and could have exercised control over trading vessels sailing into the sheltered waters of Hong Kong. Practically everything we know about the history of the Fort, which is not much, comes from the Chinese Gazetteer of the San On District (Hsin An), or New Peace County, which prior to the British occupation of Hong Kong included the Hong Kong region. According to the Gazetteer, last published in 1819, the Fort was built in the Ch'ing Dynasty in the reign of Emperor K'ang Hsi (1662–1772 CE) with the purpose of suppressing pirates and those of the rebels who remained loyal to the preceding Ming Dynasty. It was described as containing fifteen guard-houses and manned by a detachment of one officer with twenty-five men and eight cannon. The difficulty of keeping the Fort supplied and maintained on so remote an island caused its evacuation in 1810. The English name "Tung Lung Fort" is probably of recent origin; in the original translation from the Chinese it was referred to as "Fat Tong Mun Fort".

Late in 1978 I submitted to the Antiquities Advisory Board a proposal to clear, repair and restore Tung Lung Fort and received approval to go ahead. There were good reasons for my choice of this Fort: (1) it was relatively near

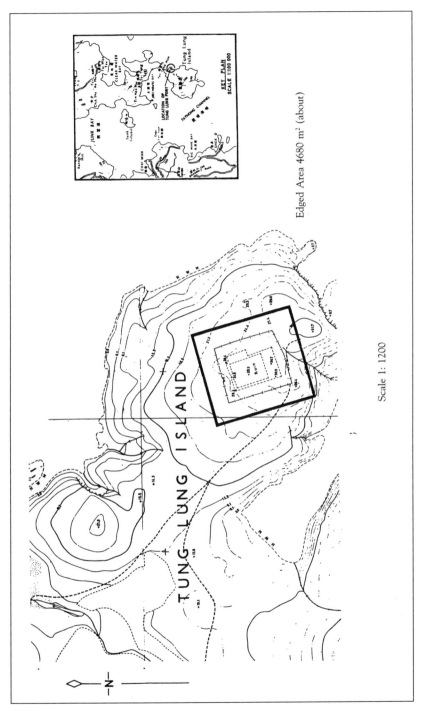

Edged Area 4680 m² (about)

Scale 1: 1200

Plan of Tung Lung Fort at Tung Lung Island.

to Hong Kong Island and Kowloon and had a good pier,[7] (2) brief inspection of the site showed considerable damage due to thick vegetation: the Fort was probably deteriorating rapidly, (3) there were strong reasons to believe that the Fort had not been previously disturbed or excavated and therefore was likely to yield first-hand information, and (4) there were at least two small habitations on the Island, one of them close to the Fort; these could be useful in providing local labour and place for storing equipment.

I assembled a small team of volunteers consisting mainly of expatriate ladies with few family commitments but serious interest in heritage work. I shall refer to them by their first names. Some were hardly novices: Heather and Pamela were fully fledged archaeologists, Alex worked at the Hong Kong Museum of History, while others — Rosemarie, Jeanne, Brian, Marion, Eileen, and Marigold — had worked with me previously on excavations or minor repair projects. I explained to the Team that the Tung Lung Fort Project would require several phases and that until we cleared the ruin of dense vegetation I could not tell how long it would take and how many phases would be required to complete the project. We arrived on the Island on 18 January 1979 to begin the first phase of the project.

Clearance

A rugged, tortuous footpath, steep in places, led to the Fort which was about one kilometre away from the pier. A small hamlet with a few cultivated fields and a small pig-farm was located on the low ground near the Fort. At the little hamlet we were able to hire four workers — three women and one man — they proved excellent and would continue working for us throughout the project. We found the Fort so thickly overgrown with wild vegetation that hardly any portion of the wall could be seen from the outside, nor could we detect an entrance. As we stood there looking at the unfamiliar, forbidding structure, trying to grasp the enormous task before us, we felt bowed down, and I must confess to having serious doubts about our ability to meet the challenge. Moments later, I uttered what must have sounded like a command to take up sickles and machettes and start cutting the vegetation. Although we wore gloves, some of us were soon bleeding from scratches by the thick, prickly vegetation.

---

7. The presence of an excellent pier, capable of docking large vessels, at an island so sparsely populated, was a mystery never resolved. I have a hypothesis, far-fetched I admit, that the pier was meant for the popular and much visited Tin Hau Temple across the bay, but was placed at Tung Lung Island by mistake.

The first phase was short, lasting only eight days. Working every day, we managed to remove most of the vegetation, outside and inside the Fort though there was still a lot of rubble on the ground. We could now appreciate the shape, the dimensions, and the condition of the Fort. It is rectangular in shape, measuring 33.5 by 22.5 metres, has a single entrance, in its north wall, and an 8-metre-thick south wall. A surprising and unusual feature is a platform measuring 4 by 15 metres abutting the east wall, which makes the Fort asymmetrical in shape. The walls, which averaged 3 metres in height, were in an advanced state of ruin with ten major areas of collapse.

No interior walls were visible, except for a single portion of pounded earth wall 90 centimetres high, but an undulating ground surface forming a pattern suggested the presence of underlying structures, perhaps internal walls. Generally, we were pleased with the results of the first phase. The Fort no longer appeared as formidable as before and seemed to beckon us to get on with more work. The mood was cheerful and all felt that interesting developments were in store ahead. The Team celebrated the "end of the beginning" with a bottle of wine on the site. After arranging with our village-workers to keep the Fort clear of vegetation, we left the Island.

We returned in November 1979 for another eight days of hard work — the second phase. New faces appeared among the volunteers — Julia, Phyl, Ulla, Brigitta, Rachel, Matthew; also the Museum of History's curator, Brian, joined sporadically and offered both work and advice. Our village workers, eager to start working again, welcomed us back warmly. There was still some residual vegetation to be cleared and a large amount of rubble, soil, and bricks from collapsed walls to be removed. Attention was also focused on the entrance which appeared badly damaged and blocked with large amounts of debris from collapsed walls. When cleared we were delighted to discover two gate pivot stones, one on each side of the entrance, and a number of wedge-shaped bricks — many still bound together with mortar — indicating an arch over the entrance, both the gate and the arch no longer present. Also revealed were the steps topped with flat slabs of stone leading to the entrance. Large heavy corner stones of the entrance were found displaced and required considerable physical effort to be moved back to their original position. Clearance of soil and displaced stones from the inner side of the west wall revealed brick-lined steps leading up to the top of the wall. Although we expected to find such steps, their exposure was greeted with obvious satisfaction. The Fort which in the beginning was for us an unknown mysterious structure was revealing its secrets as the clearance advanced. And with this, the Team's enthusiasm was notably increasing.

With the clearance of the vegetation, accumulated rubble, and stones from collapsed walls almost completed, it became my task to study the construction of the Fort and draw conclusions which could help us in the restoration. The outer walls, which averaged 2.5 metres in thickness, consisted of inner and outer vertical layers of semi-dressed stones, the space between them packed with earth and rubble. With the passage of time, penetrating rainwater washed out the fill, causing collapse of the stone walls. Although the stone arrangement seemed random, that is, not in even rows, the general pattern showed large stones at the base, diminishing in size upwards. Considering the rough, semi-dressed nature of the stones used, the walls were constructed with remarkable skill, evident in the intact portions of the walls. The remains of two brick parapets were found, along the inner and outer edges, on top of the intact portions of the walls. Since few of the bricks survived, it was impossible to deduce how high the parapets were and whether they were crenellated or not.[8] The added platform, built onto the east wall, was a mystery. If it was built to support the cannon, a different orientation of the Fort could have made the additional platform unnecessary. At any rate, its mystery made it one of the favourite subjects of discussion and speculation for the Team during its lunch breaks.

The cleared rubble contained bricks and broken roof-tiles indicating the presence of a roof at least over some portions of the Fort. Since the top of the entrance gate was missing and there was massive collapse of the walls on either side of the entrance, one was left wondering whether there was originally a gate-house on top of the entrance — a common feature in Chinese forts. Although no archaeological excavation was yet undertaken, a few finds had been collected during the clearance, including several Chinese coins, all of the Ch'ing Dynasty period. With the clearance nearly completed, I was able to examine the outer walls more closely, and in particular the original lime-mortar binding the stones. It was important in the restoration work to devise a mortar mixture which would resemble in appearance the original mortar, be strong and durable, and require a minimum of pointing so as to leave as much as possible of the stones exposed. It was also necessary to prepare a strong binding mixture for the inside of the walls in place of the original packed

---

8. Trying to solve the problem of brick parapets, I travelled to Shek Kau, a short distance across Deep Bay in mainland China, where a fort similar to Tung Lung Fort was located. The fort, half the size of Tung Lung Fort and, indeed, similarly constructed, had almost intact brick parapets topped with mortar. The parapets, of eight layers of bricks, were about eighty centimetres high and had no crenellations. It is reasonable to assume that Tung Lung Fort's brick parapets were similarly constructed.

soil. With the above in mind, I experimented with varying proportions of soil, sand, and cement, mixed and solidified as small cubes in a refrigerator tray, and tested for strength and appearance. The two selected mixtures were (i) smooth mortar for the exterior of the walls, and (ii) rough aggregate of cement mixed with pebbles for the inside fill; both proved very satisfactory (a year after completion of the project, the original and the new mortar could no longer be distinguished).[9] We were now ready for the repair and restoration work, to be undertaken at the next phase. Before leaving, the Fort was surveyed by Bill, a professional surveyor, who produced an excellent plan with successive surface levels and the line of collimation[10] clearly marked.

Repair and Restoration

We returned to the Fort in January 1980 for the third phase of the project. There was excitement in the air and the Team was in high spirits. But there were serious difficulties. There were no known sketches, plans, or descriptions of the appearance of the Fort to guide me in the restoration. We were sailing in uncharted waters and I was the skipper! Common sense and resourcefulness would be much needed. But if the details were missing, the general principles of restoration were clear to me: I had been fully converted to the prevailing philosophy of historic restoration preached to me during my attachments to the DE in England. I relayed it to the members of my Team: our aim would be to repair, consolidate, and only partially restore the existing structures. This would avoid conjecture and speculation while at the same time be aesthetically acceptable. This principle is widely followed in other countries for historical ruins, such as forts, castles, and abbeys, though not for historical buildings which may continue in use. The final result of our work would be, I hoped, a consolidated, stable historical ruin, imposing in appearance, which could be opened to the public with perfect safety.

The Royal Air Force squadron stationed in Hong Kong came to our help, generously using one of its helicopters to fly seventy bags of cement (each weighing 110 pounds) and drop them in front of the Fort. It did more by

---

9. The proportions, rounded up, were for the smooth mixture: one part of cement, three parts of sand and one part of soil; and for the aggregate: one part of cement, one part of sand and four parts of pebbles.
10. Line of collimation is an arbitrary horizontal line from which levels are marked downwards. In the Fort, the points where the line of collimation met the walls were painted with yellow arrows, so that measurements could be taken from any portion of the wall.

also bringing, as a contribution from the 6th Queen Elizabeth Own Gurkha Rifles, hundreds of cartons of Gurkha rations, which we ate for lunch with much enjoyment for months to come. A few of the volunteers had "retired" but new faces appeared — Betty, Jane, Jeanine, Alexandra, Judy, Heidi, and Thea. They and the hired workers set to work with enthusiasm. There were still heaps of stones, some large and heavy, from the collapsed walls, which had to be moved and neatly stacked for later reuse. The damaged portions of the walls were first dismantled and the interior consolidated with the cement-pebbles aggregate. They were then rebuilt with the same semi-dressed stones, each one carefully selected and fixed in place with the smooth cement-mortar mixture. No attempt was made to rebuild the walls to their original height. It was important to ensure that the repaired wall faces were flat and even. Generally, this was achieved successfully; only on one occasion, a repaired wall had to be broken and reconstructed to achieve a better result. I was interested to observe how the volunteers were becoming attached to their assigned tasks: there were, for instance, Thea's wall, Heidi's steps, Rosemary's brick parapet, and so forth. The work was progressing well, and with each damaged section reconstructed, the confidence of the workers rose. Moreover, the common objective had forged a strong feeling of solidarity among the volunteers uniting them into one friendly, harmonious team.

My own preoccupation with the Fort was bordering on obsession. The unsolved problems, the unanswered questions preyed constantly on my mind: the added platform, the excessively thick south wall and the strange stone formations on top of it, the brick parapets, the caches of large round pebbles, the roof ... I began to spend occasional nights on the Island, sleeping in the house of one of the village workers. I thought it might bring me closer to the essential Fort, perhaps even inspire new ideas, suggest possible solutions. It did not, but it did stir up my imagination. I recall standing on top of the wall on a moonlit night thinking of what it was like to be stationed in the Fort on this desolate island. A hundred and seventy or more years ago, men were living here, guarding the Fort. I imagined I could hear a faint murmur of voices; were they chatting, arguing, or perhaps gambling, while the sentries on the walls were calling to each other? I felt a strange indescribable awe creeping over me. Rousing myself, I thought: they have all gone forever; only the Fort remains — the silent witness to their past presence. I walked back to my hut; all was quiet as I went to bed — the sort of stillness one never feels in the city. I was awakened the next morning by my host's dog licking my face. In the bright and sunny morning the sensation of mystery had vanished. We stopped work early in February before the Chinese New Year and the onset of the monsoon rains. It had been a successful phase with a good deal of work accomplished. I felt that with three phases behind us, we were over the crest, as it were, with the goal now in sight.

In the fourth phase, which lasted from the end of October 1980 to the end of January 1981 (with a four-week break for Christmas), we worked twice a week instead of daily as in the previous phases. There still remained much to be done in repair and restoration of walls. At the same time my attention was diverted to several other problems which had to be addressed, predominant among them: sealing of the walls against rainwater penetration, the unsolved questions of the thick south wall, possible use of metal detectors in search of buried military ware, and the instability of the entrance steps. To prevent rainwater penetration, the top surfaces of the walls were excavated and plastic sheets placed thirty to forty centimetres below the surface, then sealed with pebbles, mortar slabs and cement. The puzzle of the two stone platforms, one round and the other rectangular in shape, on top of the south wall was the subject of much discussion, especially during the lunch breaks. I was in favour of a hypothesis that the round platform might have been the foundation of a small lookout tower, while the rectangular one, a platform for firing smoke signals. A metal detector was tried but proved ineffective. However, without it we found a number of small lead shots used in old muskets and a bronze clasp, possibly from a belt. Caches of large round sea pebbles found on top of the added platform and the south wall posed a problem. Perhaps they were used as cannonballs when the latter were in short supply.

Repair and restoration of the damaged structures was nearly completed, and it became clear that the major part of the work during the next, the last, phase would consist of excavating the interior of the Fort, which so far was limited to a single small trial pit at the south-west corner of the Fort. The excavation would involve the continuous use of wheel-barrows moving the spoil (term used for the excavated soil) out of the Fort, for which the stepped entrance was wholly unsuitable. Moreover, it had already become unstable from the constant use by the workers and required protection. A bridge built over the entrance steps seemed to be an obvious solution. I appealed to the army for help. The response came in the shape of a team of Gurkha Engineers who, in one day (in pouring rain) built an excellent wooden bridge, with a smooth, gradual curve, over the original steps. The volunteers had worked with undiminished enthusiasm throughout the phase. Many were now seasoned workers who knew what to do and needed only minimal guidance or supervision. The final objective was now in sight and anticipation was high.

Excavation

We returned to the Fort in October 1981 for the fifth — the final — phase of the project. I decided to continue with the restoration work, putting final touches and improving some of the repair work which fell short of the desired results. Excavation of the interior was entrusted to Pamela, later continued by Taryn, both fine field archaeologists, with half of the volunteer team assigned to them. New members, Lin, Beryl, Frances and Helen were welcomed by the Team. Systematic excavation during the next four months, working intermittently, revealed some of the interior layout. Layer by layer, the soil, deposited over the years since the Fort was built, was removed exposing inner walls, an outer corridor, and the original floor. By the end of the phase, five rooms were exposed along the south wall, and three on each side along the east and west walls. The plan, revealed so far, indicated that two more rooms on each side were beneath the unexcavated area giving a total of fifteen rooms.[11] This confirmed the Chinese Gazetteer's information, and although we had no reason to doubt its veracity, there was a general feeling of satisfaction at having demonstrated this point. The excavation showed that the interior walls were made of pounded earth with added rubble and tile fragments, resting on brick foundations; plaster covering the walls was still present in a few places. Most of the walls were about seventy to eighty centimetres high, certainly not their original height. Large numbers of broken roof tiles uncovered in excavation indicated a possible roof. It was assumed that it probably covered the interior rooms but not the outer corridor or the central courtyard.

Excavation yielded a large number of artefacts, not surprisingly since the Fort had been occupied for over a hundred years. They consisted of thousands of pieces of ceramics, objects of bronze, iron, and stone. They helped in part to reveal the pattern of life in the Fort, for instance broken clay pipes and various types of pottery vessels. Little of military ware was discovered even when the excavation was well advanced. This could be explained by the Fort having been evacuated in an orderly fashion and not in haste, when all useable military equipment would have been removed. Normally, in such circumstances the abandoned military structure would be damaged so as to render it useless to a potential enemy: in the present case, to pirates who might use it as a stronghold. It was disappointing that, except for a stone ink slab with two unconnected characters etched on it, uncovered in one of the rooms, no other objects with writing were discovered.[12]

---

11. It was not intended to excavate the whole of the interior, but leave about one-third of the area for further research at some future date.
12. The characters were "nine" and "wood"; their significance remained unknown.

With the interior rooms and their fragile walls now exposed, it was essential to construct a roof over the Fort to protect them, since the first torrential rain of the monsoon season would destroy the results of months of painstaking excavation. A roof of transparent plastic material was erected by the helpful Government Architectural Services in January 1982, only days before the seasonal rains started, much to our relief. There were still many unused stones left from the Fort walls. Some were now used to construct a path leading to the Fort, and a small hut outside the Fort for a possible on-site museum; in both cases the random patchwork pattern of stones was observed to resemble the Fort walls. A small stone shrine, immediately inside the Fort entrance, built during the earlier phases to propitiate the local deities and to please the local villagers, was cleaned and renovated. Our village workers, who looked after the shrine and kept it supplied with joss-sticks, were convinced that the absence of serious accidents in many days of sometimes hazardous work on top of the walls, was due to the shrine's protection.[13] Lastly, a plaque with information about the Fort, framed with left-over stones from the walls, was placed on the side of the newly built path, before the entrance to the Fort.

The Opening

Our work was completed, at least to the extent of my planned objectives. We spent ninety-six working days at the Fort over a period of three years (1979–82). More than thirty volunteers had participated at different times in the project (not all are mentioned in this article). Their contribution to the success of the project, from the beginning to the end, was immeasurable. For me, to have been in charge of the project, and to have succeeded in rescuing a neglected and nearly forgotten historical ruin from oblivion, was a source of great satisfaction.

The Fort was officially opened to the public at the Opening Ceremony on 27 April 1982, performed by the customary cutting of a ribbon by the director of urban services, who was also the chairman of the Antiquities Advisory Board and the Authority under the Antiquities and Monuments Ordinance. Government launches conveyed the many invited guests (who were advised in the invitation brochure to wear comfortable shoes) from Queen's Pier, on Hong Kong Island, to Tung Lung Island. The sudden gathering of dark-looking clouds threatened imminent rain, but after a quick appeal and offerings of more joss sticks at the Fort's little shrine, the clouds dispersed, and the Ceremony was concluded without anyone getting wet. The repaired

---

13. Indeed, during the whole of the project, there were only two minor injuries — a dislocated thumb and a sprained ankle, the latter sustained by a luckless visitor.

and partially restored Fort looked brilliant with the newly made traditional triangular banners flying from the corners of its walls. As the guests inspected the Fort, complimentary comments could be heard all around. The volunteers and I, now standing modestly in the background, felt proud and happy of our achievement. The ceremony and the reception over, everyone walked back to the pier where the launches were waiting. As I reached the top of a hill, on my way back to the pier, I looked back at the Fort and felt a little sad, realizing how much I should miss it and the Island and the warm fellowship of my Team.

Postscript (Some Twenty Years Later)

Excavation of the interior of the Fort continued sporadically for several years under the able direction of Pamela. A wooden viewing platform with explanatory captions was erected inside the Fort for visitors to inspect and enjoy the Fort in safety. With good maintenance by the government, the Fort remains in good condition. The path to the Fort has been cemented all the way. One of the village lady workers and her husband (and later her son) have been employed to oversee the Fort and keep it clean. The Fort remains very popular with visitors and parties of young picnickers, the latter often camping on the Island for the night; a private ferry from Shau Kei Wan to the Island operates on weekends. Few of the original volunteers are still in Hong Kong, but the core of the Team, who call themselves the "Tung Lung Ladies", presided by Rosemary, meet from time to time in England at reunions to rekindle old friendships and talk about the past and the happy days spent at the Fort. I visit the Fort whenever I return to Hong Kong, usually in company with some of the AMO staff and any of the former volunteers who happen to be in Hong Kong at the time. To me it feels like a pilgrimage to a place to which I had devoted probably the best efforts of my entire career in heritage.

19

TRAFALGAR NIGHT IN HONG KONG

Among some of my unusual experiences, perhaps the most unexpected episode was related to the anniversary of Nelson's famous naval victory at Cape Trafalgar. Trafalgar Night is an important and time-honoured naval tradition observed annually in October wherever there are units of the Royal Navy to be found. Officers and guests gather for dinner either on board a ship or at an officers' mess to celebrate Nelson's famous victory. There is usually a guest speaker who gives a short talk about Nelson, concluding it with a toast to the memory of the great admiral.

I could never have imagined myself in the role of the guest speaker on Trafalgar Night, yet this was exactly what happened in Hong Kong in 1984. The telephone call came one afternoon in August. It was from Captain C. G., the senior naval officer in Hong Kong. He was inviting me to be the guest speaker on 23 October, Trafalgar Night, at HMS *Tamar*, Royal Naval Dockyard.[1]

I was dumbfounded. My immediate reaction was to decline the invitation, which I did. I thanked Captain C. G. and explained that I did not think of myself as a suitable person for such an exalted role. Indeed, I had no connection of any sort with the Royal Navy, and my sole military involvement was with a local territorial unit, in which, admittedly, I was just completing my two-year appointment as the honorary colonel.[2] Captain C. G. accepted my refusal with regret. Minutes after my hasty reply, I regretted it. I always liked a challenge and this was surely an exciting one to meet. I rang back,

1. HMS *Tamar*: Name given to the stationary naval base in Hong Kong to commemorate the original ship which was scuttled in December 1941 during the Japanese attack on Hong Kong to avoid capture.
2. The local territorial unit was the Royal Hong Kong Regiment (The Volunteers).

apologized to Captain C. G. and said I hoped he would allow me to change my mind and still accept me as the guest speaker, which he kindly did.

Hong Kong in 1984 was still a British dependent territory, in effect — a colony, but the term had been discreetly and expediently dropped from usage during the previous few years; the transfer of the territory to Chinese sovereignty was still thirteen years away. At the same time British military presence had been scaled down considerably during the late 1970s and early 80s, with only token army and navy units stationed in Hong Kong. The Royal Navy contingent was tiny, consisting of a few patrol gunboats and an occasional destroyer on duty visit to Hong Kong. Captain C. G. was posted in Hong Kong several months previously. My invitation to Trafalgar Night was not entirely fortuitous. His family was musical and held regular musical soirees. We became friends after I had attended several of their soirees, both as a participant and a listener. Nevertheless, this would hardly qualify me to speak about and propose the toast to the Immortal Memory of Admiral Lord Nelson at one of the Royal Navy's most notable occasions. Obviously Captain C. G. thought otherwise.

I had two months to prepare my talk. The story of Nelson must have been presented countless times on countless numbers of Trafalgar Nights, many probably by brilliant speakers. It would not be easy to be interesting and original. The basic biographical facts of Nelson's life would have been known to every British schoolboy, let alone the naval people. I realized that in my talk I would need to make some interesting references to the Admiral's personality, while at the same time not omitting the important events of his life and, of course, the Battle of Trafalgar. Moreover, all this had to be squeezed into fifteen, at most twenty minutes. A daunting task to say the least. Among the various possible sources, I chose Robert Southey's *Life of Nelson* as my main reference book.[3] Although without naval affiliations, Southey was Nelson's near-contemporary (he was born in 1774, sixteen years after Nelson), a friend of Coleridge and Wordsworth, and a Poet Laureate; I thought he was a good choice. In any case, I liked his straightforward and elegant period style.

On the Night, I came dressed in my regimental dinner mess-kit with miniature medals. The Loyal Toast came before my talk. I then rose and, addressing my host and the attending members and guests, humbly asked my audience to bear with my ignorance of naval subjects. Below is my brief rendering of Nelson's life and achievements, based on this talk, much of it reproduced verbatim.

---

3. *Southey's Life of Nelson*, edited and introduced by Kenneth Fenwick, The Folio Society, London 1956.

Life at sea, it is generally known, demands good health and a strong constitution. I was, therefore, surprised to learn that Horatio Nelson was neither physically strong nor of robust health. It is entirely possible, I believe, that in the later age of medical examinations, his frail health might have prevented his ever going to sea at all. It is fortunate, therefore, that this simple routine procedure was not introduced until much later, or England might have been deprived of its greatest naval hero. This lack of physical strength, however, was more than compensated by a fierce determination to succeed, a courage to face every danger, and the interest and intelligence capable of mastering in the highest degree the intricacies of seamanship and naval strategy — qualities which were to bring him almost unbelievably rapid promotion. Indeed, he was promoted to the rank of lieutenant before he was nineteen (though it is reputed that he claimed he was twenty), captain at twenty-one, and admiral at thirty-nine.

The late 18th and early 19th centuries were the years of long wars with France and her allies. England was threatened with invasion. Action and danger there was in abundance. By the year 1797, when Nelson was just promoted rear-admiral, he had been in four major actions with the fleets of the enemy, in three blockade actions, took three towns, assisted in the capture of seven sail-of-the-line,[4] six frigates, four corvettes and eleven privateers, taken or destroyed near fifty sail-of-merchant vessels, and actually been engaged against the enemy upwards of 120 times, losing his right eye and right arm. This amazing list of services performed during the war had taken place even before the great battles of the Nile and Trafalgar. For a while the loss of his arm had deeply affected him, but he was thinking only of his duty. "A left-handed admiral," he wrote, "I am a burden to my friends and useless to my country."[5] But England thought otherwise, and within a year Admiral Sir Horatio Nelson hoisted his flag in the *Vanguard* and rejoined the fleet in the Mediterranean. He was soon in pursuit of the French in Egypt.

In this climate of continuing hostilities, it was not surprising to hear Nelson addressing one of his midshipmen in the following terms: "There are three things, young gentleman, which you are constantly to bear in mind. First, you must always implicitly obey orders, without attempting to form any opinion of your own respecting their propriety. Secondly, you must consider every man your enemy who speaks ill of your king: and, thirdly, you must hate

---

4. Sail-of-the-line: Old term of the era of sail; refers to big warships, two- or three-deckers, with heavy guns.
5. *Southey's Life of Nelson*, p. 110.

a Frenchman as you do the devil."[6] (At this point of my talk, the audience erupted into applause and loud cheers).

What was he really like, the sailor, the man? Like most great men, Nelson had a sense of destiny. There is no doubt that he believed himself to be fated for great exploits. He was arrogant and vain and he was fond of praise. As a young captain of twenty-seven, he was once rebuked by the governor of the Leeward Islands for presuming to give advice to an older general. "Sir" Nelson replied, "I am as old as the Prime Minister of England and think myself as capable of commanding one of His Majesty's ships as that Minister is of governing the state."[7] He was referring, of course, to William Pitt the Younger with whom he was of the same age. Although some who met him might have disliked his vanity and love of praise, to the great majority his vanity seemed inoffensive. Men who served under him loved and respected him for his courage and his humanity. "Our Nel," they used to say, "is as brave as a lion and as gentle as a lamb." Men who fought against him knew him to be gallant in action, magnanimous in victory. He had a profound sense of duty which he also had the power to inspire in others. "Joseph Conrad, a Pole by birth, well said that Nelson was a terrible ancestor for sailors, for what before his time had been heroism, he made simple duty for the future."[8]

But there was yet another aspect of his personality — a sensitive and artistic temperament, a gentleness and humanity which, to those who knew this side of his character, seemed to be the very opposite of the man of action. It also perhaps explains his relationship with Lady Hamilton, for England's great naval hero was also a passionate man who needed love, and no account of him could be complete without referring to that episode. Lord Nelson's and Lady Hamilton's love may have been the scandal of the century, but in truth it was also a tragedy in the Shakespearean mould. Emma Hamilton gave Nelson the greatest happiness he would ever know, in a harsh life of constant duty and danger without parallel in history. They were both people of great courage and tenderness, of warmth and passion. It was their misfortune that they met too late, when both were married, and in the circumstances the private tragedy of their lives was inevitable.

It is impossible in this short account to refer to all or even most of Nelson's great achievements. His complete victory on the Nile, in 1798, is not described. But the Battle of Trafalgar is, of course, central to this account. The years 1803–05 were dominated by Napoleon's intention to invade England,

---

6. *Southey's Life of Nelson* p. 57.
7. Ibid., p. 44.
8. Ibid., p. 16.

and 1805 was to be the year of decision. Much has been written about this great battle and, quite honestly, I cannot hope to fully understand it in my ignorance of naval warfare and seamanship. But this I can understand — that the English fleet consisted of twenty-seven sail-of-the-line and four frigates; the enemy's of thirty-three sail-of-the-line and five large frigates. Moreover, the enemy's superiority was not merely in numbers but also in size and number of cannon.

Nelson on board the *Victory* prepared for battle. Several miles ahead were the combined fleets of France and Spain. Every schoolboy knows Nelson's signal, which is probably the most famous and enduring signal in England's history: "England expects that every man will do his duty". Contrary to popular belief, it was not Nelson's last signal, for twelve minutes later another signal was hoisted which meant "Engage the enemy more closely".

The rest is history. It was a great victory, perhaps the most significant victory that was ever achieved upon the seas, by which all the maritime schemes of France were totally frustrated and England's shores made secure for many years to come; it was the product of Nelson's surpassing genius. But the cost was great. Nearly 1700 men fell, with them Admiral Nelson. It was an ironic twist of fate that the fatal shot came from the ship, *Redoubtable*, which Nelson had spared, supposing that she had struck.[9] It was also typical of the man that, feeling that the wound was fatal, he insisted that the surgeon should leave him and attend to those who might yet be saved. His last words were "Thank God, I have done my duty".[10]

The death of Nelson was felt in England as a national calamity. The victory at Trafalgar was indeed celebrated, but it was robbed of joy because of the loss of the beloved and revered hero. And yet one cannot help thinking that if Nelson's destiny was to die, he has chosen well. If it can be said, to quote Southey, that "the most splendid death is that of the hero in the hour of victory...", then Nelson "... could scarcely have departed in a brighter blaze of glory. He has left us a name... and an example which are at this hour inspiring thousands of the youth of England...".[11]

With the words "It is the name we honour tonight", I concluded my speech, then proposed the customary toast : "The Immortal Memory of the Great Admiral Lord Nelson".

---

9. "Struck": In naval warfare meant "lowered her ensign" indicating submission or surrender.
10. *Southey's Life of Nelson*, p. 291. According to Southey, Nelson did say "Kiss me, Hardy", preceded by a plea to Hardy to take care of Lady Hamilton, but they were not, as popularly claimed, his last words.
11. Ibid., p. 297.

20

WORKING WITH THE HONG KONG CHINESE ORCHESTRA

"Whence comes this voice of the sweet bamboo,
Flying in the dark?"

Li Po (c. 699–762 CE)

Introduction

We live in a world of sounds. Scientists may wish to tell us that sound is a product of our brain, that outside our senses sound is merely a wave motion. Who cares? What counts is that we hear sounds. For me, the silent world is unthinkable, and my heart goes out to those who are deprived, by nature or disease, of hearing. How Beethoven must have suffered when he could no longer hear his own sublime music except in his mind! Incidentally, I think I am getting a little hard-of-hearing myself, but not to sounds or music, only to conversation.

It is not difficult to imagine how early humans discovered music through their instinct for singing and dancing, how slowly, in the course of thousands of years, music developed form and structure, and evolved into art.

I have been involved in music as a participant since the age of ten, when I began studying the violin with my uncle, a professional musician. At twelve I enrolled in the school of music, which I attended concurrently with my high school, and at the age of fifteen I considered taking up music as a profession. In the end, I was persuaded to study medicine where I was likely to achieve a greater degree of success and security. I found working as a physician fully satisfying, but I had never abandoned music for more than brief periods during most of my life. Still, I never imagined that I would eventually return to music professionally, let alone as a full-time conductor of a Chinese orchestra.

Chinese Music

Music in China is a very ancient tradition, its beginning shrouded in legend and myth. Of these, the most popular one relates how around 2000 BCE a certain Ling Lun was sent by the emperor to the western mountains to cut bamboo pipes from which the fundamental pitches of music could be derived. Music was already well established during the Chou Dynasty, 1100 BCE, when according to existing records, a special minister was appointed solely to supervise rituals and music. Confucius, in the 6th century BCE, attached great importance to music and considered it one of the fundamental factors in education. It may be interesting to note that in those ancient times strict etiquette prescribed that music must not be performed: (1) in tempest and rain, (2) in noisy market places, (3) before vulgar audiences, (4) before an audience which will not sit down, and (5) before one not properly dressed. Would that we followed such etiquette today!

Instrumental ensembles, or orchestras, of different sizes have been employed in China from the earliest times, initially for official ceremonies or for royal entertainment, and later for other functions such as outdoor processions during festivals, weddings and funerals. These were inclined to use only wind and percussion instruments and were often excruciatingly loud. An orchestra was also used to accompany singers especially in opera performances, in which music was generally simple and often improvised, creating an image in the West that this was all there was to Chinese music. One Westerner who had spent many years in China wrote in 1870: "A Chinese Orchestra or band, when in full note, strikes upon the ear of a European as a collection of the most discordant sounds... It seems, when hearing them, as if each performer had his own tune, and was trying to distinguish himself above his competitors by his zeal and force".[1] One could hardly blame this "well-informed" gentleman, since much of the music heard in those times was used as an accompaniment — secondary to other performances — and lacked refinement. It seems that the fine elements of Chinese music — the traditional themes, the folk music, its pure, delicate melodies — were seldom heard. Foreigners generally remained, even in recent times, reluctant to listen to Chinese music influenced by several misconceptions, one being a widespread belief that Chinese music is pentatonic, that is using only five notes of a scale.[2]

---

1. Wells Williams, *Middle Kingdom: Survey of Geography, Government, Literature, Social Life, Art, and History of the Chinese Empire and Its Inhabitants*, New York 1883, pp. 103–104.
2. The pentatonic scale can be likened to using only black keys on the piano.

This scale was popular and often used especially in folk songs, but the Chinese have known and used the full twelve-tone chromatic scale since the earliest times. Another misconception is that Chinese music has no harmony and is played and sung in unison. Some Chinese instruments, known from antiquity, can produce two or three notes together, as chords, and so achieve harmony. But the biggest misconception of all is that Chinese music is incomprehensible to Western ears. Today there are countless Asian musicians, some among the best in the world, who appreciate and perform Western music; surely the reverse must also apply. All that is needed are interest, patience, and a desire to listen to Chinese music with an open mind, to discover and appreciate its unique style, its relative simplicity, and its special effects. Indeed, there is today a small but growing number of Western musicians and composers who are deeply involved in Chinese music and its traditional instruments. Unfortunately, Western audiences have so far been slow in embracing Chinese music.

It is sometimes asked: how was Chinese music written in antiquity? The answer is we do not know. Initially, and even in recent times, it was played from memory. It is believed, however, that some sort of a notation, perhaps resembling Chinese characters, may have been used. It is possible that in the destruction of libraries, under the great despot Shi Huang-ti in the short Ch'in Dynasty (221–206 BCE), notation, music, and perhaps musical instruments were lost. The earliest known notation comes from the Song Dynasty (10th–13th century CE) and shows a system of symbols which look like Chinese characters, but actually are artificial signs indicating simultaneously the note, the fingering, and the stroke to be used.

In spite of its long and glorious past, music in China, it must be conceded, remained relatively stationary for centuries. Fettered by tradition and used largely as an accompaniment, its development as an independent artistic expression has been a recent phenomenon. A remarkable change in Chinese music began to reveal itself in the early 20th century when, spurred by contacts with Western music, Chinese composers and musicians began to explore new pathways and experiment with different musical styles, while still retaining the essential national character of Chinese music. It was an immense leap forward — in effect a new era of modern Chinese musical art. To meet the demands of the new musical movement, a larger orchestra emerged, resembling but not copying a Western symphony orchestra. The Chinese symphony orchestra was born, no longer an accompanying body but one performing Chinese music for its own sake. It is generally agreed that the first truly modern Chinese orchestra employing Chinese traditional instruments was founded in Nanjing in the late 1930s. From there the idea spread to other major cities in China.

Hong Kong Chinese Orchestra

The Hong Kong Chinese Orchestra (HKCO) was formed in 1977 by the Urban Council of Hong Kong. With the existing Western-style Hong Kong Philharmonic Orchestra already in its third professional year, it was strongly and justifiably felt that Hong Kong with its predominantly Chinese population deserved to have a professional orchestra performing Chinese music and using Chinese traditional instruments. Its establishment was hailed as a milestone in the history of Chinese music in Hong Kong. Unlike the Hong Kong Philharmonic, which had performed as an amateur orchestra for twenty-seven years before turning professional, the HKCO was from the start a full-time professional orchestra, its members employed on contracts and their salaries paid by the Urban Council. There was no shortage of Chinese instrumental players. The post-war influx of refugees from China and a further inflow resulting from the Cultural Revolution of 1965–76 brought to Hong Kong, among others, many skilled and talented Chinese musicians. Among them was a brilliant musician and composer, NTK,[3] who became the Orchestra's first music director (MD).

In many ways a modern Chinese symphony orchestra was an experiment, each orchestra trying to achieve a perfect instrumental balance in its own way; there was no standard model, only common features. Like other Chinese orchestras which had sprung up in China and Taiwan, the HKCO had four sections — bowed strings, plucked strings, wind, and percussion — but apart from this basic structure, it tended to follow its own path of development. The HKCO started with sixty musicians, expanding to eighty-five by 1980. It was administered by a full-time managerial staff seconded from the Urban Services Department of the Hong Kong Civil Service, but the policy of the Orchestra was dictated by a special Select Committee of the Urban Council. The music director, supported by the assistant music director (AMD), shared conducting duties between them. Guest conductors were sometimes invited to perform with the Orchestra, and it was in the latter capacity that I first became acquainted with the HKCO.

My Exposure to Chinese Music

My early musical education, in the northern Chinese city of Harbin in the 1920–30s, was Western-oriented in a Russian cultural environment. At the music school, named after the Russian composer Glazunoff, the emphasis was

---

3. Initials only are given.

on the baroque and the classical musical periods, though the Russian romantic school was naturally considered important and its composers were studied and performed a good deal. Growing up in what was after all a Chinese city, my initial exposure to Chinese music was not unlike that of the "well-informed" foreigner mentioned earlier. Chinese funeral processions were common and were invariably accompanied by bands of poorly trained Chinese musicians who made loud discordant sounds. Then, one summer evening I heard the distant sound of a Chinese flute playing a sweet poignant melody. I heard it played again, the same serene melody, on several occasions. I never discovered who the flautist was or where the sound came from, but I had fallen totally under its spell.[4] Perhaps the seed of my interest in Chinese music, with a special affection for the Chinese bamboo flute, was planted then, though little happened for many years to make it grow. In Hong Kong after the War, in the early 1950s, I was conducting the amateur Sino-British Orchestra, later to become the Hong Kong Philharmonic. The principal flautist of the Orchestra, Dr C. K. Wong, a medical doctor and a friend of mine, who had been a fine exponent of the Chinese flute, formed a small Chinese instrumental ensemble. I begged him to teach me to play the traditional bamboo flute and to let me join his orchestra. This he did and he even personally made a flute for me; I treasure it to this day. Not surprisingly, I was the only non-Chinese player in his group. Although it was an amateur group with limited skills, it was for me a most enjoyable experience; and I was able to fulfil my long-held wish — to play, however inexpertly, that haunting sweet melody which I heard as a young boy many years before.

Apart from occasional recitals and the Chinese Radio broadcasts, opportunities to listen to live Chinese music in Hong Kong remained few until 1977 when the HKCO was formed. I attended its concerts as often as time permitted. I met its music director, NTK, soon after his arrival in Hong Kong, and we became good friends. Still, it was a big surprise when in 1980 I was invited to perform with the HKCO as guest conductor. With a mixture of excitement, awe, and trepidation I accepted, but asked for, and was given, six months to prepare myself. Although fully employed at the time directing the Antiquities and Monuments Office, I devoted as much time as I could spare listening to recorded Chinese music, studying the works chosen for my concert, and familiarizing myself with Chinese traditional instruments. I recall being nervous when I started rehearsing the Orchestra, but was soon put at ease by

---

4. Many years later I included this melody in my one and only composition, a medley of sketches for a Chinese orchestra, which I performed with the HKCO.

the good nature and encouragement of the musicians. Three performances (of the same programme) were scheduled and were sold out within a week, so a fourth performance was added. This success was perhaps partly due to the curiosity of having a foreign guest conductor, and partly to the inclusion in the programme of the immensely popular "The Butterfly Lovers Concerto" to be performed by a Chinese soloist on a Western violin. The Concerto, written jointly by two composers, Ho Jim-ho and Chan Kong, describes the pain and frustration of two young lovers who after death are reunited as butterflies in a fairy land. The performances took place in the City Hall in November 1980. As I walked onto the stage and bowed to the audience, I thought I heard a collective gasp from it followed by applause: the surprise at seeing a foreigner on the podium? The next moment, I was completely submerged in the music surging from the Orchestra as it followed the movements and expressions of my baton. And then it was over, followed by applause and four curtain calls, and I wished it would continue — such was the thrilling sensation of joy and satisfaction. I would in future conduct the HKCO often, but I could never forget the exultation of my first appearance.

The concert was obviously deemed by the Urban Council to have been successful, for in January 1982 I was back on the podium, a guest conductor again of the HKCO. Another successful concert, with three full-house performances, this time without an extra one. I enjoyed the challenge of my new musical experience, and was discovering ever fresh aspects of Chinese music. I liked the Orchestra and its members seemed to approve of me. More was to come, and in September of the same year, I was invited to join the Orchestra on its trip to Brisbane, Australia, as guest conductor (sharing performances with the MD) to perform during the cultural week, ahead of the Commonwealth Games. The Orchestra was welcomed with enthusiasm and great warmth by the Australian listeners for whom our concerts must have been new and interesting. A surprising and delightful discovery was of an Australian university students' ensemble playing Chinese music on Chinese instruments, directed by an American non-Chinese teacher. A combined session with the HKCO followed, in which the exchange of ideas was much enjoyed by both sides. For members of the Orchestra the visit to Brisbane was not only a rewarding musical experience, but for most of them also an exciting first visit to a Western country. For me, it meant an added appreciation of Chinese music and its traditional instruments, and a stronger tie with the HKCO.

I Join the Hong Kong Chinese Orchestra

In 1983, my tenure with the Antiquities and Monuments Office ended. Within weeks of my leaving the Office, I was invited by the Urban Council to apply for the post of assistant music director of the HKCO, recently made vacant. I accepted, was interviewed by the appointing panel, which included the music director, and was duly appointed. When I was presented to the Orchestra in my new full-time role and saw the friendly reassuring faces before me, any apprehension I might have felt vanished: I was not among strangers.

In the every-day rehearsal routine, the Orchestra differed little from its Western counterpart. Musicians rehearsed five days a week, Monday to Friday, with a total of thirty hours per week. They tuned before starting, usually to the middle A of the scale, had their mid-rehearsal break, and practised their individual parts in their own time. The Orchestra gave concerts twice a month in its regular venue — the City Hall Concert Hall — each generally comprising three performances of the same programme. The concerts were usually well attended, especially when popular works were performed; in this respect the predominantly Chinese audience was not different from a Western one in preferring works it knew best. On the stage, the Orchestra and the conductor looked very smart in their Chinese blue silk gowns with white cuffs. My duties consisted of assisting the MD in musical and administrative matters, conducting a certain number of public concerts and most of the educational (school) concerts. I was also required to train the Orchestra in various aspects of orchestral discipline normally followed by Western symphony orchestras but still relatively new to the HKCO. Language barrier was a problem initially, as only two or three members of the Orchestra knew some English, but after a while I managed well enough with my limited Cantonese and Mandarin and had no further problems in conducting or imparting my wishes to the players. There were, however, occasional amusing incidents, for instance when I pronounced "bar" (a division in music) to sound like "girl". "We shall start again from bar No. 3" would invariably set the Orchestra laughing. I did not try to correct my pronunciation: an occasional bit of fun was welcome to break the tedium of a rehearsal.

Soon after my appointment, I was dismayed to find the Orchestra deeply divided: problems, of which I was only dimly aware during my guest conducting, were now revealed in an alarming way. Divided loyalties resulted in rifts and cliques. Many musicians had known each other from China and old jealousies and personal enmities from the past had surfaced. The worst single rift was between the music director and the concertmaster, each commanding a large following in the Orchestra. Before long I witnessed ugly confrontations, some occurring during rehearsals, when members from opposing camps would stand up and shout insults at one another.[5] I had no doubt that the resulting unhappy atmosphere would adversely affect the Orchestra's performance. It seemed to me that as an uninvolved foreigner I had the advantage of being regarded by the musicians as neutral and could perhaps win their trust sufficiently to restore the Orchestra's unity and team spirit. I decided to try though as a newcomer I knew I should have to proceed carefully and tactfully. The Management must have been fully aware of the conflicts within the Orchestra and it even crossed my mind that my appointment may have had something to do with the Orchestra's problems. Was I meant, I wondered, to act as the troubleshooter? Unexpectedly, an event three months after my appointment helped to strengthen my position in the Orchestra. We were giving a concert, with the MD conducting, in the newly built Concert Hall in Sha Tin, an old market town which had recently developed into a large, well-populated satellite town. Half-way through the concert, during the interval, the MD suddenly declared that he felt unwell and asked me to take over. Although I attended the rehearsals, I had not myself rehearsed the programme. An announcement was made to the audience, and I conducted the rest of the concert without any mishaps. As the musicians and I left the stage, there were approving smiles and other signs of approbation directed at me. They were clearly impressed. It was as if I had passed a test, and in a way I suppose I had.

In 1984 the Orchestra participated in two important events: in September, the Orchestra visited South Korea to take part in the Seoul International Folkloric Festival, giving successful concerts in Seoul and Pusan with the MD and myself sharing the podium. This was the HKCO's third overseas visit (the first two being to Brisbane in 1982, previously mentioned, and to Japan in 1983, before my appointment) and no doubt helped to promote the Orchestra's international standing. The second event was the live "simulcast" (broadcasting on television and radio simultaneously) by the HKCO, the first of its kind in Hong Kong, conducted by me. Unfortunately the small size of the studio allowed only half of the orchestra to perform. The *Hong Kong Standard* wrote on this occasion: "The Hong Kong Chinese Orchestra

---

5. One of the worst confrontations between the MD and the concertmaster factions occurred during a rehearsal in the presence of a guest conductor from mainland China, to the acute embarrassment of the Orchestra's managing staff and the attending members of the Urban Council.

is now in its eighth professional season. The orchestra has been innovative in introducing new musical works in its repertoire. Over 300 pieces of new and arranged works have been commissioned since 1977. Today the orchestra has gradually achieved maturity and lovers of Chinese music are glad to see its entry into the world of music with style and flair."[6]

The trip to South Korea, while culturally successful, had an unfortunate sequel for the MD. For some time before, the management of the Orchestra had reasons to be displeased with him: there were missed, or late in starting, rehearsals; internal dissensions and general lack of discipline in the Orchestra; the MD's imperious behavior; his lack of co-operation with the management. The combined effects of these, the management claimed, interfered with the Orchestra's progress. The South Korean trip had apparently confirmed the management's suspicion that the MD was unlikely to reform. Early in 1985 the axe fell: in a "face-saving" manoeuvre, the management persuaded the MD to resign. I found myself in sole charge of the Orchestra. I was sorry to see him go. He was an outstanding musician and the inspired first MD of the HKCO. The Orchestra and the Hong Kong public owed him a great debt of gratitude. He may have been a victim of his own ego, in assuming that he was indispensable. My relations with him remained friendly to the end, but I must confess that I learned more about Chinese music and its style from members of the Orchestra than from him. There was, of course, an initial upheaval in the Orchestra when the MD's resignation was announced, with sharply varying reactions, but it settled down quickly and without complications. Although now effectively the acting MD, I declined the title, out of respect for the former MD, who still had a big following in the Orchestra and whom I too respected and admired. I remained as before — the AMD.

I Take Charge of the HKCO
What was my reaction to finding myself, a foreigner with a different background and only partial knowledge of the intricacies of Chinese music, in charge of a Chinese orchestra? It was a mixture of apprehension and excitement: apprehension as to whether I should be able to cope with such a responsibility. Clearly, the management decided that I would, when it dispensed with NTK's services. But I also felt excited at the challenge before me, and at being in a position to introduce a number of changes I thought were needed before a new MD was appointed. In the event, this appointment was not made until almost two years later.

---

6. *Hong Kong Standard*, 28 September 1984.

Eight years after its foundation, the HKCO's basic structure was reasonably well established and was not affected by the changes which I gradually introduced. These included a different seating arrangement of the instrumental sections, increasing the number of bass instruments, revising music scores, special training sessions, and many others of minor impact. I have no doubt that collectively these reforms improved substantially the sound balance and overall performance of the Orchestra. Another change, which appealed strongly to members of the Orchestra, was to extend solo appearances, previously limited to the concertmaster and one or two other players, to many members, some of whom were of a virtuoso standard. In this connection, I especially remember one member of the flute section who amazed and thrilled both the Orchestra and the audience with his incredible technique and brilliant sound achieved on a tiny, three-inch flute with only three holes known as the "houdi" or mouth-flute. I cannot claim that the old feuds were fully resolved, but I do believe that the Orchestra functioned much more harmoniously (no pun intended) as a team than before. Discipline was restored, rehearsals started on time and as a rule proceeded smoothly. We were working happily together and I felt that I had the Orchestra's trust and confidence.

Orchestral Structure and Instruments
The Orchestra's four sections — the bowed strings, the plucked strings, the wind, and percussion — each with a distinctive tone colour, combined to produce a rich, well-balanced sound. Western-style cellos and double basses, introduced into all modern Chinese orchestras, made up for the lack of bass sound in old traditional ensembles; the HKCO went even further, fashioning their sound boxes to resemble the Chinese violin. I grew especially fond of the plucked strings because of their delicate, harpsichord-like sound. In the wind section, the shang, a pipe mouth organ, and the bamboo flute each provided a very attractive sound. Even the suona, loud and strident in inexpert hands, produced a beautiful sound when played, with an amazing technique, by the Orchestra's capable musicians. Modern Chinese compositions demanded ever increasing skills from performers, and the HKCO members practised hard to attain them. As for the percussion, I must confess to a partial defeat by the bewildering number and variety of drums, gongs, bells, cymbals, wooden blocks, and many others. In spite of this large number and variety, the Western timpani (kettle drums) has earned a permanent place in the percussion section of most Chinese orchestras including the HKCO. To meet the demands of

modern Chinese compositions with their greater complexity, some traditional instruments have been modified. Like the bowed strings with the added hybrid cellos and double basses, the traditional shang was joined by a family of newly designed shang of varying sizes, from a small treble to a large bass shang. The ancient, refined seven-string chin, the delight of the purists, has become all but obsolete, and replaced by the modern twenty-one-string guzheng, and there have been plans to add pedals to the dulcimer-like yangqin.

A list and descriptions of the Chinese instruments is in the Appendix.

Repertoire

The Orchestra's initial repertoire was small, but it grew rapidly as local and overseas Chinese composers, encouraged by the Urban Council's commissioning policy, submitted their compositions. Some were original, others were arrangements of traditional melodies or folk songs, whose origin had long been forgotten. I was required to look through the submitted compositions and make recommendations, a task for which I did not consider myself fully qualified. I was fascinated by some of the works' attractive, exotic names, such as, for instance, "Reflection of the Moon in Water", "Little Sisters of the Grassland", "Song of the Homebound Fisherman", "Romance of the Eastern Sea". Some composers had received early training in Russia and the influence of the Russian romantic school was only too obvious. Occasionally I found a composition carelessly or hastily written which did not merit acceptance into our library, but on the whole, the submissions were praiseworthy. I was particularly impressed by the efforts of the Hong Kong Chinese composers whose works showed originality, inventiveness, and sometimes daring, avant garde style. As a vehicle for new and modern compositions, the Orchestra was in the front line of expounding and promoting contemporary Chinese musical expression. Though an unlikely judge of the repertoire, I was, however, able to contribute some technical improvements. Every orchestral composition includes a conductor's score, showing all the playing instruments. In a Western music score these are arranged in a standard order, from top to bottom: woodwind, brass, percussion, strings. Chinese scores did not appear to have a standard order, which made them difficult for a conductor to follow. I also discovered that not all composers were familiar with the ranges of the Chinese instruments, so that some parts were found to be unplayable. It was simple for me to prepare and circulate the necessary information, with a request to abide by it, to all likely composers known to the HKCO.

Concerts

The years 1985 and 1986 were for me happy and rewarding. The Orchestra and I enjoyed a good working relationship, and I was gaining steadily in confidence conducting Chinese music. The concerts were successful and things were running smoothly. I knew, of course, that a new MD would be appointed sooner or later, but in the meantime I was in charge and I enjoyed it.

I discovered that the Urban Council, in addition to the HKCO, also sponsored and financially supported the Hong Kong Chorus. Unaccountably the two had never performed together. I decided it was time to bring this about and in February 1986 I conducted a joint concert of the HKCO and the Hong Kong Chorus in which the highlight was the six-movement "Hong Kong Vocal Suite" composed by a well-known Hong Kong composer Fu Yam-chi.

School Concerts

From the start of my appointment, I conducted most of the school concerts. The schedule was irregular depending on the availability of the Orchestra and the requests from schools. During school vacations there were few concerts, but in term-time we sometimes gave as many as three or four performances in one week in different schools. I enjoyed conducting these concerts for one can hardly find a better audience than that of children. We covered most of the schools in the Territory including the English-speaking schools. A concert usually lasted about an hour, at the end of which children were allowed to come up to the stage, examine musical instruments, ask questions and generally mingle with the players. One problem encountered was the size of a stage: in most of the schools it was small, allowing only a portion of the orchestra to perform. With the Orchestra now reaching ninety, I divided it into three ensembles of roughly equal size and equal performing ability, designating them Ensembles 1, 2 and 3, who then took turns performing. The idea was popular, as it allowed two-thirds of the Orchestra off duty at each performance, but the designation was not, as it could be taken for rank or grade, that is that ensemble No. 1 was better than No. 2 and so on. Naming them A, B, and C had the same effect. It was a question of "face". To satisfy the "face saving" principle, I finally named the three groups Red, Green and Yellow and everyone was happy. Wisdom of Solomon!

New Music Director

I had been in charge of the Orchestra for nearly two years before steps were taken to appoint a new MD. There was no question of considering me for the post, nor did I want it. It was, therefore ironic, if not absurd, that a shortlist of three applicants was given to me for my comments and recommendations; all three were known to me and had appeared previously as guest conductors with the Orchestra. The new MD (KNC),[7] who was, in fact, my choice, was appointed at the end of 1986, and I resumed my duties as AMD. My working relations with the new MD were polite but not close. We went about doing our respective jobs without interfering with each other, though my workload, of course, had become substantially less.

Concerts in Beijing

In September 1987 the Orchestra was invited to perform in Beijing, at the China Art Festival. It was a significant milestone for the Orchestra and a sign of recognition by China of the important role the HKCO played in the development and promotion of Chinese music. The visit to China was immensely exciting: for the HKCO players it was a home-coming, even if some had left China in inauspicious circumstances. For me, apart from performing Chinese music in the capital of China, there was the added excitement of meeting several prominent Chinese composers who until then were only names on musical scores. The concerts, which the MD and I shared, were very successful. The MD, who was also a competent composer, conducted his own composition which was very well received. When I stood on the podium to conduct the smart-looking HKCO, with a large audience of Chinese people behind me, I was aware how unique my position was: a foreigner conducting a Chinese orchestra in a programme of Chinese music in the heart of China. In the interval I was taken to meet Mr Ji Peng-fei, a senior Chinese minister in charge of China–Hong Kong affairs. In my blue silk Chinese gown, I must have looked strange to him for he turned to his aide and whispered (which I understood): "He does not look Chinese", to which the aide replied: "No, he is a foreigner", and a thought suddenly crossed my mind that a hundred years ago he would have probably said "he is a barbarian". And perhaps I still was, alone amidst thousands of people who belonged to a noble ancient culture.

Good Things Come to an End

A few months after our return from Beijing, my tenure of four years with the Orchestra ended. I did not plan to continue. It was very hard work with hardly any time left for my other activities, among which archaeology still played an important part. At the same time I could not recall another period

---

7. Again, initials only.

in my life more challenging or more rewarding, nor could I remain unmoved by the uniqueness of my position — perhaps the only full-time non-Chinese conductor among the existing Chinese symphony orchestras.

The relationship between a conductor and an orchestra, ideally based on mutual respect, is of paramount importance and one on which the quality of performance largely depends. I believe that in my four years with the HKCO we had achieved a very satisfying rapport. I learned to appreciate the many fine qualities of the musicians, among these — their artistic integrity and dedication to their music. We learned from each other. I was able to impart to the players some aspects of orchestral discipline and behavior, of which they were previously unaware, and gradually improve their morale and esprit de corps. From them I gained a wealth of invaluable insight into Chinese musical style and instrumental expression.

Were there any disappointments? Alas, yes; notably one: during the period when I was effectively acting director, the Orchestra recorded its first disc. Although I was perfectly capable of directing the Orchestra for this important first event, politics dictated that a Chinese conductor be employed for the task. While I could understand the motive behind this, I could hardly remain unaffected by this decision which I regarded as unjust. I returned to the podium of the HKCO as guest conductor a few times after my retirement, the last time in September 1991 in the newly built Hong Kong Cultural Centre, at Tsim Sha Tsui, Kowloon. For that concert I arranged two works of Bach, one of them a full concerto of three movements for yangqin (a Chinese dulcimer) based on Bach's clavier concerto in D Minor. The management wanted to call the concert "From Bach to Bard" but I declined. Perhaps I had in mind the shortest musical review I ever saw many years before in the *New Yorker* which went: "...(name) played Bach. Bach lost". Instead we called the concert "A Tribute to Bach". At this concert I also conducted the first performance of a composition called "Rising", by the non-Chinese Australian composer, Tony Wheeler, who had devoted many years of his life to Chinese music, becoming a composer and a fine performer on several Chinese instruments.

In 1993 I moved permanently to Australia and gradually lost touch with the HKCO. From occasional news reaching me, I gathered that it continued to be a dynamic ensemble, exploring new frontiers in music with the responsibility of bringing Chinese traditional and modern music not only to Chinese listeners but also to an increasingly interested cosmopolitan audience.

Postscript

In 2006 unexpectedly came an invitation from HKCO to conduct at its 30th anniversary concert in 2007. It was exciting news: I had not been forgotten. The concert, scheduled for the 23 June 2007, was titled "Old Friends". I was to share the podium with five other conductors, formerly associated with the Orchestra. At the rehearsal, I found the Orchestra in great form and the musicians received me enthusiastically. I was delighted to discover that more than half of them I knew from my old days with the Orchestra. The concert was a splendid event. As I stood on the stage, ready with my baton, I was presented by Barbara Fei, my old friend from the Canton visits fifty years earlier,[8] looking as elegant and attractive as ever. Then I was conducting, lost in the music. It was a most thrilling experience to be back at the helm of this marvellous orchestra, even for the few minutes allotted to me.

---

8. Described in "Sino-British Club of Hong Kong and Its Legacy".

APPENDIX

Instruments of the Hong Kong Chinese Orchestra
(In Mandarin; Cantonese transliteration in brackets)

1. Bowed Strings

Erhu (yi wu)

The most popular of the bowed instruments and the mainstay of the string section, the erhu is a 2-stringed instrument with the bow clasped between the two strings. It has a range of about two octaves and its player can develop a very high degree of skill. The sound box is traditionally covered by a snake skin which gives the erhu a distinctive tone colour.

Zhonghu (chung wu)

The zhonghu is larger than the erhu but otherwise very similar. It is also lower in pitch than the erhu and adds to the range of the orchestra.

Gehu (gak wu)

The gehu is a modern instrument — a hybrid: it has four strings and its tuning and technique are the same as those of the cello, but its body is made to resemble the erhu. The sound box is covered with a snake skin giving it a tone quality different from a cello.

Bass (or di yin) Gehu (dai yam gak wu)

The bass gehu, like the gehu, is tuned and played like the double bass. Both the gehu and the bass gehu further extend the range of the orchestra.

Erhu (yi wu)

Zhonghu (chung wu)

Gehu (gak wu)

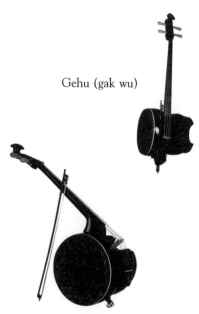

Bass (or di yin) Gehu

2. Plucked Strings

Pipa (pei pa)

The leading instrument of the plucked strings, the pipa is of ancient origin and became the dominant instrument in the Tang Dynasty (618–906 CE). It has four strings and is shaped like a pear. It is used both for solo and accompaniment, and has a beautiful delicate yet clear tone, well suited to all forms of Chinese music.

Liuqin (lau kam)

The modern liuqin — a small instrument with four strings — is a relatively recent version (about 100 years old) of the original ancient form which had two strings. The liuqin has a higher pitch than the pipa and has lately become popular for solo playing.

Ruan (yuen)

The ruan is a short-necked, lute-like instrument with four strings. It has been used in Chinese music for over 1000 years, and possibly as far back as the Han Dynasty (206 BCE–220 CE). It has been gradually improved, and the range extended by having ruan of two sizes, medium and large.

Sanxian (saam yuen)

The sanxian is a very long-necked instrument with three strings and a snake skin stretched over the resonating box. There are different sizes of sanxian and all have a rich pleasant tone. It is widely used for accompaniment and solo work.

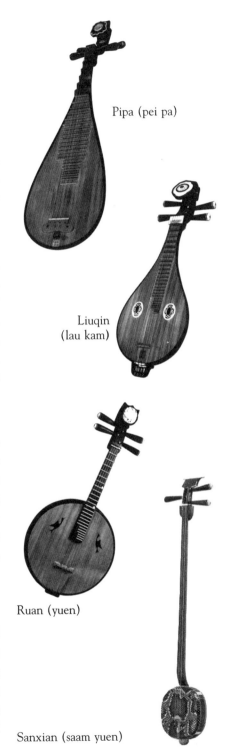

Pipa (pei pa)

Liuqin (lau kam)

Ruan (yuen)

Sanxian (saam yuen)

3. Wind Instruments

Di (tek) and Hsiao

The di is the traditional Chinese bamboo flute, held horizontally, which has changed little since ancient times. Made in different sizes, they are pitched in different keys. A unique feature of the di is the presence of a special hole covered by a thin piece of rice paper, which adds a gentle "buzzing" quality to its distinctive tone. It is a beautiful solo instrument with a very pure tone, but is also used extensively in orchestras.[9]

The hsiao is a vertical variety of bamboo flute, said to date from the Han Dynasty. The tone is soft and delicate and less reedy than that of the di.

Di (tek) and Hsiao

Sheng (shang)

The sheng is one of the oldest Chinese instruments, reputedly used for over 3000 years. It is, in fact, a mouth pipe-organ using 17–36 bamboo pipes of varying lengths. The pipes are placed in a circle and can be played as single notes or together as chords. It has a reedy yet soft and clear tone. It was said about sheng that it could sound like the cry of the phoenix bird and that its shape resembled a phoenix with folded wings. It is possibly the oldest instrument, based on the organ principle, in the world, and may well have influenced the development of the reed organ in 17th century Europe. The HKCO uses several sheng of different sizes, from a small soprano to a large bass one.

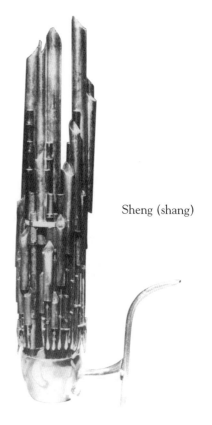

Sheng (shang)

---

9. The HKCO had seven di players, the biggest number in the wind section.

Guan (koon)

The guan is a vertical tube fitted with a reed mouth-piece. It has a small range and a reedy tone, and tends to sound harsh when played inexpertly. The HKCO has three guan of different sizes.[10]

Suona (sau lap)

The suona is a double-reed instrument derived from an ancient prototype called "la-ba". Its body is made of wood except the bottom part, which opens out like a trumpet and is of metal. There are several sizes of suona. Its tone is bright but inclined to be loud and harsh if played inexpertly.

Guan (koon)

Suona (sau lap)

10. I must confess that I have never developed a liking for the guan. Its range is too small and it seems to add little to the collective tone colour of the wind section. Moreover, few players seem to be able to achieve on it a pleasant tone.

4. Percussion

Chinese orchestras use a very large assembly of drums, cymbals, gongs, tambourines and wooden blocks. In addition, modern Chinese ensembles have adopted the concert tympani. All the instruments are used very effectively in orchestral works.

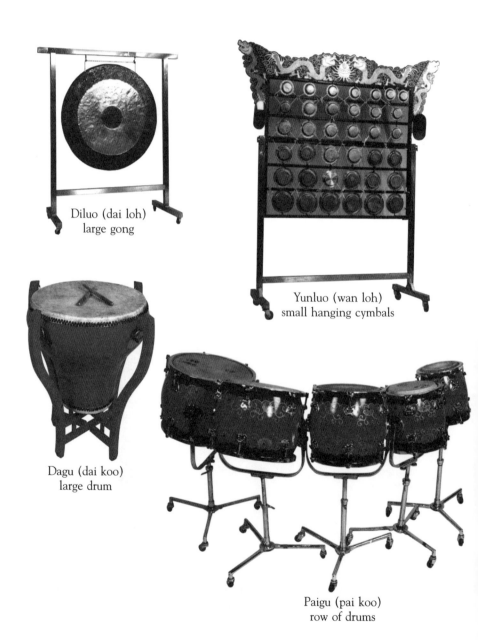

Diluo (dai loh)
large gong

Yunluo (wan loh)
small hanging cymbals

Dagu (dai koo)
large drum

Paigu (pai koo)
row of drums

5. Other Instruments

Guzheng (koo tsang)

The modern guzheng is a much modified descendant of one of the most ancient and refined Chinese instruments, the 7-string chin, which is still a favourite among scholars. The modern guzheng is larger than the chin and usually has 21 strings stretched over a wooden frame with movable frets. It is still a lovely instrument with a clear and mellow tone and a large range.

Yangqin (yeung kam)

The yangqin is a comparatively late instrument, apparently introduced into China in the middle of the Ch'ing Dynasty (17–20th century CE), possibly derived from the Western zither. It has been called a "butterfly harp" because of its shape, but it is not a harp but rather a sort of dulcimer played by hammering strings with thin bamboo sticks. The sound produced is graceful and not unlike a dulcimer or a harpsichord. Yangqin is an important instrument in a Chinese orchestra.

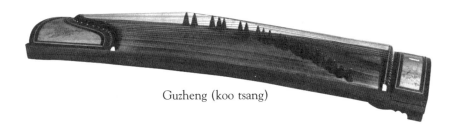

Guzheng (koo tsang)

Yangqin (yeung kam)

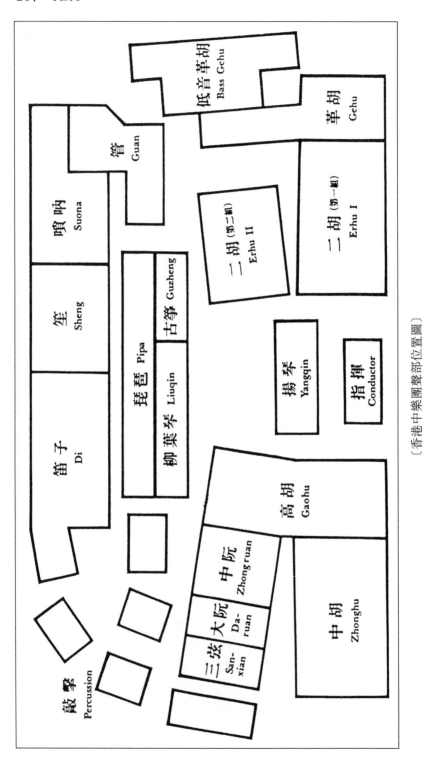

〔香港中樂團聲部位置圖〕

Hong Kong Chinese Orchestra: Layout plan of instrumental sections (1987).

15.1 Crowning the Inca pageant, Cuzco, Peru, June 1960. The massive pucara wall and the hill above are crammed with spectators.

15.2 Cuzco, Peru, June 1960. "The Inca" holding a staff stands on the artificial platform to receive homage from kneeling soldiers.

15.3 Cuzco, Peru, June 1960. "The Inca" is carried in a litter around the open ground. The colourful clothes worn by the carriers are reputed to be the original Inca attire.

15.4 Cuzco, Peru, June 1960. The procession of musicians playing on a mixture of old and modern instruments.

15.5 Cuzco, Peru, June 1960. People are strolling around the Plaza de Armas.

15.6 Cuzco, Peru, June 1960. The famous Stone of 12 Angles.

15.7 Inca pottery: the sherd on the left shows painted geometric designs; the other one, showing plant-like design, is probably of a later, Spanish, period.

15.8 Cuzco, Peru, June 1960. Llamas resting on the ground.

15.9 On the way to Machu Picchu, Peru, June 1960. A brief stop amidst magnificent scenery.

15.10 Machu Picchu, Peru, June 1960. One of the sharp lofty peaks above the city.

15.11 Ruins of Machu Picchu, Peru.

15.12 Machu Picchu, Peru, June 1960. Inez and I photographed perched on a reputedly sacrificial stone.

17.1 Easter Island/Rapa Nui, 1970. Two Nicos and two Rositas in front of their house at Hanga Roa.

17.2 Easter Island/Rapa Nui, 1970. Rano Kau: Nico junior and I on a tractor during a visit to the Orongo bird-cult site. Samuel, who took the photograph, drove the tractor. Nico would have loved to drive it, but was not allowed.

17.3 Easter Island/Rapa Nui, 1970. Ahu Vinapu: the finest ahu on the Island, it belongs to the Early Period. I took the photograph with Samuel and Nico junior. The precisely fitted large stones are a marvel of construction.

17.4 Easter Island/Rapa Nui, 1970. Ahu Tahai: I pose as a human scale next to this fine moai. Only one was restored from the original several. The red topknot was specially made at the time of the restoration.

17.5 Easter Island/Rapa Nui, 1970. Ahu Akivi: I pose in front of the seven giants, all painstakingly restored by William Mulloy and his local team. Herman Hotu who took this photograph had assisted in the restoration.

17.6 Easter Island/Rapa Nui, 1970. Hanga Roa: a familiar scene in the late afternoon, when people gather at the little harbour to meet the returning fishermen and buy fish and crayfish. Note the casual fearless way the child is sitting on a horse, in the foreground. Children are completely at home on horseback.

17.7 Easter Island/Rapa Nui, 1970. Moai Kavakava: the traditional carved wooden figurine of an emaciated, bearded man (front and profile), supposedly representing the starved state of the first settlers on Rapa Nui after their long sea journey in search of a new island home. Carved in different sizes, this one is eleven inches high.

17.8 Easter Island/Rapa Nui, 1970. Rano Raraku: general view of this magnificent mountain quarry. On the left, the tracks of our tractor.

17.9 Easter Island/Rapa Nui, 1970. Rano Raraku: scattered moai near the bottom of the mountain. The soil creep had buried some of them up to their necks. Ready for transportation to the ahus, these moai appear to have been abandoned as if due to a sudden calamity. Signs of past excavations can be seen around the moai in the foreground.

17.10 Easter Island/Rapa Nui, 1970. Rano Raraku: Samuel (right) and I pose next to one of the moai in the foothills of the mountain.

17.11 Easter Island/Rapa Nui, 1970. Rano Raraku: I pose in front of an unfinished giant lying in its rock cradle. Finished, it would have been around sixty feet tall. This great quarry was the source of nearly all the moai on the Island.

17.12 Easter Island/Rapa Nui, 1970. Ahu Te Pito Kura: Samuel is standing on the perfectly spheroidal "navel of the earth", dubbed "120" in white paint by the late Fr. Sebastian Englert.

17.13 Easter Island/Rapa Nui, 1970. I am about to explore one of the Island's caves.

17.14 Easter Island/Rapa Nui, 1970. Herman Hotu poses next to the red moai, the only one of this type on the Island.

18.1 Tung Lung Fort, Hong Kong. Phase 1 (January 1979): view from the south, the Fort before clearance is largely hidden by thick vegetation. (Photograph courtesy of the Antiquities and Monuments Office of the Leisure and Cultural Services Department).

18.2 Tung Lung Fort, Hong Kong. Phase 1 (January 1979): myself, facing a thick "jungle" of vegetation inside the Fort at the start of the clearance.

18.3 Tung Lung Fort, Hong Kong. Phase 2 (November 1979): general view of the Fort after partial clearance. Note the original sharp, well-constructed corner (north-west). It was the best-preserved corner of the Fort. (Photograph courtesy of the Antiquities and Monuments Office of the Leisure and Cultural Services Department).

18.4 Tung Lung Fort, Hong Kong. Phase 2 (November 1979): the entrance steps into the Fort partly cleared. Fused wedge-shaped bricks from the collapsed arch over the entrance are seen in the foreground. (Photograph courtesy of the Antiquities and Monuments Office of the Leisure and Cultural Services Department).

18.5 Tung Lung Fort, Hong Kong. Phase 2 (November 1979): brick steps are revealed leading up to the top of the wall. (Photograph courtesy of the Antiquities and Monuments Office of the Leisure and Cultural Services Department).

18.6 Tung Lung Fort, Hong Kong. Myself acting as the paymaster: the hired workers receiving their pay at the end of a working day.

18.7 Tung Lung Fort, Hong Kong. Army helicopter landing near the entrance to the Fort to deliver bags of cement. (Photograph courtesy of the Antiquities and Monuments Office of the Leisure and Cultural Services Department).

18.8 Tung Lung Fort, Hong Kong. Interior of the Fort after completion of the project, 1982. Photograph shows excavated areas with rooms and inner walls.

18.9 Tung Lung Fort, Hong Kong. Phase 5, end of the project (April 1982): happy and proud of their achievement, team members pose for a photograph on the wooden bridge over the entrance to the Fort (not in order): Taryn, Jeanne, Judy, Darren, Helen, Matthew, Ulla, Heidi, Jeanine, Brigitta, Rosemary, Lin. I am standing on the extreme left. At the extreme right, wearing a helmet, is the new custodian of the Fort who is the husband of one of the village workers. (Photograph courtesy of the Antiquities and Monuments Office of the Leisure and Cultural Services Department).

18.10 Tung Lung Fort, Hong Kong. Fort after completion of the project, 1982. Photograph shows the constructed stone path leading to the entrance of the Fort and the information plaque, framed in stone, depicting a short history of the Fort. (Photograph courtesy of the Antiquities and Monuments Office of the Leisure and Cultural Services Department).

18.11 Tung Lung Fort, Hong Kong. Some of the ceramic material recovered at the excavation of the interior of the Fort, displayed at a special exhibition 1984/85.

20.1 Myself as guest conductor of the Hong Kong Chinese Orchestra in Brisbane, Australia, September 1982. Only a portion of the Orchestra is visible.

20.2 Conducting the reduced Hong Kong Chinese Orchestra at the Radio Television Hong Kong studio in the first live "simulcast", 1 October 1984.

20.3 Conducting the Hong Kong Chinese Orchestra in the City Hall, 1985.

20.4 Conducting the Hong Kong Chinese Orchestra at the Festival of Asian Arts, 1986.

20.5 Conducting the Hong Kong Chinese Orchestra in Beijing, September 1987.

20.6 I return to conduct the Hong Kong Chinese Orchestra as guest conductor, 23 June 2007.

21.1 Monica and Paul (facing the camera) in front of The Old Curiosity Shop, in Portsmouth Street, Central London, August 1963. Made famous by Charles Dickens in his story by that name, the Shop is popular with tourists.

21.2 Monica and Paul in front of the Tower of London, August 1963. This historic English fortress, on the south bank of the Thames, built in the late 11th century, is now a museum, an important heritage structure, and a tourist attraction.

21.3 Jonathan Bard punting with Monica on the River Cam, Cambridge, August 1963. I do not remember whether it was Paul or David (face unseen) sitting behind Monica.

21.4 Villa Luciano, Ischia, viewed from the road leading to Maronti Beach, August 1963.

21.5 The family on Maronti Beach, Ischia, August 1963.

21.6 The children are posing among the impressive remains of Pompeii, August 1963.

21.7 Paul and David in one of the streets in Pompeii, August 1963. The ruts made by heavy carts millennia ago are clearly visible. Also note an ancient "pedestrian crossing" of large stone slabs.

21.8 The House of the Fawn, Pompeii, August 1963. An exquisite bronze statue of a fawn was revealed in the excavation of this elegant house. At the back a large peristyle can be seen.

21.9 Tomb of Theodor Herzl (1860–1904), Mount Herzl, Jerusalem, September 1963. The simple tombstone with only his name upon it, is the final resting place of the founder of modern Zionism.

21.10 Site of the ancient Caesaria, Israel, September 1963. (Left to right) David, Monica, Sophie and Paul pose among the ruins.

21.11 On the way to Galilee, Israel, September 1963. David is having a ride on a camel, while Monica (on the left) watches.

21.12 One of the main streets in Kathmandu, Nepal, September 1963. The number of temples, even in this short stretch of the street, is truly astonishing. On the extreme left, an itinerant musician with a four-stringed instrument, the saringhi, can be seen; he is also the subject of Photograph 21.15.

21.13 Kathmandu, Nepal, September 1963. Paul and David examining the Land Rover, which was our transport during our stay, with local children looking on. Curious Nepalese children nearly always followed us wherever we went.

21.14 Kathmandu, Nepal, September 1963. Mr Upadia with the children near one of the temples.

21.15 Kathmandu, Nepal, September 1963. An itinerant musician (also seen in Photograph 21.12) with the saringhi, which I bought from him for 10 rupees, posing with the children. Note the local children watching us.

21

MY FAMILY

"I threw my cup away when I saw a child
drinking from his hands at the trough."

Attributed to Diogenes, 4th century BCE

Children

I love this quotation. For me, it captures the essence of childhood, its
innocence, its naturalness, its inborn sense of wonder, as yet untouched by
the real world. We had a friend in Hong Kong who used to visit us with
his little dog. The children loved this dog and played with it. One day our
friend came alone. He looked sad and told us that the dog had died and we
all felt sorry for him. When he came again, a week or two later, Monica,
then aged five, asked him: "Is your dog still dead?" The innocent children,
how I wished I could delay or hide from them the sad, painful aspects of life,
which sooner or later they must learn and accept. We tend to underestimate
children's intelligence, their extraordinary capacity to see into the heart of
things, their sense of humour. A friend who came for dinner said to Paul,
who was about six at the time, in that adult condescending manner: "Well,
little man, have you brushed your teeth?" and Paul replied: "What, are you
a dentist?" I found it hard not to laugh.

Background

In my other essays I frequently referred to my "ancestral" family. This essay is
about my personal family, my wife and especially my children. I met my future
wife, Sophie Patushinsky, in Hong Kong in 1938. Her medical studies, begun
in Shanghai, were interrupted by the Japanese invasion and war in China,
and she was sent by her family to continue them at Hong Kong University.
Sophie had a similar background to mine: born in Harbin, daughter of
Russian-Jewish parents of merchant class who were driven from Russia by the

Revolution. They moved to Shanghai in 1920 when Sophie was two years old. Unlike mine, however, her primary and secondary education was entirely in English, though she spoke Russian fluently since it was spoken at home. We were married in Shanghai in September 1941. Sophie's and my parents were present, the latter having arrived from Argentina to attend my brother Leo's wedding a few months earlier. In Europe and in Russia the war was raging and its extension to the Pacific was thought imminent. I had already joined the Hong Kong Volunteer Defence Force as a medical officer in the Field Ambulance. Anxious to be with my unit, if and when the war broke out, we returned hurriedly to Hong Kong. In the event, we only had two and half months of married life before Hong Kong was attacked by the Japanese and, after eighteen days of fierce fighting, surrendered. I went into captivity and did not see Sophie for three years and eight months. The fighting and the imprisonment are described in "The Battle for Hong Kong" and "Behind Barbed Wire" essays.

After the war Sophie and I were repatriated to England, where Sophie completed her medical course and I was engaged in various refresher courses and short-term jobs. We liked England, but prospects were poor. In 1947 I accepted an offer to join a doctor in general practice in Hong Kong. I sailed for Hong Kong in September 1947, and Sophie followed in January 1948, immediately after obtaining her medical degree. After eight years, dissatisfied with general practice, I joined Hong Kong University to take charge of its newly established University Health Service. The post-war years, in Hong Kong and England, are described in the "The Post-War Years" essay.

Our three children were all born in Hong Kong — Monica in April 1948, Paul in December 1950 and David in July 1953. Like most European children in Hong Kong, they went to English-language kindergarten, primary and secondary schools. Like most European households we had a Cantonese nanny, generally known as "amah".[1] Most amahs spoke pidgin English, but ours had worked previously in Saigon and spoke pidgin French. When she attempted to use it with the children, we politely but firmly directed her to use Cantonese only. As a result the children grew up knowing some common-usage Cantonese. Sophie and I also learned to speak (though not from our amah) a fair amount of Cantonese, but to my everlasting shame, I never acquired a full fluency in it. At home English was spoken, since both Sophie

---

1. Amah: A term widely used in the Far East for a woman who looks after children. The origin of the word is not clear, but reputed to be from the Portuguese "ama" or "ana", perhaps originating in Macao, formerly a Portuguese colony.

and I, although fluent in Russian, were more comfortable with English.[2] When, in 1956, I joined the University staff, we moved into the University campus and were given a large, comfortable, old colonial-style house. At the time, the University was still small, with a total student body of barely five hundred. Most of the staff were accommodated around the main campus, on the well-wooded slopes above the Main University Building. For the children there were many playmates: many families had three, four, or five, and in one case six children. After dinner our children often disappeared for an hour or so to play "spies", in the darkening woody compound centred around the lily pond. What the game was about I never discovered, but a friend, who had eavesdropped once, said he overheard the children conducting a mock trial of one Dr Bard accused of subjecting them to painful jabs, no doubt the preventive inoculations.

Having a nanny allowed Sophie and me to work full-time unhindered in our respective medical fields. Sophie, after finishing her internships in Hong Kong, went into general practice, gradually specializing in gynaecology and obstetrics. However, we spent many weekends with the children, either on the beach, in summer, or hiking and walking in winter. My strong interest in archaeology led me to spend many weekends and holidays in archaeological field work, but even then the family was not entirely excluded. Indeed, it was during one of our joint field excursions, in 1958, that I discovered a new archaeological site on Lantao Island.[3]

There were sports at the school and, with private lessons in swimming, all three became good swimmers. As in many families, music was introduced. Monica studied the piano and reached a fair degree of proficiency, but later in life also took up the cello. Both Paul and David were taught piano and violin, but did not continue. However, the interest and appreciation of music remained, which in my view was a worthwhile result. At school the children were performing at an average level, though Monica tended to rise above it. Myself an avid reader in childhood, it irked me to find that my children were not. Even without today's television and computer games, there were many distractions and many playmates on the campus. Once, in desperation, I locked Monica in her room with Dickens's *Little Dorrit*. I am not proud of

---

2. Among the children, only Monica complained of not being brought up speaking Russian as an added language. She tried to learn it, but never progressed beyond a beginner's stage.
3. Located at a place called Man Kok Tsui, the site proved to be very rich in neolithic/bronze-period artefacts. It was excavated by the University Archaeological Team in 1959.

my act; it was a foolish thing to do. In any case, Monica has grown up a thoughtful well-informed person. It was fascinating and a source of pleasure to observe how our children were growing and developing their own distinct personalities, and how these characteristics were changing with the passage of time. Monica was a happy uninhibited child to start with, full of fun and very gregarious. Paul on the other hand was growing up as a quiet, gentle and sensitive little boy, but with hidden strength and pluck. When Monica was once in some minor trouble on the beach, Paul, although younger, rushed to help. David, as a small child was the most mischievous and often a worry, for we were never sure what his next prank might be. Together with a friend from the house next door, they made a dangerous combination when it came to practical jokes. It was rumoured that between the two of them they were responsible for the broken glass of most of the University campus lampposts. It is amazing how these individual personalities changed over the years, sometimes very markedly. Monica gradually changed into a shy but quietly confident person. Paul grew into a confident and self-assertive boy, but perhaps the greatest change was in David, who became a warm, kind and compassionate young man without a hint of any anti-social tendency. Overall it seemed to me that our children were growing up as normal healthy average children with no outstanding talents or outstanding drawbacks. Could one ask for more? I think not.

For some years, Sophie and I took our overseas holidays separately, partly because one of us would stay with the children, and partly because our priorities in travel were different. I travelled widely, which is reflected in some of the essays, often combining a trip with a meeting of student health officers. Sophie took her holidays either in Japan with close friends of ours living there, or in Australia with her family, who had migrated there from Shanghai in the early 1950s. But 1963 was to be an exception when we travelled abroad as a family. I want to devote the rest of this essay to that trip.

In my essay "The Beauty Pageant" I described my time in 1963 with the Counselling Bureau at the University of Minnesota. At the end of my stay there, late in July, I did not return immediately to Hong Kong but flew to England, where I met Sophie and the children who had arrived from Hong Kong. We planned to spend our holiday travelling together. For the children it was their first time in England. How different, I mused, was their childhood from mine. They had a different mother tongue and a different adopted country — both achieved in one generation. I was keen to show them all the famous landmarks which had thrilled me seventeen years earlier, when I saw London for the first time.

London

We rented a flat on Bayswater Road opposite Hyde Park and then began our sightseeing tours: Dickens's Old Curiosity Shop, the Sherlock Holmes Museum on Baker Street, Madame Tussauds wax museum, Trafalgar Square, Buckingham Palace and the Tower of London. There was so much to see. The children were excited to see the places about which they had only read before. It was all so different, so big, so breath-taking compared to Hong Kong. They asked many questions, but I can only remember a few, for instance: David wanted to know if people were still beheaded in the Tower of London, and Monica asked if we could see the Queen.

We spent some time with the recently discovered English Bards; they had three boys roughly the same age as our children. Basil and Ena Bard were born in England, but Basil's grandparents came to England in the 1880s from the same region of Poland as my paternal grandparents. The clan connection was strongly suggestive, but in the end it did not matter as we had become close friends anyway.[4] Visits to Oxford and Cambridge were most enjoyable, where Basil and Ena's eldest son Jonathan took Monica punting on the river Cam.

The musical *My Fair Lady*, based on Bernard Shaw's *Pygmalion*, opened that year in London and we managed to get tickets. It was in a small theatre in central London, in Haymarket I think. During the Ascot Race scene, when Eliza Doolittle forgets her newly learned manners and diction, and shouts: "Come on, Dover! Move yer bloomin' arse", David turned to Sophie and very loudly said: "Mummy, what a rude lady!" I am sure the whole theatre must have heard it: there was laughter, but I could not be sure whether it was at David's or Eliza's words, perhaps both.

After two hectic and very enjoyable weeks, we were ready for our next holiday destination. We decided on Italy. It was the middle of August. The travel agent informed us that the tourist season was still on and it would be difficult to find a good place, but he could book us for three weeks on the island of Ischia. He explained apologetically that the only available place was a *pension* on the southern coast of the Island, the less popular area, whereas

---

4. Dr Basil Bard, scientist and barrister, had a habit, when visiting new places, of looking up "Bards" in the telephone book. When visiting Hong Kong, in 1956 I think it was, he found my name and, over a cup of coffee, we discovered the connection, albeit somewhat tenuous. Incidentally, another Bard migration from Poland occurred in 1905, when three of my father's brothers migrated to the USA, where they changed their name, for reasons which are not altogether clear, to Barrett.

the centre of activity — the hotels, the shops and the entertainment amenities — was on the northern coast, at the port of Ischia. We accepted and set off for our island holiday.

Ischia

Ischia is located just off the Gulf of Naples and is reached from Naples by a ferry or a hydrofoil, about an hour's trip. Its sister island, Capri, the more famous and much written-about, is about fifteen kilometres south-east of Ischia, and on a clear day can be seen from the latter. Disembarking at the small port, we could indeed see the bustling activity all around, with many hotels massed along the waterfront and crowds of holiday-makers. When we settled down in our small guest house, called Villa Luciano, we had good reason to be grateful to the travel agent for placing us there. It was a charming small villa, located on high ground among several scattered houses, loosely called Testaccio. Above was the village of Barano, and all around us beautiful countryside with olive groves and vineyards. A good way below lay the Beach of Maronti, where we would spend many days sunning and bathing in the sea.

At the *pension*, we were met by Peppi and Amelia, the owners, who immediately made us feel at home. Both of middle age, Peppi was a thin, spare man with an angular face and a twinkle in his eye, while Amelia was of more generous proportions. Their two teenage sons, Franco and Giorgio helped in the running of the place, while little Regina, about eight years old, and obviously the favourite, also helped if she could. In the kitchen, Giovanni, a young chef, ruled. The guests ate at separate tables, on the large open verandah. We soon got to know everyone. Among about five families, there were an elderly German couple; two brothers from Naples, both dentists; and a family from Portici, a small village outside Naples, Professor Esposito, his wife and three teenage daughters. Each morning as the guests were having breakfast, Peppi would walk among the tables inspecting and chatting. He always stopped at our table and asked David: "You feela good Devi?", and David would reply "Yes, Mr Peppi, and how are you?" Around mid-morning we would be ready for our daily trip to the beach. Loaded with towels, straw mats, drinks and sandwiches, we would walk down to Maronti Beach, about a twenty-minute walk, where we would hire two beach chairs and a tent. Being brought up in Hong Kong, surrounded by water and beaches, the children were good swimmers and loved it. In a flash they would be in the sea, coming out only for an occasional drink or a sandwich. Monica at fifteen was an attractive teenager, and drew many admiring glances from the boys on the beach. Sophie and I, comfortable in our beach chairs, were usually reading after a quick dip in the sea. To get back to the Villa — a steep climb — we took a bus. After a cup of tea and a short rest, Sophie and I sometimes walked up to Barano — a pleasant stroll as the day cooled down. The boys, still full of energy, might be playing around, while Monica as the eldest would try to keep them in line. The holiday in Ischia turned out very relaxing and pleasant, and being together as a family felt wonderful. In the evening, after dinner we would chat with the other guests, while the boys might be playing some games, and Monica socializing with the older boys at the Villa. We became especially friendly with the two brothers (dentists) and the Esposito family. Both extracted from us a promise to visit them on the mainland. Professor Esposito was actually a school teacher; apparently in Italy it was common to title teachers "professor". Sometimes there was a party with music and dancing. The boys did not want to dance with little Regina, and she would pull at my sleeve, shouting in her strangely husky voice "Balare, balare!" (dance, dance). On several occasions Franco and Giorgio took Monica to a fiesta at the port.

I brought from America a couple of frisbees for the children.[5] Paul and David were already quite good at it, having practised throwing them at Hyde Park in London. One day Paul and David started throwing and catching the frisbees in the Villa's grounds. It created a sensation; the frisbee apparently was still a novelty in Europe. Franco and Giorgio joined in. Then Giovanni, unable to resist, left his cooking and rushed out with his cooking apron still on and also joined in, Peppi and Amelia shaking their heads and remonstrating with him. In no time, the frisbees were flying all around with the guests laughing and ducking out of the way.

In the evening we sometimes watched the lights of a ferry in the far distance as it made its crossing from Ischia to the mainland. At the Villa we all agreed that whenever anyone left the Villa to return home, we would wave to each other: those who remained, from the verandah, and the departing ones, from the ferry, though both unseen in the darkness. When the brothers left to return to Naples, and two days later the Esposito family, we at the Villa dutifully stood on both evenings by the verandah's parapet, staring into the dark until the lights of the ferry came into view, then waved, hoping that they would be doing the same.

---

5. Frisbee: A plastic disc, about twenty-five centimetres in diameter. Deftly throwing and catching it became a popular pastime when it was first introduced in the 1960s. It is still played.

It was early September and our turn to leave. We had spent three very
enjoyable weeks wallowing in the warm relaxing and friendly atmosphere of
Villa Luciano, which I knew we would remember for many years to come.
As we were packing our bags, Peppi, Amelia, their boys and the guests of the
Villa came to say goodbye and we all hugged each other. Giorgio was taking
us in his tiny scooter-car to the port for an early dinner and the evening trip
on the ferry. As we were standing outside in the street waiting for Giorgio,
the bus passed by on its way to Maronti beach. The friendly driver, obviously
realizing that we were leaving, stopped the bus, got out and shook hands with
each one of us. Not a single passenger raised an objection to this delay. On
the contrary they all smiled with obvious approval. That evening we stood
on the deck of our ferry, as it sailed towards Naples, staring into the dark
where we thought Villa Luciano would be and waved to our unseen friends
at the Villa as we hoped they would too.

In Naples on the weekend, we rang the two brothers. They arrived shortly
afterwards in a large car and we all piled in for a drive south of Naples along the
Amalfi Coast. The area is renowned for its beauty and abundance of popular
resorts. Strangely enough I confess that I recall little of our drive, except
that the coast was indeed beautiful, but not in a wild untouched sense, and
that the children were somewhat bored, except when they were eating large
portions of pasta. I suppose nothing much happened during that excursion,
except for admiring the sights and eating. Both brothers spoke tolerably good
English, but I cannot recall the subjects of our conversation. Perhaps they
were of no import. Still, all in all, it was an enjoyable day.

The next day we went to visit the Esposito family at Portici. A charming
village, Portici is about ten kilometres east of Naples, on the coast facing
the Bay of Naples. We arrived there late in the morning and were warmly
welcomed by the family. The Espositos lived in a large two-storey, old-looking
house with wooden shutters. The visit would long remain in our collective
memory as "The Day of the Big Italian Lunch". The lunch began with thick
soup and two courses of pasta. Unfamiliar with Italian customs, especially
how they entertain guests for lunch, we partook generously of these courses
assuming that there was no more to come. Both the professor and his wife
were probably too polite to warn us. Indeed, there was a great deal more to
come, as dishes of meat, chicken and other culinary delights kept arriving
at the table — nine courses in all! After the fifth course it became akin to
torture, as we struggled to eat, trying at the same time to appear appreciative
of the efforts which had been made by the Espositos to entertain us. At last

the lunch was over and the Bard family was too full to talk or move. The professor then announced that we would all retire for a two-hour siesta, after which we should drive up to Mount Vesuvius. A siesta was certainly what we all needed. The shutters were closed, the house was plunged into darkness and we went to bed, still feeling uncomfortable from gross overeating.

Somehow we all managed to squeeze into the Esposito family's not very large car, though one of the daughters I recall chose to remain behind, and drove towards Vesuvius. Rising to an elevation of some 1200 metres, only a few kilometres from Portici, Mount Vesuvius's majestic appearance dominates the landscape of the Bay of Naples. Most people know of the mountain's catastrophic eruption in 79 CE, when it destroyed the two Roman cities of Pompeii and Herculaneum. Less well known, as Professor Esposito related to us, is its frightful history of many other eruptions, some almost as bad as the 79 CE, with the last major eruption as recent as 1944. Yet all around it could be seen towns and villages existing apparently unconcerned. I asked Professor Esposito how he could feel safe living within the sight of this volcano which has repeatedly devastated the country around it, and he replied: "We don't think about it", which I thought was a very philosophical answer. We drove to about half-way up the mountain and then walked a little further. It is obviously still an active volcano, as smoke can be seen issuing from its centre — not a reassuring sight I thought. But one could understand how people would not want to leave what had been their home perhaps for generations, and continue to live under the shadow of a possible disaster.

My children were interested to hear about the destruction of the two Roman cities, and so we decided to visit Pompeii. Herculaneum, I was told, was not open to visitors. In the evening, at the hotel, I told my children all I could remember from my school studies and subsequent reading about the terror and the agony of the people of Pompeii as they sought to escape the deadly red-hot lava engulfing their city and the hot ash raining on them from the sky, nearly two thousand years ago. One appalling fact emerged: the children, even Monica at fifteen, knew absolutely nothing about ancient history; the subject was apparently not taught in English schools, at least not in Hong Kong.

The next morning we hired a taxi which took us to Pompeii, about a twenty-kilometre-ride from Naples. The site is open to visitors and, of course, very popular with tourists. Several decades of intensive excavations through solidified lava and ash had uncovered the buried city which was a favoured resort place for rich Romans. It felt strange walking through the narrow streets of this dead city which two thousand years earlier pulsed with life and pleasure. Villa after villa was revealed with rich frescoes, colour still appearing fresh since it was sealed in volcanic ash two millennia ago. There were marvellous floor mosaics, columns of public buildings, and ruts in the streets made by carts with heavy loads. I must confess I was shattered. The impression was unforgettable — wonder mixed with awareness of a great tragedy. It was also a revelation of what archaeology could achieve. Sophie, a practical, down-to-earth person, took it in her stride. The children, however, were impressed though not for long. It was not surprising, since children generally relate everything to their immediate experience. For them, in the end, it was another day of fun, a day to be enjoyed.

The next day we travelled by train to Rome, where we spent three days, visiting the usual tourist sites and eating lots of pizzas. Three days are woefully inadequate for this great city, so it was a hectic rush to see the Colosseum, the Forum, the remains of a few ancient temples, St. Peter's and the Vatican. I had visited Rome before, but for Sophie and the children it was the first time. Rome was the final resting place of England's two great poets — Keats and Shelley, and so I took the children to the cemetery where the poets are buried; they lie side by side. English was not my mother tongue, but it was my children's. The most poignant epitaph is on Keats's tombstone, which without mentioning his name reads, in part, "Here Lies One Whose Name was writ in Water".

Israel

Our next destination was Israel, where we flew for a two weeks' stay. My brother Leo and uncle David, with their families, had migrated to Israel in 1948 soon after its establishment as a state. Leo had moved on to Argentina to join father in the late 1950s, but David was still in Israel. He seemed to have made a successful transition in profession from music to optometry and now had an optical shop in Nathanya, a small town on the coast, north of Tel Aviv. He booked a flat for us in Nathanya. This was my third visit to Israel, but the first for the family. I have always felt a surge of emotion when arriving in Israel, as the land where momentous events in the history of my people took place. How can one feel otherwise? Here Joshua broached the walls of Jericho, Samson was betrayed by Delilah, King David fought Goliath and established his capital in Jerusalem. But soon, emotions give way to the reality of everyday life. Nathanya proved to be a pleasant town with a holiday atmosphere, an excellent beach, where our children rushed almost before we had properly settled into our flat.

I made contact with several old classmates from my Harbin days, who had migrated to (at that time) Palestine after finishing school, in the early 1930s. As in my previous and subsequent visits, I have always had a passing feeling of guilt at not having followed their example. Together, as youngsters, we were members of the Betar.[6] I was still a Zionist at heart, yet I had done nothing to help build Israel as a state. I was impressed by the way they said, quite naturally, that they could not imagine living anywhere else. It seemed that they had found their true home. A visit to the modern Jerusalem was still an inspiring occasion, but the old walled city, the historical East Jerusalem, was in Jordanian hands and we could only observe it from the distance. On the nearby Mount Herzl we visited the grave of Theodor Herzl, the ideological father of modern Zionism and visionary who foresaw the rebirth of the Jewish state in its ancient homeland. The tombstone is impressive in its stark sombre simplicity, with just one word on it in Hebrew — "Herzl".

On the coast between Nathanya and Tel Aviv, lie the ruins of the Roman town of Caesaria.[7] The rising sea has gradually submerged part of the town. As we wondered among the ruins, admiring ancient columns and occasional marble statues, all headless by the way, we saw archaeologists still working on a sector of the site.[8] We were told later that a few years previously, a French archaeological team, working on the submerged ancient harbour of Caesaria, found a tablet with an inscription in Latin: "Pontius Pilate, Procurator of Judea" — the first positive historical proof of his existence.

One day we went to Galilee to visit a kibbutz, a communal settlement and a typical feature of Israel. It was most inspiring and I hoped an interesting experience for my children. The scenery in Galilee is spectacular and, when not intruded upon by some modern feature, gives one a true feeling of the ancient biblical land. But the most exciting visit was to the ancient fortress of Masada, by the Dead Sea, where the Jewish Zealots in 72 CE made their last stand against the Romans, and where they committed mass suicide rather than fall slaves to the Romans. Rising some four hundred metres above the arid plain, and flat at the top, Masada presents a spectacular appearance. A narrow serpentine track leads to the top. In the still hot September weather, we slowly trudged up. The Jewish general and historian of the period, Josephus,

---

6. Betar: A Zionist Youth Organization.
7. Caesaria was actually built by Herod the Great in the 1st century BCE.
8. The reason, not widely known, why so many statues on Roman sites are headless is that when Christianity prevailed as the official religion of Rome, many statues were "beheaded" as relics of Roman pagan polytheism.

gives us a vivid description of the siege of Masada in his book *The Jewish War*.[9] I did not know at the time that a distinguished Israeli archaeologist, Yigael Yadin, would begin that year (in October) excavations at Masada which would confirm much of Josephus's story. Hot and exhausted, we came down from Masada and went to look at the Dead Sea. Famous for its very high concentration of salt, the Dead Sea has no living creatures in it. One cannot sink in it. The children had a great time, floating on it like corks. I found it an unpleasant sensation as the skin felt as if coated in oil. It occurred to me that I had not instilled in my children the same national spirit as I possessed at their age. I consoled myself with the thought that, Israel now being a historical reality, it was no longer necessary.

Teddy, a relative of Sophie's, and his wife Rasha, have lived in Israel (Palestine before 1948) most of their lives, and it was a particular pleasure to spend some time with them. On the day we were invited to their home for Shabbat (Sabbath) eve, we were spending the afternoon on the beach at Nathanya. When it was almost time to get ready to drive over to Teddy and Rasha's, I saw David running up to us, blood dripping from his mouth; he had torn his lip on an old wooden plank with a nail in it, which he picked up on the beach and was using as a surfboard. Monica and Paul were hovering around, anxious about David. Brief examination revealed the wound was minor, but required a stitch or two. A friendly man next to us pointed to a medical clinic a short distance from the beach. We hurried there with David holding a handkerchief to his mouth. The nurse on duty informed us that as Shabbat eve was approaching, the doctor was off duty and could not be called! Calmly I told her that I was a doctor and that I could stitch the wound myself. No, this was impossible, she said, since I was not a local doctor. A short argument ensued during which I tried hard not to raise my voice, but eventually demanded, in as stern a voice as I could muster, a needle and thread. It worked. I stitched up David's lip and he took it like a little trooper. I was left with an impression that Israeli first aid facilities needed improvement. We made Shabbat eve at Teddy's in time.

A warmhearted and interesting evening was further enhanced by the presence of Teddy's father, Dr Kaufman, who had a few years previously arrived from Soviet Russia. And what a harrowing tale he had to tell about

---

9. Josephus was charged with the defence of a fortress in Galilee. Realizing the futility of resistance to the Romans, he surrendered and went over to the Roman side, adopting the Roman name of Flavius Josephus. Regarded as a traitor, his book contains, in large part, justification of his actions.

his experience in the Soviet gulag. Dr Kaufman was a well-known doctor in Harbin in the 1920s and 30s, a leader of the local Jewish community and a prominent Zionist. In 1945, at the end of the Second World War, the Soviets joined the Allies against Japan; Soviet troops drove the Japanese out of Manchuria and occupied Harbin. Shortly afterwards, the Soviet authorities called a meeting of various prominent Harbin citizens, ostensibly to discuss matters of common interest. Instead, the men were arrested and, without even goodbye to their families, put on a train and sent forthwith to Russia. Some were executed, others like Dr Kaufman were sent to a gulag, where they suffered starvation, disease and humiliation. He spent ten years in Russia, some of them in "internal exile", which meant that he had some freedom of movement within a restricted area, where he was also allowed to practise medicine. Because of Israel's intensive diplomatic efforts for his release, he was eventually freed and allowed to go to Israel.

After two weeks in Israel, Sophie flew back to Hong Kong, as she did not want to stay away from her practice too long. I decided that the rest of us would stop in Nepal for a few days before returning to Hong Kong. While in the USA, I met a Nepalese psychologist, Mr Upadia, who was also visiting the States. He invited me to visit Nepal whenever I had the opportunity. This I thought was one. I sent a cable to Mr Upadia telling him that I should be arriving in Kathmandu with three children and asking him to book us into a hotel. His reply was an enthusiastic welcome. We left Israel at dawn. As we sat outside the airport building, with uncle David, his wife Sarah and a few friends, watching the sunrise, I wondered if our stay in Israel had any special effect on my children. They clearly enjoyed the travel and the new experience, but somehow I doubted whether there was a strong emotional impact at being in the land of their remote forefathers. And if there was not, was it my fault?

Kathmandu

We flew to New Dehli, in India, from where a small aeroplane of Indian Airlines took us to Kathmandu, the capital of Nepal. Mr Upadia met us at the airport, took us to the Hotel Himalaya and then left promising to return the next morning. It was the dingiest, the dirtiest, the worst hotel I had ever seen. When Monica sat on one of the beds, it promptly collapsed. The toilet was at the end of a dark corridor and was in a shocking state. We spent the rest of the afternoon exploring the centre of the city and took a peek at the only other hotel, The Royal. We found it only marginally better than the Himalaya. At a quick meeting convened in the street, we decided to remain in the Himalaya, since moving, we thought, might offend Mr Upadia. Kathmandu is an imposing city, but many buildings looked dilapidated and in need of repair. There were temples everywhere; more, it seemed, than ordinary buildings. There appeared to be no souvenir shops, not even postcards of Nepal or Kathmandu which could be bought. Clearly the country was not yet ready for tourists, and, indeed, we did not see any. We walked into a cafe and ordered tea and cakes. The tea came with milk, strong and sweet; I recognized it instantly — British army tea. The proprietor who served us the tea was a retired Gurkha soldier. The Gurkhas are Nepalese mercenary soldiers who, by arrangement with the Nepalese government, have been recruited by Britain since the early 19th century. Famous for their use of curved kukri daggers, the Gurkhas are tough, utterly loyal and fearless fighters. Much appreciated by the British, they are generally feared by the enemy. Initially commanded by British officers, they are now led mainly by Gurkha officers.

The next morning Mr Upadia arrived in a Land Rover with a driver; this was to be our transport for the next few days. The children were delighted as we drove exploring the city further. We stopped often and tried to talk to people. They seemed very nice, always smiling and very curious about us. Again we were amazed at the multitude of temples. Mr Upadia explained that the Nepalese practise Hinduism and Buddhism, the two intermingling, and often worshipped in the same temple. The country was very poor, perhaps because so much effort and money was spent on temples, he added. Hindus venerate the cow and these animals were seen wandering around the city, which prompted the boys to ask why, but Monica was apparently aware of Hindu custom, and immediately explained that the cow was a symbol of motherhood. This veneration also extends to the respect for all living things.

During one of our rambles in the city, I noticed an itinerant musician playing on a crudely made wooden instrument with four strings, not unlike the Chinese violin. The tone of the instrument was pleasant. A small crowd gathered around us and someone speaking English explained that the instrument was called a saringhi. I thought the saringhi would make a good souvenir and offered to buy it. The musician immediately agreed to sell it for ten rupees. No doubt he would be able to make another one easily. I still have the instrument, though I have never tried to play on it.

Nepal is a kingdom, ruled by an old dynasty.[10] Mr Upadia informed us that the present king, Mahendra, was away on a foreign tour, and that we could

---

10. That was then. Monarchy was abolished in May 2008, when Nepal became a republic.

visit the King's Palace and gardens. Considering the surrounding poverty, the Palace was an ostentatious place of luxury, while the gardens were spacious and well looked after. The children were thrilled to play with tame animals like deer, which came to us unafraid. The children asked Mr Upadia why there were so many monkeys, especially around the temples, and he replied that monkeys were also regarded as sacred animals. He then took us to a small clearing in a wooded area and started making strange crowing sounds. In a flash, as if from nowhere, we were surrounded by hundreds of monkeys clamouring for nuts. Fortunately Mr Upadia had seen to it, and produced several packets of nuts which the children proceeded to feed to the hungry monkeys. Suddenly we saw many of them, snarling and yelling, chasing one monkey. It was an interloper from another tribe, explained Mr Upadia.

As we were in Nepal, we decided that we should at least make a symbolic effort to climb the foothills of the Himalayas, and pretend that we are attempting the Everest. Mount Everest is actually about 150 kilometres from Kathmandu. At any rate, the children were excited at the project and Mr Upadia said he would provide us with a sherpa, a local guide. Imagine our surprise when the sherpa turned out to be a boy no older than about ten, David's age, or so he seemed. This was our fourth day in Nepal and the weather, previously bright and sunny, had become dull and the sky overcast. Nevertheless, we set out and were soon hiking up a narrow rocky footpath led by the little boy. Above us, in the distance, we could see occasionally through gaps in the clouds, the snowy peaks looking splendid, but so unreachable. Still we walked. After about two hours, we slowed down considerably, while the little sherpa-boy was running up and down making circles around us. I am sure he climbed twice the distance we did. After a short break for a snack, we resumed our climb but finally had to stop. I reckoned we might have climbed about three thousand feet, not a big achievement, but the children were very happy — at the mere idea of climbing the Himalayas!

The descent back was at times even harder than the climb. We arrived back at our hotel exhausted, but still managed to go out for a meal with Mr Upadia, who was much amused at our "attempt at Everest". The next day it started to rain heavily and we were practically grounded.

As the weather had not improved, we decided to cut short our stay and arranged to leave the following day, our sixth in Kathmandu. Our destination was Calcutta, where we were due to pick up our international flight to Hong Kong. For some reason, which I cannot remember, Mr Upadia was unavailable. A bus picked us up at the hotel. It was the oldest, most rickety bus I had ever seen. It was full of passengers. The journey to the airport was nightmarish. The bus moved slowly, creaking at every joint. It stopped several times, the water tank steaming, and each time a little lad dashed out with a tin can, collected some water, filled the radiator, and we would start again. I feared we would never reach the airport, but we did eventually, after a harrowing journey. The weather was foul, with the sky completely overcast and occasional rain. A rumour had spread among the passengers that the flight might be cancelled. We sat in anxious expectation looking at our small plane, of the Royal Nepal Airlines, standing on the tarmac. Then the captain came out, looked at the sky, shook the flaps of the plane (I wondered why), shook his head and said "We fly." There was a communal grunt of relief.

End of Journey

We flew above the clouds among spectacular snow-covered peaks; occasionally it seemed too close for comfort. The crew was wonderful. My children, the only ones on board, spent the whole time in the cockpit, enjoying themselves immensely. We were obviously flying at no great altitude, as I recall one of the crew in the cockpit opening a window and throwing out his cigarette, something one would never expect in a modern airliner! Above Calcutta, the cloud blanket seemed impenetrable and I was wondering how we were going to descend. Perhaps this was also in the mind of the pilot, for we seemed to be circling for a long time, though he may have been waiting our turn to land. Whatever it was, suddenly there appeared a hole in the clouds and we could see Calcutta below. The plane seemed to dive through the hole and soon we were landing on the ground. This may all sound unreal, but that is how I remember it. We thanked the crew for their special treatment. The Grand Hotel in Calcutta was an indescribable luxury after the Himalaya in Kathmandu. In the evening we sat down for a marvellous curry dinner served by no less than five waiters. Very early in the morning we were driven to the airport for our flight to Hong Kong. While we were looking at the planes on the tarmac, the Nepalese crew of our previous day's flight walked past. We all shook hands and the Captain told us to watch his plane fly by. We did, and as the plane flew above our heads it dipped its wing in a farewell salute to us, which we thought was a wonderful gesture. I shall always carry the happiest recollection of that crew and the people of Nepal generally. Soon we were on the plane flying back to Hong Kong, the end of our travels.

The children missed a few weeks of schooling, but I believe had benefited a good deal in perceiving new countries, meeting new people and gaining new impressions.

Postscript

Monica finished her school in 1966 with excellent results in A Level examinations, and was the head girl in her final year. It was decided to send her to Australia, where she was accepted by Sydney University, and where Sophie had her family. After a year at Sydney University, she begged us to allow her to transfer to a university in England. We conceded and she chose the University of Sussex, where she read Social Anthropology and Psychology. There was a gap of several months between the academic years of Sydney and Sussex Universities, during which Monica travelled with a girlfriend across Russia by the Trans-Siberian Railway, then across Europe and finally England. She graduated in 1971, took a Master's degree in 1974, and worked for the local County Council as a social worker. She specialized in psychotherapy and since 1985 has had a private practice as a psychotherapist. She is married to Michael, has one daughter, Antonia, and they live in London.

For some time Sophie and I had been unhappy with the boys' progress at their secondary school. After a good deal of thought, discussion and soul searching, we decided to send the boys, one at a time, after they reached the age of thirteen, to a boarding school in Australia. Having Sophie's family there — mother, sister, aunt and uncle — ensured that the boys would have a warm welcome and healthy home food at the weekends, which in our view was essential for their comfort and happiness. Both were accepted by The Scots College in Sydney, and both did well in their studies and sports.

Paul proceeded to Sydney University where he graduated from the Faculty of Law. He has a busy law practice in Sydney, is married to Mary-Ellen, also a lawyer, and has four children (from two marriages), Alexandra, David, Jonathan ("Jono") and Rachel. They live in Sydney.

David, after school, enrolled in the School of Optometry at the University of New South Wales, following his grandfather's and uncle's profession. He graduated in 1978 and soon after joined a private firm of optometrists, where his work and pleasant personality won him praise and many friends. The following year he married Katrina, a fellow student at the University. Six weeks after their marriage, on 3 August 1979, while driving at night, they had an accident. Katrina survived the crash, but David succumbed to his injuries and died a week later without regaining consciousness. He was twenty-six years old. We lost a prince of men. He is remembered in the David Bard Scholarship which we have set up at the School of Optometry which he so loved. There are gaps which are never filled, wounds which never heal, pain which never stops.

Sophie continued with her practice, specializing in gynaecology (women's diseases) and obstetrics (midwifery), and by all accounts was a popular doctor. Often, when introduced to someone, I would hear: "You must be the husband of Dr Sophie Bard; she delivered our children, you know." Sophie was an intelligent, active, gregarious person who enjoyed life, dinner parties, meeting friends, and playing bridge and poker. She was a very competent bridge player, winning many trophies. She liked the comfortable life with household help (who would not?), yet was tough in adversity, as shown during the Japanese occupation of Hong Kong, when she walked for miles, often at great risk to herself, bringing food parcels to prisoners-of-war and civilian internees in the camps. Many, including myself, probably owe our survival to her efforts. In the 1980s she gradually wound up her practice, taking occasional locum jobs at the Hong Kong University Health Service. She retired completely from medical work in 1992, as we were making preparations to leave Hong Kong permanently for Australia. But already the early signs of Alzheimer's disease were becoming apparent. It was especially tragic that her terminal illness had struck at the time when she stopped work and was preparing to enjoy her retirement with her family. It was not to be. She knew the diagnosis and the hopeless future in store, but was very brave about it. It took many years of slow decline, as the dreadful disease slowly and relentlessly destroyed her mind and personality. She died in 2006 at the age of eighty-eight, ending a partnership of sixty-five years, not always smooth, but for the most part loving and rewarding.

Finally, briefly about myself. In accordance with the University's policy of compulsory retirement at the age of sixty, I retired in 1976 after twenty years with the University's Health Service. The University graciously conferred upon me the honorary Doctorate of Letters (D.Litt, honoris causa). I did not return to medicine, nor did I actually retire. After a short break of three months, spent in England, there followed two full-time jobs in Hong Kong: first, as head of the government's Antiquities and Monuments Office, titled executive secretary, Antiquities and Monuments, or ES(AM), 1976–83, and second, as assistant music director of the Urban Council's Hong Kong Chinese Orchestra, 1983–87. Both positions were arduous, challenging and immensely satisfying.[11]

---

11. Described in the "Old Chinese Fort Rediscovered" and "Working with the Hong Kong Chinese Orchestra" essays.

INDEX

Note: Numbers in bold denote an illustration.